Net Attitude

WHAT IT IS, HOW TO GET IT, AND WHY YOU NEED IT MORE THAN EVER

Net Attitude: What It Is, How to Get It, and Why Your Company Can't Survive Without It was published in 2001 by Perseus Publishing. *Net Attitude: What it is, How to Get it, and Why it is More Important Than Ever* is a 2016 republication of the 2001 book with a new preface and a synopsis preceding each chapter.

John R. Patrick

Foreword by Stewart Alsop

Attitude
LLC

ISBN: 0692417311
ISBN 13: 9780692417317
Library of Congress Control Number: 2015913873
Attitude LLC, Palm Coast, FL

New Praise for Net Attitude

2016

"John Patrick is one of my favorite thinkers. John is one of the Web's original wise men, a bright spirit and intellect who shares his rare understanding of technology and the web, its many dimensions and limitless potential. In *Net Attitude* he lays out a clear path for anyone who is determined to succeed on the Internet and, as he demonstrates, it all begins with attitude."

Lou Dobbs, Host, Lou Dobbs Tonight, Fox Business Network

"John Patrick remained optimistic about the Internet during and after bursting of the Internet Bubble in 2001. Now you get to read how John was right then, how he will be right again, and how you can prosper with the right 'net attitude.'"

Bob Metcalfe, Professor of Innovation, The University of Texas at Austin

"*Net Attitude* is a creative and useful mix about Internet technology, every day living, and a vision of the future. It was true in 2001, and it is true today. John Patrick covers the full spectrum of communications and information in a highly pragmatic and very readable way. Patrick's recurring theme that attitude is the ultimate differentiator between success and failure gives life to the technologies, ties them together, and makes the book a must read."

James D. Robinson III, General Partner and co-Founder, RRE Ventures, Former Chairman and CEO, American Express Company

"John is a renowned Internet seer and advisor. His first book was required reading at my first web-tech company. Much of what he predicted has come to pass and his insights and outlook for the web are valid more than 10 years later. His new *Net Attitude* is a must read for anyone seeking to understand where the web is going."

Chris Forbes, CEO of HireArt, former CEO or Knovel Corporation

2001

"Intelligence is mostly point of view and the rest is attitude. John provides a charming and easy-to-read cultural primer and travel guide for citizens of the world of atoms who plan to visit or emigrate to the land of bits."

Nicholas Negroponte, Chairman and Co-founder of MIT Media Laboratory

Also by John R. Patrick

Health Attitude: Unraveling and Solving the Complexities of Healthcare (2015)

Net Attitude: What It Is, How to Get It, and Why Your Company Can't Survive Without It (2001)

Dedication

This book is dedicated to my loving wife, Joanne. Her patience enables me to find time to work on books.

Preface

I wrote *Net Attitude*[1] during the summer of 2001. Facebook, Google Plus, Instagram, LinkedIn, MySpace, Pinterest, SnapChat, Twitter, YouTube, and almost all of the nearly 200 sites in Wikipedia's "List of Social Networking Websites" did not exist.[2] Total e-commerce sales for 2001 were just one percent of total retail sales.[3] Amazon and eBay were emerging but quite small compared to today.

As of June 2001, there were 479 million Internet users in the world representing 7.9% of the population.[4] At the end of 2014, there were 3.1 billion users representing 42.4% of the world's population.[5] When I wrote *Net Attitude*, Internet use was in its infancy. Despite growing usage of Amazon and eBay, most websites were dysfunctional. You could "Click here to buy" and be presented with a page displaying, "Click here to download a form. Fill it out and fax it to us". Other sites had pages displaying, "Click here to get a list of retailers carrying our product". Slightly more advanced websites displayed, "Enter your zip code to get a list of the retailers nearest to you". Some "Click here to buy" links even displayed, "Please visit our retail location Monday to Friday between 9 AM and 5 PM". Such website messages are hard to imagine today, but many websites still are difficult to use.

Airline, hotel, and restaurant websites can facilitate your reservations, but often provide no way to copy the reservation to your smartphone calendar. Some websites provide a link to add the reservation to your Outlook calendar but don't seem to recognize millions of people use Apple, Yahoo, or Google calendars. Some airlines allow you to put the reservation on your device, but they create a continuous appointment starting from takeoff time and ending at landing time, like one big meeting. These sites provide the confirmation code but not the airline name or flight number. They apparently think you only use their airline.

Most webpages accepting input from a user have data fields such as name, address, phone number, and dates. If you enter 203-648-9026, an error message may tell you dashes are not allowed. If you enter 2036489026 at another site, you may get an error message telling you dashes are required. Likewise, the same thing would happen with dates, social security numbers, and account numbers. These frustrations are not caused by unavailability of technology. If the website database needs dashes, technology can easily add the dashes in an intelligent manner. Similarly, if the database does not allow dashes, technology can remove them. The lack of such solutions is not a technical problem. All it takes is an attitude which gives high priority to the user experience, a net attitude.

A net attitude is a different way of thinking. It involves moving out a bit closer to the edge – where things are somewhat uncertain; where you don't have the control you would like to have, but where innovation is happening continuously. On the edge is not a place to live, but a place to visit often to get a sample of the culture integral to a net attitude. In today's world of rapidly evolving technology, it is essential to get and maintain a net attitude. All of us need it more than ever.

Many of the 2001 user interface challenges still exist in websites today, 14 years later. The premise behind my book, *Net Attitude*, was usability problems were not technical, they were attitudinal. I described the Internet as being about "Power to the People". A net attitude advocated an outside-in point of view as opposed to an inside-out point of view. The people, I wrote, are out there and website developers need to walk in their shoes. Many websites of multi-billion-dollar organizations had websites built for them, not for the users.

Another example of not adopting a net attitude is the following. When you click to get more information on a site, you are presented with a form requiring your contact information and often much more – almost like a survey. The form does not include an email address and doesn't copy yours. In other words, the priority of the site is to get information, not to give information. Some websites of major companies have, "Chat with us". You click and are asked to enter information such as your name, account number, email address. You are then required to enter a description of your problem or the reason for your request for the chat session. Then, the site responds, "Thank you for your inquiry. We will get back to you in 2-3 business days". This is a chat without net attitude. And, what is a business day? Amazon and the U.S. Postal Service deliver packages on Sunday. A net attitude recognizes e-business is global, nine to five is meaningless, and every day is a business day.

In 2001, I perceived a significant void – a need to help organizations of all types learn the culture of net attitude, how to develop it, and maintain it. Fourteen years later, the need is as great as ever. In 2001, I said we were just two percent of the way along the journey to a net attitude which could simplify our lives and make things easier. As of summer 2015, I would say we are only at 10-15%. Some sites are quite advanced, but many, especially in healthcare, are at a very early stage.

The original book, *Net Attitude: What It Is, How to Get It, and Why Your Company Can't Survive Without It*, had 14 chapters. *Net Attitude: What it is, How to Get it, and Why it is More Important Than Ever* presents those same chapters, each prefaced with a short synopsis. I summarize what I thought in 2001, where I was right and where my predictions may have missed the mark. While technology has changed dramatically in 14 years, reading *Net Attitude* will likely convince you the philosophy of net attitude is needed more than ever. *Net Attitude* also provides numerous lessons from stories about the early development of the web.

All businesses have websites and a social media presence. The ones with a strong net attitude are successful and growing. The goals of *Net Attitude: What It Is, How To Get It, And Why It Is More Important Than Ever* are to share the 2001 perspective, provide the keys to developing a net attitude, and provide ideas on how to build an organization that achieves unparalleled results.

2001 Preface

In late 1993, while I was part of the IBM corporate planning department, I began to experiment with the Internet. I heard that a group of engineers in the company had built a "gateway" that enabled access to the Net using an office PC. I got connected and became captivated by the "gopher", a program that allowed you to browse through files in computers outside of IBM that were also connected to the Internet. Most of these computers were at universities and government laboratories. Being able to type the "dir" command on your PC and see what directories (folders) and files were on your PC was no big deal but to be able to do that on a computer thousands of miles away was amazing to me. A few months later I installed a program called Mosaic that enable me to see the world wide web for the first time; not just seeing the files on another computer but seeing colorful and graphical documents that had links in them that allowed you to click and "hyperlink" to a document in another computer somewhere thousands of miles away It is hard to describe how amazing this was. I got very excited about it. I saw it as revolutionary; something that would change everything forever. I had been using online banking and proprietary online services since sometime in the 1980s and I saw the web as something that everyone would use instead.

Then along came Dave Grossman, a young IBM computer scientist at Cornell University's Theory Center, who was part of a team helping the university to exploit their IBM supercomputer. The web intrigued Grossman also and he was following its development intensively. One day during the Lillehammer Winter Olympic Games he discovered that Sun Microsystems was creating webpages showing game results on webpages. The data came from systems that IBM was maintaining as part of its sponsorship of the Games! Grossman found out that

Irving Wladawsky-Berger, then head of IBM's supercomputer business, Abby Kohnstamm, new head of marketing, and I, among others were engaged in a corporate strategy review in Armonk. He further found out that an IBM Research team had setup a high-speed connection to the Internet in the same building where the meeting was being held. He drove to Armonk from Cornell, hooked up a large computer display, and gave all of us a demonstration of the web. It was an eye opener.

I couldn't spend enough time with Dave, learning more about the web. The more I learned, the more excited I got. While many people saw the web as entertaining, Dave saw it as making data universally accessible through the browser. He convinced me that this would turn the world upside down – that the web was going to redefine information technology. I soon found there was an underground community of engineers and scientists in IBM engaged in many product and research efforts based on the Internet. Together we formed a grass roots effort and launched ibm.com in May 1994. In June two of my colleagues, Jerry Waldbaum and Jane Harper, and I went to Internet World in San Jose, California. Most of technology demonstrations were from little known companies. IBM, Microsoft, Oracle and other major companies had nothing to show. I met Alan Meckler, then chairman of Mecklermedia, who had organized the event and with Jane and Jerry's urging, I signed up for the largest booth Alan had for the next Internet World conference to be held in Washington, D.C. that coming December, 1994. Alan invited me to give a talk during a breakout session at the conference and I shared my enthusiasm for "The Future of the Internet" publicly for the first time. That became my theme for the next six years as I gave dozens of keynote speeches around the world.

After my talk in December 1994 a lot of people called and wrote and emailed asking for copies of my presentation so I decided to build a website to share my views. Over 150,000 visitors have since stopped by at ibm.com/patrick and asked questions, offered suggestions, or simply said thanks for sharing. I was inspired by these visitors and their messages and each time I received an email I said to myself, one of these days I am going to write a book. I thought it would be a book about the many personal experiences I had with my website, the people who visited, and the things they said, but over the years I came to realize the tremendous impact that the Internet was going to have on our business and personal lives. I also began to see that the technology would be tremendously important but that there was an attitude factor that would be at least as important. In the early days I got the attitude from Dave Grossman and David Singer and other colleagues but as time went on I began to develop a lot of the attitude on my own. I began to witness, first hand, the differences between organizations that seemed to have this net attitude and those that didn't. I hope that this book will help more organizations get a net attitude so they can be highly successful (at whatever they do) on the Internet.

Foreword

By Stewart Alsop

I was right! So was John Patrick. I re-read my foreword to his original book, written back in the dinosaur days of 2001, after the Internet Bubble burst and before the economy collapsed and before the demand economy arrived, leading to multi-billion dollar private valuations for new-age companies. His thesis was you have to have attitude about how the Internet can be used in order to use it well and effectively. It turns out he was right. And my foreword still stands pretty good, 14 years after publication. So I asked John to let it stand. I hope you agree.

Tude. Attitude. Attitude is everything! At some level, I believe, attitude is everything anywhere in life. But, for sure, attitude is everything when it comes to the Internet. And that's what this book is about. Internet Attitude.

I've known John Patrick for a long time, since before the Internet came along, back when he was just an IBM executive. I remember that even back then he was good at "business development" -- that meant he got out of the office and talked to other people including both customers and people who worked for other computer companies. Perhaps because he was a good schmooze artist and a smart guy, he saw the possibilities of the Internet early on. (If he hasn't told you somewhere else in the book, go visit his website at IBM: http://www.ibm.com/patrick, where you can find out a lot more.) Anyway legend has it that he got involved in the Internet so early that he ended up having the IBM webserver under his desk. He was among the prime movers inside IBM who recognized that the company should be visibly involved with the Internet and evangelized the use of the Internet to the rest of the company. IBM, of course, had been involved in the development of the Internet itself, mostly in its research labs. But its research labs were often isolated from the mainstream of the company's real business: serving customers. Patrick was the guy who got the Internet to become part of the company's business. (He ended up as Vice President of Internet Technology for the whole corporation.)

All of that was attitude. Patrick has a lot of it himself. Odd, since IBM wasn't always known as a place where people with a lot of attitude survive and prosper. But good for the company, because attitude is everything on the Internet. And totally appropriate to have a guy with a lot of attitude write a book about Internet Attitude.

Here's the attitude. The Internet changes everything. It changes the way business gets done with customers and between business partners and suppliers. It changes the way we live and enjoy our personal lives. It changes the way we get educated, manage our governments and public policies, entertain ourselves, produce creative stuff, everything. It changes everything.

My personal experience: I grew up in the magazine business, mostly as an editor. I love magazines. Magazines are toast in the Internet era, mainly because of attitude problems. People who publish and edit magazines think of magazine readers in terms of very large groups, demographic groups or psychographic groups or special interest groups. That magazines are toast is ironic because they were first medium that could be targeted. Before cable television, before radio networks, before any other medium, magazines figured out how to create a targeted environment that was designed for just sailors, for instance, instead of everyone who had a boat, regardless of whether it was a sailboat or a powerboat.

Now magazines are toast because there's a better way to target even more specific groups of people. There's even a way to target individuals as a group. In fact, it really isn't appropriate to think of "targeting" because the very notion is founded inside the context of large mass markets, one where marketers need to hone in to targets. But magazine people think targeting, and can't conceive of a different way of doing it. They just can't get their minds around the idea that you could write for one person at a time, or that computers could handle managing the interaction with an individual one at a time. They don't have the attitude.

To have the attitude, you have to embrace the Internet and all of the new abilities it gives you, even if they challenge the most fundamental principles you learned at home, in school, at work, or even on the street. Here are the few basic, immutable principles that I've been able to discern that are relevant to the Internet:

Personalization: The idea that you can target media to an individual is now embodied in the phrase "one to one marketing", popularized by consultants Don Peppers and Marth Rogers in a book by that name several years ago. Before that it was known as narrowcasting, as opposed to broadcasting. But it's not just media or marketing. On the Internet, the fundamental promise is that you can be the single most important entity whenever you are interacting with it. Computers can remember information about anyone. Computers can use that information to present only the most relevant data to any individual automatically. The networks that connect computers into the Internet can deliver that information to you wherever you happen to be. This is personalization: It is a still a very difficult thing to accomplish. The technology is still primitive. We haven't done very much personalization yet so we still don't really know how to do it. True personalization requires integration, which is the hardest thing of all to do with computers – to get various computer systems to cooperate even if they weren't designed to do so. You'll get example after example from Patrick as you read Internet Attitude about how personalization could work if we had the technology and knew how to apply it. It's just a matter of time – and attitude.

Interaction: Before computers came along and got hooked up to the Internet, media were static or passive. In other words, media people – writers, producers, editors, musicians, actors, etc. – made something that you consumed. A movie might involve several senses, but you got to consume it without talking back. The Internet is interactive. That means consumers can talk back. This is a very, very difficult part of the Internet Attitude for almost everyone to adopt. Whether you are a business person or a creative person or both, you've been trained to control your environment. Having everybody talk back to you all the time seems both overwhelming and chaotic and precisely the opposite of what you were trained to do.

For instance, one of the most central effects that the Internet has had in business is to give individuals the ability to look inside companies in a way they were never able to previously. So, when a company put up a site on the World Wide Web for the first time, the senior management had to decide who controlled the information about the company: was it the marketing department? Or customer service? Or sales? Or information technology, which traditionally controlled everything about computers? This led to internecine warfare inside a lot of companies because each department viewed it as crucial to their particular mission and didn't want to give up control to another department. Each had a legitimate need. Many companies still haven't resolved this conflict, haven't even understood that it gets resolved by understanding that the issue is interaction and that the customer has the right to interact. Have you tried looking up the email address for any real human being on any corporate website? In my experience, 90% of companies still won't tell you how to send an email to one of their executives. Companies act like they are scared of their customers. That's not Internet Attitude.

Real timeliness: The Internet happens in real time. This was a big challenge for my colleagues in the publishing business, where life is defined by how long it takes to produce and distribute your publication: daily newspapers, weekly or monthly magazines, or even books, which take at least a year. Unlike older media, there is no logistical reason – other than the time spent thinking about or creating the communication – for Internet communications to take time to produce and distribute. Real timeliness takes the concept of interactivity and cranks it up a notch. Not only does Internet Attitude call for letting customers look inside your company, but it sets an expectation that you will actually respond to customer communication right away, in real time. I bought a pair of shoes from Rockport.com and they didn't fit. I sent an email to the address shown on the Rockport.com website for authorizing returns. I never got a response. My wife took the shoes to the shipping store, so I got a credit on my credit card. But I'll never buy from Rockport.com again, since they don't apparently read or respond to email to an address they publish on their website. They should not have created a website unless they were prepared to respond to customers in real time. They don't have Internet Attitude.

The technology of the internet – computers and communications integrated and broadly available – can lead to threats as well as opportunity: invasion of privacy, widespread spamming, computer viruses. Part of Internet Attitude is to recognize that we are in a major transition as a society and to embrace the threats as equally as the opportunities, to understand that we will ultimately figure out how to handle the impact that the Internet will have on our society and not to run away from it or try to stop or slow down the change because of the threats.

Enough already. Patrick knows Internet Attitude. He's written a book about it. Read the book and get the attitude.

Table of Contents

Preface ··· ix
2001 Preface ·· xiii
Foreword ·· xvii
Table of Contents ··· xxi
Part One Rising Expectations ·· 1
  Chapter 1 We Haven't Seen Anything Yet ···················· 3
    2:30 And Counting ·· 5
    The Heart of the Problem ··································· 6
    Who Accommodates Whom? ································ 7
    Millions Of E-Businesses ···································· 8
    E-Backlash ··· 9
    The Next Generation of the Internet ······················ 11
    Next Generation Attitude ·································· 13
    Goals ·· 14
    What To Expect ··· 15
  Chapter 2 Power to the People ···························· 17
    We Are At The Very Beginning ····························· 19
    Customer Choice Is Power ································· 21
    The Intel Story ·· 22
    People Power In Midland, Malaysia, And Kosovo ··········· 23
    The Power To Vote ·· 24
    The People And Their Money ······························ 26
    Power To The People Happening Everywhere ·············· 27
    What Is Napster All About? ································· 27

Chapter 3 The Customer Is Always Right ·························· 33
   Systems That Don't Talk To Each Other ···················· 35
   Click Here To Send A Fax, Fill Out A Form, Or Get Our
   Phone Number And Hours ······························ 37
   Down For Maintenance·································· 41
   Guitars And Chickens ································· 42
   Listen Carefully; Our Menus Have Changed ·············· 43
   For Your Own Protection······························ 45
   Peanuts And Potato Chips······························ 46
   It Is Not All Gloom And Doom ························· 49
   And Now To The Future ······························· 51
Part Two The Next Generation of the Internet ··················· 53
   Chapter 4 Fast ·· 55
    The Packets Don't Care ······························ 56
    Adam Smith's Invisible Hand··························· 57
    So Who Is The Winner?································ 59
    From Wired To Wireless To Optical ···················· 60
    Where Does The Bottleneck Move To? ·················· 62
    So What Do We Do With The Speed? ·················· 63
   Chapter 5 Always On ·································· 67
   Chapter 6 Everywhere ································· 77
    AOL In Your Kitchen?································· 84
    Becoming Mainstream?································ 84
   Chapter 7 Natural ····································· 89
    It Isn't Just For Kids Anymore ························ 90
    Learning On-Line····································· 96
    Universities Go Online Too ···························· 97
    Sprechen Sie Deutsch································· 99
    An Agent At Your Service····························· 100
    Music Makes The World Go 'Round ··················· 101
    Radio Goes Digital Too ······························ 103
    Pictures Too! ······································· 104
    And of Course There Will Be Video ··················· 105
    Speech Says It All···································· 105

The Next Generation of Speech Recognition ···················· 106

Accessible To All ······································· 107

A Browser That Talks to You ····························· 108

Limitations In Today's Computing Interaction ················· 108

Convergence At Last·· 109

Chapter 8 Intelligent ······································ 113

A Bold New Standard·· 114

How Is Your Vocabulary? ···································· 115

Contracts Talking To Each Other···························· 116

Taking The High Road ······································ 116

E-Marketplaces Will Change How Business Is Conducted ········· 117

Portals for Our Every Need ································· 119

Specialized Portals··· 119

Community Portals – Hanging Out ·························· 120

Knowing What You Know ···································· 120

Content Isn't What It Used to Be··························· 121

Life Sciences – The Next Frontier··························· 123

Autonomic Computing·· 125

Chapter 9 Easy·· 129

Who Builds Websites, Anyway? ····························· 131

The High Priests Et Al······································ 132

Browsers Are Great For Browsing ··························· 134

Freedom from The Browser··································· 135

The Next Generation of E-Business·························· 137

The Early Days··· 137

The Web ··· 138

The Application Web·· 138

An Even Faster Evolution of E-Business ···················· 141

Penguin To The Rescue ····································· 142

Three Shifts ·· 143

Who Needs It?··· 143

The Community··· 144

Is It Real? ··· 145

The Ultimate Test ··· 146

Embedded Computing · 147
Making Things Easier · 148
Chapter 10 Trusted · 151
Privacy · 152
A World Where Everything Is Connected · · · · · · · · · · · · · · · · · · · 154
Privacy, Confidence, And Trust All Go Together · · · · · · · · · · · · · · · 154
The Cookie Monster · 155
Platform for Privacy Preferences · 156
Internet Security – The Glass Is Half Full Not Half Empty · · · · · · · · · · · 157
It's Not The Technology · 158
Who Are You – Really? · 159
Digital Ids to The Rescue · 160
Authentication (You Are Who You Say You Are) · · · · · · · · · · · · · · 163
Authorization (Who Can Do What) · 164
Confidentiality (Only The Intended Recipient
Can Read Your Messages) · 165
Integrity (You Both Know Nothing Got Changed) · · · · · · · · · · · · · · 165
Non-Repudiation (No One Can Deny
A Conversation Or Transaction) · 165
Back to The GE Wire Transfer · 166
Open Standards Need To Continue To Rule · · · · · · · · · · · · · · · · · 167
So Many Issues; So Little Time · 168
Part Three Attitudes for success · 169
Chapter 11 Getting an Attitude · 171
A New Vocabulary Is Needed · 172
Just Say NO to ALL CAPS · 174
Communicate, Communicate, And Communicate · · · · · · · · · · · · · 175
Staying Connected to The Real World · 177
"Outside-In" · 178
Name That Product · 179
The Call Centers We Love · 180
Groovin' With Peer-To-Peer · 180
Think Globally and Act Locally · 181
Chapter 12 Organizing to Get Things Done · · · · · · · · · · · · · · · · · · 185
The Skunk Works · 186
Small Teams With Maximum Freedom Of Action · · · · · · · · · · · · · 187

Impedance Matching ··························· 188
Fail and Fail Often ··························· 188
alphaWorks ··························· 189
We Are All in This Together ··························· 190
Planning Ad Nausea ··························· 191
Just Enough Is Good Enough ··························· 192
Avoid The One-Size-Fits-All Approach ··························· 192
Trial by Fire ··························· 193
Kasparov 1, Deep Blue 0, Website In The Ditch ··········· 194
Make Easy Things Easy! ··························· 196
Think Integration ··························· 196
Build On a Framework ··························· 198
Where Is The Leadership? ··························· 199
You Are Not Normal ··························· 200
Entrepreneurs Don't Know It Can't Be Done ··········· 201
Chapter 13 Get A Taste of The Culture ··············· 203
Dad, You Should Know More ··················· 204
What Is Normal? ··························· 206
Extreme Blue ··························· 206
Talk To The Kids ··························· 207
ThirdAgers ··························· 208
Chapter 14 What to Do Next ··················· 209
First and Foremost, Communicate, Communicate,
Communicate ··························· 209
Outside-In ··························· 211
Think Big but Start Simple and Grow Fast ··········· 212
Information Technology Infrastructure ··········· 213
Internet Culture ··························· 214
Epilogue ··························· 217
Acknowledgements ··························· 221
References (2001) ··························· 225
Notes (2016) ··························· 227
Index ··························· 229

Part One

Rising Expectations

Net Attitude describes a way of thinking which can help an organization take maximum advantage of the Internet's capabilities. If you have a net attitude, you can exceed the expectations of your customers or constituents. The challenge is people have continuously rising expectations. The bandwidth available today is 100 times what was available in 2001, but people want even more. The new Apple Watch has amazing capabilities not dreamed of in 2001, but people are already asking it to have additional functions. The first three chapters of Net Attitude discuss the nature of people's expectations and two key elements of an effective net attitude: "Power to The People" and "The Customer Is Always Right". Having a net attitude is as relevant and important today as it was in 2001.

CHAPTER 1

We Haven't Seen Anything Yet

The first chapter of Net Attitude described the need for the Internet. It opened with an example of my experience closing a financial transaction which almost was derailed because of a quagmire of paperwork and faxes. There were good technical reasons why the fax machine should be history by 2015, but unfortunately, the example describing an antiquated process for completing a simple real estate transaction still gets repeated everyday. As discussed in my 2014 book, Health Attitude,⁶ the only consistent way to transfer information from a patient folder from one physician to another physician is to fax it.

Doctors are buried in faxes – as many as 1,000 per month. Dr. P. J. Parmar, a family doctor, said, "Fax is a technology that should have disappeared along with beepers. Oh wait", he said, "Medicine is the only field that still uses beepers."⁷ Fax machines remain the lingua franca of healthcare.

Chapter 1 described the seven characteristics I identified as emerging in the Next Generation Internet: Fast, Always on, Everywhere, Natural, Intelligent, Easy, and Trusted. I no longer use the term "Next Generation Internet", but the seven characteristics continue as a useful framework for examining past, present, and future capabilities of the Internet.

*The focus of a net attitude then and now is on the customer. Net Attitude
helps you understand how to get connected to bring your constituencies to
you at the least cost and sustain the relationship. The social media tools
today dwarf what was available in 2001, but the communications philosophy remains the same. I said in Net Attitude that the only prerequisite for
reading the book is a strong desire to meet the rising expectations of people
growing up on the Web. This prerequisite is the same today.*

I t was a hot summer afternoon about 2:00 PM and I had a problem. I was at
590 Madison Avenue in a conference room on the ninth floor discussing the
future of the Internet with some IBM customers. I glanced at my watch and
realized that I had until 3:00 PM to wire some money to my attorney for a personal transaction. The money was in a money market fund at GE Capital. I called
there to see if they could get the funds wired before my deadline. The folks at GE
were very cordial and said it was no problem to wire money because I already had
standing instructions that could enable me to wire funds to my bank at any time.
I told them this transaction was not to my bank but rather to my attorney. In that
case, they said they would have to fax me a form to set up new instructions. I said
I had all the information and could give it to them over the phone. They insisted
they needed to fax me a form. I said that I could tell that the conversation was
being recorded and because they already asked me my social security number,
home address, mother's maiden name, date of birth that surely they knew that I
was who I said I was. I asked if I could just give them the information. "What is your
fax number?" was the only response I was going to get. 590 Madison Avenue is not
where my office is located. I was borrowing an office for this meeting in New York
City and I had no idea where the fax machine was let alone the fax machine number. So, I scurried around the ninth floor looking for a fax machine where I could
receive the form. I was fortunate to find a helpful administrative person who told
me which machine to use and he gave me the number. I called GE back and shortly
I had the form. I excused myself to the customers telling them I would be just a
few more minutes. Wishful thinking as it turned out. Filling out the required data
for my attorney was easy but filling out a form with my personal data that they
already had in their system was annoying. Then I got to the bottom of the form. It
was labeled "Signature Guarantee".

2:30 And Counting . . . .

A lump forms in my stomach and I am getting nervous. It is 2:30 and I have only until 3:00. Even though I knew what "Signature Guarantee" meant I had this naïve feeling that maybe I could talk GE out of it. After all, someone had already asked for my personal data on a recorded line and confirmed all my security information. I called to confirm what I feared. I would have to go to a bank and get my signature guaranteed. Horrors! A bank! Not my favorite place to visit. I called information and asked for the nearest Chase Manhattan Bank. The address I got was just a block away. Relief. I raced for the elevator and ran down the street. On the big glass door was posted a sign: "We have moved to a new location". I raced around the corner and down the street to the new location. Beginning to sweat. I went into the bank and got in line behind quite a few other people. At the head of the line was a person who was talking to the teller. Not sure what they were talking about but the teller was thumbing through a Rolodex! A Rolodex? Here we are in the new millennium and I am standing in an office of one of the largest banks in the world and the teller is using a Rolodex? This does not bode well for my signature guarantee much less for electronic signatures! Finally I got to the head of the line and made my simple request for a signature guarantee.

"That won't be possible" said the teller. "The branch manager is out to lunch". It is now 2:45. "You don't understand" I said, I need this in a hurry". "You don't understand" the teller said, "the branch manager is out to lunch". Now I am getting very nervous. "Get in the line to your far left and you will be first in line when she gets back". It must have been my lucky day for as soon as I got in the new line the branch manager returned. She looked at my driver's license and put the official bank stamp on my wire transfer request form. I rushed out the door back to 590 Madison Avenue, up the elevator to the ninth floor, back to the conference room sweating profusely to apologize to the customers again and tell them that for sure I will only be a few more minutes. I placed a jubilant call to GE Capital. It is 2:55. "One other thing, Mr. Patrick", as she explained that they would also need a fax of a Federal Express or Airborne shipping label to verify that I had purchased an overnight fare to send them my wire transfer request form. GE wanted to make one hundred percent sure that they were going to get a piece of paper with real ink on it. I said that was ridiculous and they said "maybe so but we won't wire the money until we see this additional fax". "Then you will wire the money?" I asked.

"Yes, as soon as we see that second fax". "How about if I don't actually send you the overnight package?" I asked. The woman explained that if I was dumb enough to purchase an overnight Federal Express shipping label and then not ship it that it would be my problem. I ran down the hall, got a blank (free) Airborne shipping label, filled it out, faxed it to GE Capital and then called them yet again. It is now 2:59. Still sweating. GE was happy and wired the money. I was exhausted. I threw the Airborne shipping label away. I figured if a wire transaction is this hard to do it should be next to impossible to undo. This fiasco was not e-business.

The story is not about GE. In fact GE is a model company in many ways and is making a rapid, focused and effective move to become a highly advanced Internet technology-enabled business from top to bottom. I am sure they will be success-ful. My sad tale of woe could have been through a similar experience at almost any financial services company in the world. Many would have been much more difficult.

The Heart of the Problem

Why couldn't my wire transaction have been a few mouse clicks on a web-page? Is it a technology problem? Definitely not. It would not be much more com-plex than clicking to buy a book or reserving a hotel room. Encryption technology and digital ID technology are available from numerous companies that could have secured the transaction. Is it a legal problem? Some would say so but if GE was willing to accept a fax then they have already agreed to accept an image of my signature. That same image could easily be created from my laptop or from a web server. No, the problem is not technical or legal; it is an attitude problem. Net Attitude – or lack thereof. Net Attitude is about preparing your organization, the people that are part of it, and all its systems and processes, to take advantage of everything the Internet has to offer. The Internet has changed not only how peo-ple communicate but also has changed their expectations of what is possible on-line and at the same time created a strong distaste for many of the old-fashioned business processes that exist today. Whether a consumer or a corporate purchas-ing agent, people's expectations for what an e-business should be able to do for them are expanding by the day. Currently, most websites don't even come close to meeting those expectations. In many cases people leave websites without buying anything or signing up for anything because they couldn't find what they wanted or the server crashed or they clicked for more information and were told, "Call us

Monday to Friday during our normal business hours of nine to five!" In some cases they are even told "Print out this form and fax it to us".

Who Accommodates Whom?

The issue starts with how you define e-business. Some would say an e-business is an electronic business where you can "click here to buy"; i.e. e-commerce. E-commerce is a key part of being an e-business but it is just one part. An e-business is an electronic business that reaches all constituencies of a business – not just those who want to buy something. It includes buyers, suppliers, stockholders, employees, business partners, the press and financial analysts who follow the company. An e-business not only reaches this broad constituency but it provides all transactions and interactions that any constituent may need. Buying something, selling something, getting a price, checking the status of an order, signing up for the local blood drive, changing employee healthcare benefit choices, listening to a quarterly analysts briefing, participating in an electronic meeting, or collaborating on a new product design in a virtual laboratory.

The bottom line is about Accommodation. Organizations of all kinds have a fundamental decision to make. Choice number one is to accommodate the Internet, but continue to do business the way they have been doing business. "Yes, we are really into the Internet. We have an e-commerce website." While "accommodating" the Internet, they tacitly embrace their old vocabularies, old attitudes, and old ways of doing business. Choice number two is to become an e-business and embrace the Internet as the *primary* relationship mechanism -- not an alternate mechanism -- with all constituencies; while accommodating the way they have been doing business until they are able to morph those old attitudes and processes into more Net based ones. Primary relationship mechanism. That is a very big commitment. It means that the Internet is not an alternate distribution mechanism or an additional channel for customer support or a supplementary approach for simulating a new product design collaboratively with engineers on another continent. It means the Internet is recognized as the new medium for all communications and is the primary way in which the organization relates to all of its constituencies. It doesn't mean it is the only way but it means that the strategies of the organization are all built around the Net. Customers will be judging organizations based on their on-line presence; they are already beginning to make decisions about whether or not to do business with companies based on their on-line experience with them, whether or not they have a physical presence. There isn't time for a six-month corporate task force to study this. Nor for multi-year business process reengineering projects. Consumers and business customers are getting impatient. They know what is possible and they expect it. Time is of the essence.

Millions Of E-Businesses

The next evolutionary stage of the Internet will allow for the creation of millions of new e-businesses. They will include consumers selling directly to other consumers -- consumer-to-consumer e-business or c-to-c. They will also include businesses that provide information and products to consumers -- business-to-consumer or b-to-c. They are often called e-tailers and their process e-tailing. The b-to-c e-businesses will be of all sizes. Very small businesses like the Italian jeweler in Verona, whose family has probably been making fountain pens for decades, who is now operating an e-business selling pens to buyers around the world. (They probably didn't do an IPO to bring their website public and their market cap is probably modest, but every single day they are selling fountain pens and likely making a handsome profit.) The handful of giant b-to-c companies, such as Amazon and eBay, will likely succeed but there will be a much larger number of e-businesses that are extensions to existing businesses. The extensions will give those existing companies new reach. They will all become global and, if they set the right price and have great customer service, they will be successful by any measure. E-tailing is very much alive and well around the world

While I am very optimistic about the future for these business-to-consumer e-businesses, the biggest part of e-business will be e-businesses that provide products and services to other e-businesses – business-to-business (b-to-b). However successful business-to-consumer e-business may become, business-to-business e-business is going to be five to ten times bigger. Meanwhile, behind the scenes there is something even more profound beginning to develop -- a vibrant, multidimensional agora, enabled by electronic connections that include consumers, public sector and industrial buyers, suppliers, designers, customer service representatives, and specialists of all kinds. They will all be participants in electronic marketplaces (e-marketplaces) that facilitate information sharing, standards creation, collaboration, and commercial transactions.

The e-marketplaces will be a form of trading hub and they will exist in every industry as the major players get together and form relationships. It won't just be the top X companies in an industry but perhaps will include geographic or even ethnic clustering of companies, forming their own e-marketplace as a way to share their buying power. They will expect other e-marketplaces to be responsive to their needs. E-marketplaces will become an important and fundamental aspect of most industries; some will become companies themselves and compete with others in the industry. Companies who are not part of an e-marketplace and who choose to stand by and watch the phenomena emerge may find themselves paying fees to an e-marketplace and being disadvantaged.

E-Backlash

During the last months of the year 2000 we began to see many failures of "Internet" companies. In fact, webmergers.com reported that at least 210 Internet companies folded in the year 2000. The Wall Street Journal ran a headline about the failure of a European e-tailer called boo.com that said, "Boo.com's Collapse Further Darkens E-Tailing Picture". The implication is gloom and doom. Actually, business failures are not a new thing. According to data from The American Bankruptcy Institute, there have been an average of more than 60,000 business bankruptcy filings in the U.S. per year since 1980. The failures have nothing to do with the Internet. Business failures are caused by not properly segmenting your market, not setting the right price, not having a great fulfillment system for whatever it is you deliver, or not having world class customer service. Those will be the factors that always separate the winners from the losers.

It surely isn't the Internet that caused the business failures. A business not using the Internet is like a business in the 1990's that didn't have a fax machine. The last months of 2000 and continuing into 2001 have seen an e-backlash not seen before with Internet startups laying off thousands, some closing up shop completely, and market capitalization of many dropping from hundreds of dollars per share to pennies. The layoff of twenty people, the acquisition, merger, or the restatement of goals by an Internet startup company makes front-page news. Some of the headlines make it sound as though there have never been any business failures before. If there weren't business failures we should really be alarmed because that would mean that perhaps not enough innovative ideas are being tried. The Internet provides a way to try business ideas at a much lower cost and with a much greater speed than has ever been possible before, so we should expect that not all the new ideas will turn out to be good ones.

We may see some existing "brick and mortar" companies fail too -- because they studied the Internet too long. Some may not be able to come to grips with the reach, the range, and the disruption to traditional business models made possible by the Internet. Some may not be able to face the gut-wrenching changes needed in their distribution channels or in the way they would have to provide customer service and support. In other cases it may be the decades long dependence on agents such as securities or insurance brokers, that became sacred. Some of the CEOs used to be such agents for their company and they may not be able to bear seeing their former colleagues be eliminated or redeployed.

The good news is that the bold (some of them too bold) ideas that got launched in the form of large numbers of Internet startup companies or "dot coms" have shown *all* companies the tremendous reach, range, and potential of the Internet. The result is that *existing* organizations of all kinds have gotten the wake-up call and have leapt to action. Some of the world's largest retailers, banks, airlines, and electric utility companies are becoming the pace setters. Many from the throng of people who left these established companies to join startups are now returning to their former employers and sharing what they learned out on the "frontier".

In late 2000 we saw a backlash with the business models and profitability of pure Internet companies. It may last awhile. In fact, it is possible that the Internet has so penetrated every business and institution that there may not be much room for a pure Internet company. Every company is, or should be, using the Internet in what they do. The original pure Internet companies were the pioneers and showed the way; hence the huge initial valuations in spite of no profits. But, once everyone else started following, and started to leverage the Internet, those same companies no longer looked so pioneering; they just looked like bad businesses with no profit. This is why the bubble burst. A close examination of the statistics will show that e-businesses are alive and well even though the pure Internet business segment may not be. Once everyone is using the Internet, you need a much better business model and a lot better execution to survive in the marketplace. Irving Wladawsky-Berger, co-chairman of the Presidential Information Technology Advisory Committee, says, "We are still in the early stages of the revolution, and much more needs to be done to make the technology highly usable and reliable. Somehow the high valuations caused people to forget how much more there is to be done."

The Next Generation of the Internet

The Internet we use today is undergoing a massive evolution -- bringing about far more change in the next few years than in the last ten. The Next Generation of the Internet, or NGi, will make today's Internet seem primitive! Many parts of the NGi are here already. Everyone doesn't have it yet but millions do. There is no arrival date but each day we get a step closer. Not only will the Next Generation Internet be orders of magnitude faster but it will also be Always on, Everywhere, Natural, Intelligent, Easy, and Trusted. The impact of these characteristics on organizations of all kinds will be dramatic. Many people expect or hope that the NGi is going to bring us incredible speed for surfing the web. Speed is in fact one of the characteristics of the NGi but all seven characteristics are profoundly important.

I abbreviate the Next Generation of the Internet as NGi for a reason. The capital letters of next generation are to signify that the focus is on what is coming next because it is so profound. The word Internet is generally capitalized to signify the collection and interconnection of many networks around the world into a single Internet. I use the small i in NGi to signify that the Internet will become such a natural part of our lives that we will take it for granted.

Fast: Adam Smith's invisible hand is at work on bandwidth (the speed of the Internet). Competition among cable, telecom, satellite, and other media to provide Internet access, as well as technology advancements will assure the rapid expansion in bandwidth. Using the NGi will be a dramatically different experience compared to using the Internet of today. High quality full-screen jitter-free video will enable experts to appear on video walls in hospitals and classrooms from thousands of miles away.

Always on: no more logging on; you will just be on. You don't log on to the power grid to use your toaster; you won't long on to the Internet to tap the vast resources that it offers. They will just be there. We will begin to think of the Internet as a powerful communications network that is not just for surfing the web, but since it will be Always on, we will use it to monitor real time data from weather stations, industrial processes, and even medical monitoring equipment attached to real people.

Everywhere: the Era of the PC as the center of the web is over. Mobile phones, kiosks, PDA's, pagers, and new wireless devices will enable the Internet to be everywhere; not just where our PC is. Digital signatures will enable us to wire money, transfer securities, and sign contracts electronically from wherever we are: at home, on a train, walking down the street, or from an airplane moving at 500 miles per hour. When we walk down the Champs-Elysees in Paris our mobile phone will vibrate and remind us that we are walking by a store that happens to have that rare wine we have been looking for.

Natural: envision a real-time multilingual intercom for customer service. Integrated telephony and voice recognition within webpages will enable us to ask a question of customer service in the language of our choice and have that question be routed to the most knowledgeable expert who will answer the question in their native language and then enable us to hear the answer in our own language. All forms of media, in fact our entire collection of pictures, sound, and movies, will be able to be carried around in our pocket

Intelligent: A new web standard called XML (extensible markup language) will add context to webpages that will enable people to find things and will enable application software programs to be seamlessly integrated with each other. Finding things on the web will no longer be an exercise in frustration. Instead of millions of matches, we will get a few relevant ones. A new design for computers called autonomic computing will enable systems and networks to become self-healing much like the human body.

Easy: A software system developed by a student in Finland, called Linux, is changing how computers will operate. From Beijing University to Taiwanese entrepreneurs, Linux is taking Asia and the rest of the world by storm. As more and more computers use Linux and more and more students come from school with Linux skills, it will make e-businesses much easier to build and maintain. A new approach to creating software applications, called "web services", will allow websites to do much more than "click here to buy". The result will be that websites will do much more for us and we will stand in fewer lines in the physical world and have to endure fewer telephone call centers that want to control us. Fulfillment models at our favorite retailer's website will result in the staple goods we need just showing up outside the garage door when we need them.

Trusted: Security is not going to be the biggest issue. Authentication is. Who is that web server you are dealing with? How do they know it is really you they are doing business with? The NGi will use Digital ID's so that we can have authentication; i.e. be able to establish that we are who we say we are and without having to go to a Notary or a bank. We will also know that websites we visit really are who they say they are. We will be able to send messages to friends and businesses that only they can read, be assured that no messages were changed, and allow our financial transactions on the web to stand up in a court of law. Once we establish who we are we will also be able to establish the level of privacy we would like to have.

The potential of the Internet is much greater than meets the eye. As the Internet evolves to the NGi, it will be so pervasive, reliable and transparent that we will take it for granted. It will be part of our life—like electricity or plumbing. We know that the Internet is already transforming business, education and entertainment. Even larger changes are coming as the Internet becomes more reliable and robust. Net Attitude will help you get comfortable with the seven characteristics of the NGi and allow you to start planning for how to take advantage of them.

Next Generation Attitude

To build a successful e-business requires insight about what the Next Generation Internet will make possible and an e-business strategy that is deeply embedded into the fabric, the culture, and all the operational systems of the company. Also required are a solid business plan, a robust technology plan, and in-house or outsourced human resources with all the latest skills. But even having all of these things at your disposal is not enough to build a successful e-business. In fact, all the technology and money on the planet won't enable you to meet people's expectations if you don't have the right attitude. It is essential to have a "next generation" attitude imbued in management at all levels of the organization --company, university, hospital or government – so they are prepared to think and act in new ways that meet the rising expectations of customers and constituencies.

Part of net attitude is looking to the future, following the Internet standards, and anticipating new technology -- but a bigger part of it emanates from the grass roots thinking that was part of the evolution of the Internet itself. It is a way of thinking that is extroverted in nature – very people-oriented. A net attitude is hard to describe but you will know it when you see it. Young people tend to have it but it is not really an age thing. An increasing number of seniors have it too. The masses of people in the middle layers of large organizations often don't have it. It is not that there is anything wrong with them as people; it is just that the bureaucracies of large organizations have shielded them from the new way of thinking and in some cases Darwinian instincts have caused them to bring up their own shields. A net attitude includes the ability to think globally but act locally, to think big but start simple, to think outside-in instead of inside-out, be able to accept "just enough is good enough", engage in "trial by fire", transform to a model of "sense and respond" instead of the traditional model of "plan, build, deliver". These new ways of thinking will all be discussed in more depth.

Goals

This book will give you the background and insight to enable you to adopt a net attitude. It provides the cultural insight that the author has gained from years of participation in the center of the evolution of the Internet. Net Attitude explains the new attitudes of your future customers. It provides commonsense examples and personal vignettes executives and managers can relate to. It explains the importance of talking to teenagers and seniors, the two segments of the population that "totally get it" even if the middle management layers in companies and universities and government agencies sometimes don't. It describes the role of the "Skunk works" and how to set one up in your organization without breaking too much glass. Bottom line, Net Attitude tries to help you think like an Internet startup while capitalizing on your existing strengths.

What To Expect

Net Attitude will provide you with a view of each of the seven emerging characteristics of the Next Generation Internet: Fast, Always on, Everywhere, Natural, Intelligent, Easy, and Trusted. Each of these characteristics is profound and *Net Attitude* provides the practical examples that will help you understand, apply and capitalize on the incredible capabilities that are just ahead. The focus of *Net Attitude* is the customer; be it a consumer or a corporate purchasing agent. *Net Attitude* tells you how to "get connected" in a way that will bring your constituencies to you at the least cost and form lasting relationships. *Net Attitude* focuses on the human and management aspects that are important to get an e-business started and links them to how the evolution of the Internet is changing the game. It will also help you get the right mindset for e-business. The only prerequisite for reading this book is a strong desire to meet the rising expectations of people growing up on the Web. The economies of the world are rapidly transforming to Internet digital economies causing a major shift of power from institutions to people. Think outside in. Outside is where the people are. They have the power. *Net Attitude* will help you walk in their shoes.

CHAPTER 2

Power to the People

I was passionate about the concept "Power to the People" in 2001 and remain passionate today. My vision on this topic was accurate. When Intel introduced its new Pentium computer chip in 1994 an error was discovered in how the chip performed certain kinds of arithmetic calculations. Intel covered up the facts. When someone learned the details and posted them online, Intel admitted the flaw and disclosed more details. The company subsequently had another product defect and immediately announced it publically. They adopted a net attitude. Most companies today know better than to hide issues from the public. I described in 2001 how "Power to the People" had an online influence in Midland, Pennsylvania, Malaysia, and Kosovo. I said as long as there is information available the Internet would provide a way to share it. It is so obvious today with social media, but the concept was not widely understood before I wrote about it

One area where my 2001 predictions were especially accurate was in the field of music. I predicted people would be willing to pay for a custom "play list" of their favorite music. I said the music industry could expand by offering more choices than it had previously. I said the music industry had the power to create brilliant new business models and marketing relationships and, if they did so, they could take the music industry to new levels. I said people would gladly pay for the value created. This forecast turned out to be true. Cable TV and Hollywood executives would be well served to read Net Attitude and the principles espoused about "Power to the People". They currently are facing exactly what the music industry faced in 2001.

In the original book, I mentioned future capabilities such as accident-avoid-ing cars, universal access to information and knowledge, entertainment on demand, learning on demand, telemedicine and geriatric robotics. I dis-cussed the latter two in detail in Health Attitude: Unraveling and Solving the Complexities of Healthcare.[8] The others have been manifested by the Google Car, BMW haptic feedback in the steering wheel, ubiquitous WiFi, voice search on mobile devices, Massive Open Online Courses (MOOCS), and Apple's Music service.

I acknowledged a dark side to "Power to the People" where the Internet allowed terrorists the potential to create "cyber wars" by unleashing crip-pling computer viruses and jamming military computer systems through electronic radio-frequency interference. I said this ability could poten-tially enable terrorists to disrupt anything that functions electronically. Unfortunately, this turned out to be true.

In some respects it seems like everything has happened, that everybody is con-nected, that we are almost finished with what is going on with the Internet and that nearly everyone is using it. The truth is we've only just begun. The number of people actually doing something on the Internet right this very second, as a per-centage of the world's population, rounds off to a very small number. There is almost nobody connected! Let's take a look at the numbers. By the time this book reaches your hands there may possibly be a half billion people using the Internet. If you as-sume that on average half of them are actually doing something at any point in time (while the other half is sleeping) then that would be two hundred fifty million peo-ple. The world's population is over six billion. The two hundred fifty million people would round off to about four percent. You might argue that for some segment of the world's population that is well educated and lives in a well-connected part of the world that the percentage of that segment using the Internet is very different than four percent. Lets take twenty something year old graduate students living in Palo Alto, California for example. Perhaps ninety percent or more of them are using the Internet. However, even for this demographic, if you look at what things that could be done on the Internet that they are actually able to do on the Internet, you find that it is a very small percentage.

We Are At The Very Beginning

According to Mike Nelson, former White House technology advisor, the Internet Revolution is less than 3 percent complete. No matter which metric you use, he says, it is clear that we are at the very beginning. Nelson's numbers follow....

1. Number of people using the Internet: 3-5% of the world's population
2. Amount of time people spend connected to the Internet: less than 3% for most normal people
3. Speed of the Internet connection being used by most people compared to what is available from new technologies such as cable modems: about 3%. In 3-5 years, broadband Internet connections one hundred time faster than today's dial-up connections will be commonplace and no more expensive than a telephone line is today.
4. Amount of data on the Internet compared to what will be there: tiny percentage. According to IBM Research, the amount of data stored on the Internet will increase a million-fold between 2001 and 2010, to millions of times the amount of information in the entire Library of Congress.
5. Number of computer applications on the Internet that people find very useful: hard to measure but likely a very small percentage.
6. Number of devices the average person has connected to the Internet compared to the number they will have within the next few years: about 3 percent. Today most people use 1-3 devices to access the Net, usually a PC or a cell phone. In the not too distant future, each of us might have 50 to 100 devices that somehow connect to the Internet.

Try your own math. What percentage of websites really meet your needs? For those websites that you really love, what percentage of the things that site could do for you is it actually doing for you? What percentage of the banner ads that you see are compelling and valuable enough to you to click on them? No matter how you look at it, we are the very early stage of the impact that the Internet will have on our business, professional, and personal lives.

In five to ten years we will likely see:

10 times as many people using the Internet

100 times as much speed when we use the Internet

1000 times as many devices connected to the Internet

1,000,000 times more data on the Internet

There are some related things going on that are at the beginning too. Every day we pick up a paper or magazine or surf our favorite website and we read about some aspect of the transformation from an economy to an e-conomy. In fact, many CEO's that I've talked to around the world say "John, I have heard e-nough about this. But the fact is we are at the very beginning of that evolution too. It is not a "new" economy but rather an incredible transformation of the existing one. It has just begun.

In the technology area, we are clearly at the beginning compared to where we are headed. The fundamental laws of physics have not been exhausted and continued rapid progress will be made in the size, functionality, and cost of all forms of electronic devices. Today's PC monitors display approximately a half million "pixels". Each one can display a combination of red, green, and blue colors and the human eye sees the whole screen as a single high quality image. Soon we won't think it is so high quality anymore. IBM Corporation recently introduced a new display measuring twenty-two inches diagonally that displays nine million pixels. A picture shown on it looks like the quality of a magazine cover. Doctors will be able to detect the smallest of imperfections in an x-ray or mammogram using these displays. Continued dramatic increases in the capacity of magnetic storage devices will make it possible to have these high quality images on personal computers and the high speed networks that are emerging will make it possible to transfer the images as easily as we send emails today. The functionality and power of handheld devices will soon approach what were recently considered to be very powerful computers. The story goes on. Everything will be smaller, faster, cheaper and larger in capacity.

Wires and cables connect today's world of computers. Starting with the wires and cables surrounding our PC at home to the briefcase or backpack full of cables we carry with us to the Internet itself there are wires and cables everywhere. That is changing. A new technology called Bluetooth will soon allow devices that are within roughly twenty-five feet of each other to recognize each other and transfer data back and forth using radio signals. No wires. Walk in the house with your notebook computer and music you downloaded from the Internet automatically gets transferred to your home digital sound system. Wireless Internet antennas will soon be built into the case of notebook computers and "connectivity" will be available to you in virtually all hotels, airports, train stations, and public areas.

Changes are also happening in the software arena. A new form of computer software is beginning to change the way computers will be programmed and who will write the programs. The best example of this is Linux, software written by a young Scandinavian student, which will have a dramatic impact in the years ahead. For software, like hardware, we haven't seen anything yet compared to what we are going to see.

If you look further out, say fifty years, the possibilities are mind-boggling. Raj Reddy, a professor at Carnegie Mellon University in Pittsburgh, discussed the impact of infinite memory and bandwidth at a presentation in late 2000. He talked about capabilities such as accident-avoiding cars, universal access to information and knowledge, entertainment on demand, learning on demand, telemedicine and geriatric robotics. He even discussed more esoteric capabilities such as teleportation ("Beam Me up Scotty"), time travel and immortality becoming possible. Obviously these raise a number of social and ethical questions. Professor Reddy says that as we find ways to transform *atoms to bits*, that is, substitute information for space, time and matter, that many of the constants of our universe "will assume a new meaning and will change the way we live, work and govern ourselves. Some of us will have superhuman capabilities, like getting a month's worth of work done in a day."

Customer Choice Is Power

What does the incredible rush of new technology mean for us as people? In many ways the Internet is about the massive transfer of power from institutions to people. I am not talking about anarchy, people marching in the streets, or

Tiananmen Square in any way. I am talking about the empowerment of people who now have the ability to click a mouse button or mobile phone button or PDA button to express their desire to engage in entertainment, e-commerce or education or to communicate and collaborate globally. It is the power of a click. Many organizations are missing the point that they no longer have the power they once had, that the simplicity and the ease of a click make it easier for customers to simply click somewhere else.

Recently, one of the major stock exchanges announced that they were going to hold a meeting at which they would take a vote on whether or not to extend the hours of the day during which people can trade securities. Meanwhile, every computer in the world is virtually connected to every other computer in the world in a real time global network with many millions of users. How can there be any doubt that it is imminent that people will be able to trade stocks whenever they want?

After hours markets are starting to spring up and new forms of trading are being introduced on the Internet. In a highly connected world does it make sense that if you are in Europe or Asia and your stockbroker is sleeping in America that you can't trade any securities? The Internet makes it possible and many trading systems are online and have proven themselves over the past few years. Why can't the trading be done anywhere, by anyone, at any time? Rules. Rules set in a world where the power has been concentrated in large organizations. A small group of people on a board in New York City think they have the power to decide what their customers can do and when they can do it. If the rules don't change then people will switch to another exchange or financial services provider, or a new competitor will arise that will deliver what the people want when they want it. There is no stopping it. "Power to the People".

This is just one of the many examples of where organizations will soon realize that that they have lost power. From a people perspective, it used to be that you couldn't have much of an impact individually. You had to rely on politicians or lobbying organizations to influence a large company, a government or a movement. The Internet changed that. There are many examples of where individuals using the Internet have been able to have a dramatic impact in helping change the rules.

The Intel Story

When Intel introduced its new Pentium computer chip in 1994 an error was discovered in how the chip performed certain kinds of arithmetic calculations. It had to do with how the chip converted "floating point" numbers (e.g. 123.876423) for use in certain calculations. The result was that the Pentium chip made a math error on certain calculations. Most people would never see the error and in fact some engineers said that the error would likely occur only once every 27,000 years. However, the company was less than forthcoming about the problem -- they reasoned that not many people would be affected since the problem occurred so rarely and only during sophisticated number crunching,

Reports began to appear on the web and Internet newsgroups began to alert people about the math bug. Intel seemed indifferent, and did not come forth quickly with any plans to recall the chips. The flood of negative reaction from customers, who voiced their dissatisfaction via the Internet, quickly changed Intel's mind. In fact, the dissemination of information and open discussions of the problem on the Internet changed Intel's course of action; they apologized to their customers, and spent a lot of money to fix the problem. Adam Mayers of the Toronto Star wrote a column called "People power rules in Intel's hard, expensive lesson". He said, "Among the many outcomes is to affirm a power many people think they've lost." Intel's humbling was about people power, the power of individuals, not lobby groups."

In the year 2000 Intel began shipments of its Pentium 4 chip. Personal computer makers received an improper piece of software for use with the new chip. None of the Pentium 4 chips with the incorrect software reached consumers and arguably the error was inconsequential. But being sensitive to their previous experience with the Internet and knowing the incredible power of the people, Intel was quick to make a full disclosure of what had happened. Lesson learned! Net Attitude adopted!

People Power In Midland, Malaysia, And Kosovo

When the financially distressed district of Midland, Pennsylvania was forced to close its high school, local people took control and created a cyber school. Students are learning and taking tests over the Internet. Each student is assigned to a cyber school staff member who keeps track of the student's progress and grades his or her exams over the Internet. As parents in many parts of America consider creation of "charter" schools based on local priorities, the Internet becomes an incredibly powerful tool to implement their vision.

Many countries around the world have strict rules over the publishing of content. For example, in Malaysia, newspapers and broadcasters have to abide by the prohibitive interpretations of the law of defamation, or they risk having their licenses forfeited. But the Malaysian Prime Minister pledged to have no censorship on the Internet in order to make Malaysia the center of the cyber world. As a result, the Internet is providing a channel for the people to voice their views without having to fear punishment.

In 1999 there was considerable strife in Kosovo. Part of the strategy by the government was to control information so that the people would not know exactly what was going on. Journalists were expelled from the country. The independent radio station, B92, in Belgrade was closed down. Local media was either shut down or censored. But the radio station set up a website and began to publish text, audio and video. They reported when air raid sirens were going off. Up to the minute news was provided to the population. There was no way to shut down the Internet site because the government didn't know where the server was. If they had known and shut it down another server could have been put back online. As long as there is information the Internet provides a way to share it. "Power to the People".

The Power To Vote

The Year 2000 presidential election in America shows the potential, if not the need, to enable "Power to the People" via the Internet. In prior years there was considerable online campaigning and online fundraising. This has been supplemented with discussions about the elections being exchanged in chat rooms and e-mails. There were even "vote-swapping" sites which enabled supporters of Ralph Nader in battleground states to agree to vote for Al Gore in exchange for a Nader vote in another state! The practice was upheld in the courts. The Net allowed people to participate in new and interesting ways providing them information when they wanted it and how they wanted it. This included early exit-poll data that has traditionally only been available to the media elite. The Pew Research Center for the People and the Press and the Pew Internet and American Life Project, in a report released in December 2000, said that four times as many Americans used the Internet to keep up with political news during the 2000 presidential race as did in 1996, and almost half of those voters said the information they found online affected their choice of candidates. The logical extension of this is to utilize the new medium (the Internet) for the actual vote.

It is certainly possible to envision online voting becoming a reality in the near future. People expect that they are casting a vote for the candidate they want and that their vote will be accurately counted. Although recounts should not be needed in an electronic election, if needed they will be done in seconds not weeks. The issues will not be technical. There is no question that electronic kiosks could do the job. For those not able to go to a kiosk the Internet can provide the security and privacy that people expect. Strong encryption and digital ID's far surpass the integrity of the manual methods of today that include the subjective counting and recounting we saw during the 2000 election in Florida.

How would this work? One example is that Voters might have their signature matched with a voter registration card and then receive a PIN that would activate their digital signature. This would enable voters to cast their vote online. Hopefully, electronic voting standards will evolve soon to allow for consistency that people will trust. America's experience with the year 2000 election is already spurring this to happen sooner rather than later.

The more difficult questions will be whether the political leaders of the country can agree on a national set of standards for how the votes will be counted and recounted if necessary. There will be many debates about the cost of building a national online election approach. It will not be inexpensive. But, how much did it cost for the legions of lawyers and weeks of delay that we witnessed in Florida? Clear presentation of the ballot will be critical. A confusing e-commerce shopping cart is one thing but the electronic equivalent of the Florida "butterfly" ballot is another. Surely, a clear way to display ballots can be devised which people could trust.

We won't have to wait long to see things unfold. Companies such as election.com and votehere.net are already conducting electronic elections. The early implementations have been for voting by corporate shareholders, unions, and large organizations of all kinds. The Sierra Club, the Boeing union, and Cornell University have already used online elections. The International Corporation for the Assignment of Names and Numbers (ICANN) is a global non-profit organization that provides certain administrative controls over the operation of the Internet. In 2000 they practiced what they preach by using a very sophisticated Internet election to establish the "at large" directors for the board. People voted from all over the world.

The People And Their Money

Perhaps one of the best examples of people gaining new power from the Internet is in the financial services sector. In effect the Net has allowed people to eliminate the middleman. No longer is investment a "hidden art" that takes place beyond the view of average investors. People get timely and relevant information about their investments -- and the actual trading process -- rather than relying on "tips" from brokers who may have a financial interest in the stocks they tout to their customers. The Internet has led to the emancipation of the individual investor and leveled the playing field for all. A new U.K. company called The Investors Noticeboard is planning to connect individual buyers and sellers of shares directly on the Net, eliminating the broker completely!

Shopping for cars has seen power returned to the people. Buying a car from a dealer can be a very unpleasant and uncomfortable experience for many people. When being told about the "dealer cost" they often wonder if they are getting the complete story. Or they sometimes feel pressured to buy options, services or financing they don't really understand or want. Now, because of the web, things have changed. People can get access to complete information. They can make comparisons at home while under no pressure. They can buy directly from a manufacturer, from a car buying service, from a dealer, or buy their car at an online auction. Instead of feeling powerless in the showroom many people now feel empowered. Since many dealers make much of their profit from their service operations they are more than happy to provide the buyer with after the sale service and support.

Nicholas Negroponte at MIT told a story during the early days of the Net that really makes the point. He described a woman who was looking for a very specific model black Volvo. She went to a dealer and got a price. Then she went to the Net and did some research and then went back to the dealer. The dealer assured her that she had the best price possible. Then she posted the details about the car and the price she had obtained in a discussion forum and asked if anyone else would be interested in the same exact car at the price she had negotiated. Then, according to Nicholas's story, she went back to the dealer. "Are you sure that is the best price you can give me?". "Yes madam it is", said the dealer. "Well, there is one other piece of information I neglected to give you", said the woman, "I would like to buy ten of them." Story has it that she got a better price. So, who had the Power? The car manufacturer? The dealer? Or, the woman buyer?

Power To The People Happening Everywhere

The emergence of eBay and other auction sites is yet another form of people getting more control because of the Net. It started out as the world's biggest garage sale but has evolved into enabling proprietorships of one person each. It is a form of "Power to the People". Job searches are much more in the hands of individuals now than ever before. Direct access to all of a company's current job listings, plus recruiting services and employment marketplaces are enabling people to take their careers into their own hands instead of waiting for their manager to promote them. Before the Net companies would make an announcement about some new corporate policy or health care offering and then say, "For information, see your manager". Those days are gone. People don't need to ask someone else. They take the matter into their own hands, go to the company intranet, and become informed to the degree they choose.

What Is Napster All About?

Perhaps the biggest shift with regard to "Power to the People" since the Internet itself is a new kind of technology called "Peer to Peer" (P2P). When Sean Fanning, the nineteen-year-old wiz kid who created Napster, appeared on the cover of Time Magazine, it was clear that something big was happening. On the surface it appears that Napster is a tool for getting digital music over the Internet without paying for it. The reality is much deeper.

"Peer to Peer" in not a new idea. The Internet has always enabled one computer to communicate directly with any other computer but not typically as equal participants or "peers". The preponderance of communications on the Internet is more of a "client – server" model. The servers tend to be powerful computers with very large storage capacity. The "clients" are mostly PC's (although that is changing fast – more on that later). The client goes to the server and requests information. You click on a link at your PC and a webpage gets downloaded from the server to your PC. P2P is a different model. With P2P I connect directly to your PC over the Internet or you go directly to my PC and we exchange information. Napster is a program that was written to facilitate P2P. A user can go to a central directory at a server on the Internet and find out that a certain webpage or document or music file is on someone else's PC and that person is making it available to anyone who wants it. The user can then connect directly to the other person's PC and download the file. Another P2P program, Gnutella, has no central directory on a server and instead allows you to search for a file you are looking for across the whole Internet and then download it from a person's PC that has it.

P2P is empowering to people for the same reason that carsdirect.com or eTrade are. It takes out the middleman. Although, with P2P there doesn't need to be a server, servers will continue to play many roles and they certainly are not going to go away. In fact with the growing number of users and content on the Web, e-businesses are requiring more and more powerful and scalable servers than ever (the ability to scale means that these servers can ramp up their processing power when they need it). At the same time, however, PC's are getting very powerful and very large in storage capacity. Today's PC are one hundred times more powerful and have one thousand times more storage than they had less than twenty years ago. This expanded capability plus the advent of very fast Internet connections now being offered by telephone and cable companies means that large amounts of information can be stored, searched, and distributed directly from PC to PC. This is a new and important model. It won't replace the existing model but it represents a big complement to it. Over time its significance will grow and people will be increasingly empowered.

Now, back to Napster. One of the types of files that can be shared from PC to PC over the Internet is an MP3 file. It is a form of digital music. What is digital music? It starts with analog music. When you go to Alice Tully Hall in New York to hear a string quartet you are listening to analog music. If you want to listen to it later at home you need to have a way to capture it, store it, and replay it. In the "old" days this was done with vinyl records and later with acetate tape. Today it is mostly done with CDs (compact discs) but increasingly music will be stored in the form of computer files such as MP3.

Analog music is captured with recording equipment and then placed on the CD in CD-DA or digital audio format. This is done by electronically sampling the sound 44.1 thousand times per second and capturing two characters (bytes) of information about the characteristics of that second. That results in 88.2K bytes of data for a second of music. Multiply X2 for stereo and you have 176.4K bytes of data per second. Multiply X60 and you get 10.584 megabytes per minute of music. A CD holds about 660 megabytes of data so that gives you approximately 62 minutes of music. OK, so what is MP3? There is a group of experts (from IBM and other companies) called the "moving pictures experts group" which created a standard called MPEG. MPEG has various "layers" which specify how audio or video can be compressed. Compression removes bits from the sampling process that are not essential or even recognized by the human ear. A brief pause in a song, for example, can be eliminated or compressed and then decompressed later when it is played. The result of compression is that a much smaller amount of data needs to be stored. MPEG layer 3 describes a particular standard for achieving high quality sound with compression. It results in a compression ratio of roughly eleven. In other words with MP3 you can store roughly 11 hours of music on a CD. It also means that CD music can be stored on a PC in about one eleventh of the space required if it were not compressed. It further means that now that it is compressed it has become practical to send it over the Internet in a reasonable amount of time. The result is that Napster, which was designed to share PC files, instantly became a very convenient way to share MP3 music files.

MP3 is changing how people think about digital music whether they are consumers, artists, producers, or broadcasters. The recording industry, understandably, has reacted very negatively toward Napster and other music sharing programs on the Internet. They view it as stealing and have been aggressively trying to shut down websites they view as contributing to theft in any way.

Other people say that intellectual property "wants to be free". There certainly is an argument that artists may choose to give away their music over the Internet, generate a lot of interest in it, and then charge $100 per ticket for their concerts. That is a valid model but not the only model. If an artist or music company wants to protect their music they should be able to do that too. IBM recently introduced a "watermarking" technology that enables music to be encoded with a digital "watermark" that identifies the owner of the music. Attempts to copy or distribute the music without proper payment are next to impossible. But the real issue isn't just whether and how to protect the music. The real issue is the evolution of new business models for the distribution of music. Napster has caused a lot more visibility of this issue.

People are not fundamentally dishonest. There are exceptions of course but most things in the world get bought not stolen. The Internet has provided a new distribution channel for music. Music is particularly well suited to digital distribution because it can be played immediately after being received in essentially its original fidelity. The PC can be easily connected to good quality speakers or even connected as an input to your stereo system just like a tape deck where the playback is as good or better than FM Stereo or original CDs. Some audiophiles claim they can tell the difference but most of us can't.

The distribution model has evolved from record to tape to CD but the business model of the music business has changed very little. I have a collection of Mozart CDs. Someone has decided how to package them. One CD has Symphonies 40 and 41. Another has String Quartets 17 and 19. Why can't I buy just the 40th Symphony and the 17th String Quartet? A rock star CD has ten songs on it. How about if I only want to buy two of those songs? If a CD costs $15 for 10 songs why can't I buy two songs for $3? With MP3 music a person can download more than ten hours of their favorite tracks of music and then use a CD "burner" to copy that music onto a CD. The CD the person created is now their personal selection of a favorite artist or maybe twenty artists.

Would people be willing to pay for a custom CD or a custom "play list" of their favorite music files? Is it possible the music industry could actually expand by offering more choices than have previously been available? How about a model where I get to download ten of my favorite tracks for free if I agree to send them to ten friends. Each friend receives an email from me with link in it. They click on the link are taken to a server that allows them to download the music. When they first try to play the music a small dialogue box appears on their PC that says "These selections were recommended by your friend John. Click here to enter your credit card number to purchase them. You will receive a ten percent discount if you agree to forward the invitation you received to ten of your friends". Yes, people have the power to steal music. But the music industry has the power to create brilliant new business models, subscription services, music tips, and marketing relationships and if they do so they can take the music industry to new levels and people will gladly pay for the value created.

Peer-to-peer is not just about music. A new company called Groove Networks was launched in 2000. They offer a free (for now) download of a PC program called Groove. It allows P2P communications and includes various tools to facilitate sharing. For example, the local soccer moms might set up a Groove "conversation space". Each soccer mom can see this space on her PC. When one mom posts a new soccer practice date or schedules a mom's meeting on the calendar, the information is distributed to all the other moms who can then see it on their PCs. The Adams Family might set up a family calendar. I set up a conversation space for collaboration on this book. My editors and other trusted advisors have secure access to the space to see any recent writing. There is also a space for discussion where comments and critiques were, and still are, shared. The "Power to the People" aspect comes as workgroups in companies find they can setup secure spaces to share discussions, files, presentations, calendars, and contact lists. Previously they may have wanted to set up some new collaborative area but may have found that they had to get approval from the corporate Information Systems department first. Central servers provide many valuable functions that will continue to be important but for some basic sharing tasks the P2P approach may become quite empowering.

"Power to the People" does not mean anarchy. It does not mean people marching in the streets. It does mean that people have the power to press a mouse button or a cell phone button and expect to be heard and have their expectations met. Corporations, universities, governments, and other large institutions have power too -- but they will lose it unless they use it to satisfy the rapidly expanding expectations of people. Institutions need to listen very hard to what people are saying and figure out what their needs and wants are. Those enlightened organizations that listen to the people will be greatly successful and those who don't will be imperiled if not extinct.

There is a dark side to "Power to the People". The Internet has allowed terrorists the potential to create "cyber wars" by unleashing crippling computer viruses and jamming military computer systems through electronic radio-frequency interference. This could potentially enable terrorists to disrupt anything that functions electronically. In light of this, the United States Army is actively participating in the creation of a strategy to protect against potential adversaries who might abuse their power on the Internet.

CHAPTER 3
The Customer Is Always Right

The third chapter was about a concept I learned from Stew Leonard, a grocer in Connecticut. A sign at the door of his stores says, "Rule #1, The Customer Is Always Right; Rule #2, If The Customer Is Ever Wrong, See Rule #1".[9] I explained how a net attitude can be expanded on the Internet using Mr. Leonard's concept. This chapter is replete with examples which can be applied across today's competitive landscape.

In 2001, I suggested call centers and the Internet should be integrated. "Click here" to get your problem solved and if that doesn't solve the problem, "Click here" to talk to someone. A number of companies have adopted the principle. Amazon is the most advanced in completely adopting the principle. Many other companies do not include a phone number anywhere on their site. Adoption of the customer is always right is a fundamental of net attitude and essential to be a winner in todays highly competitive markets.

While there are some notable exceptional websites, the bottom line is many businesses today are not meeting customer expectations. I described an initial burst of excitement about surfing the web in 1995. Over the next five years the Internet became faster, more reliable, and reached larger numbers of people. New Internet startups or "dot coms" emerged with some great ideas (but not always great business models). Companies in existence for a long time "web enabled" internal mainframe processes. E-commerce flourished. However, by the end of the millennium I believe many users of the Internet began to become disillusioned and frustrated. They couldn't find what they wanted or were let down when their expectations were on the rise.

Fast forward to today and expectations continue to rise. Banks, airlines, hotels, and healthcare providers are online but some are not exploiting the Internet to the degree they could. How does an organization address the widening gap between client's expectations and companies service delivery? The answer starts with a change in attitude.

As people have gained newfound power from the Internet their expectations haven increased significantly. They know the potential exists to greatly simplify their lives and they expect this to happen. Their patience will be short when it doesn't. How good of a job are companies, governments, universities, hospitals, and other institutions doing at meeting people's expectations? Unfortunately, I would have to say, on average, not very well at all. Although there are many reasons for optimism that the web can and will meet the rising expectations of people, at this stage most websites don't even come close.

Let's get specific. The American Customer Satisfaction Index for e-commerce companies was published in late 2000. It resulted from a quarterly survey conducted by the National Quality Research Center at the University of Michigan Business School, Ann Arbor, in partnership with the Milwaukee-based American Society for Quality and the CFI Group, an Ann Arbor management-consulting firm. The survey showed that consumers found large disparities in quality of service and, although there were some standout successes, many websites fell far behind in keeping their customers happy.

Patrick Barta of the Wall Street Journal reported that satisfaction levels are low enough "to cast doubt about many sites' ability to survive." He went on to say that American consumers "appear to be only marginally more satisfied with e-commerce sites than they are with the U.S. Postal Service." The index's director, Claes Fornell, says E-commerce "companies that don't provide a positive customer experience will get much less repeat business and therefore be forced out of the marketplace". It is generally accepted that getting a new customer is at least five times more costly than keeping an existing one. The survey showed that more than twenty five percent of consumers were not satisfied. The bright spot was Amazon.com, which had a satisfaction score of 84, the highest of any site. Even more alarming than the satisfaction score of this survey is how many people leave websites without completing the transaction at all because they couldn't find what they were looking for or the site did not work properly. In his January 2001 issue of the Release 1.0 newsletter, Kevin Werbach described a survey done by user-experience consultants Creative Good. The consultants ran a test with over 50 consumers on eight leading online retail sites. Forty-three percent of the purchasing attempts ended in failure, because the users literally couldn't figure out how to complete the transaction. The satisfaction, or lack thereof, also goes beyond the web. People who become dissatisfied with a particular brand on the web will translate their feelings to the "bricks and mortar" part of that brand. They will conclude that if the e-business part of a company doesn't know how to satisfy people then their company doesn't know how to satisfy people.

Systems That Don't Talk To Each Other

There are several categories where websites let people down. One of them has to do with integration of systems. Some recent personal experiences may serve to illustrate what this is about and why people are frustrated as a result. It was a Friday night when my wife and I decided to go to New York the following weekend for an impromptu opportunity that arose. I went to the website of a major hotel chain and checked my frequent guest points balance and looked for an award for a one-night stay. I have plenty of points and, sure enough, I found an award code for a one-night stay at a very nice property in New York City. I could have made an online reservation but a prior experience convinced me that they didn't have the process streamlined yet so I called the 800 number and asked the person if a room was available for that following Friday night. "Yes sir", she said, "I can confirm that for you". "Great" I said. "Is there anything else I can do for you, Mr. Patrick?" "Yes, I would like to pay for the room using Award code XYZ".

"Oh", she said, "I can't do that". I asked if I was talking to an answering service or the hotel chain itself. "This is the hotel chain", she said, "but this is the reservations department and I don't have access to any frequent guest data". I explained that I was looking at the coupon in my browser and asked if there wasn't some way she could help me use it. "Oh, no problem, Mr. Patrick", she said. "Just call us back on Monday morning". She went on to explain that I would need to call them by long distance, no 800 number, and that I could call anytime during *their* normal business hours of nine to five Monday through Friday. She said that when I called I could just simply give them my credit card number and for just $35 they would send me the coupon (which I was looking at in the browser!) via overnight express mail. Now is that a "stick in the eye" or what? The problem is lack of application integration. The frequent guest system and the reservations system don't talk to each other. They are applications that were likely built in different decades and which operate on different and incompatible computer systems. The examples abound.

I ordered three items from an on-line catalog at cdw.com. It was actually a good shopping experience. The FedEx shipping was a relative bargain at $5.49. The next day I received a phone message saying that one of the items I had ordered had been discontinued but that the other two items were shipped. This was quite disappointing since the discontinued item was the most important of the three things I ordered. I called the customer service department and asked why the website was offering an item that had been discontinued. Lack of real time inventory or out of stock conditions is one thing but offering discontinued items for sale seemed like a real process problem. "Oh", said the customer service representative, "our website is two to three months behind on updating for discontinued items. We are working on that". The result was I had to order a substitute item and pay additional shipping. Problem: no integration between the inventory system and the web e-commerce system.

Recently I went to the United Airlines website to accept a special offer. It was very smooth. A few clicks and I was finished. Then I got a message that said, "You have selected 10,000 Mileage Plus bonus miles. Your miles will be credited to your Mileage Plus® account in approximately 6 weeks. They are yours to use as you please. Thank you again for this opportunity to reward you for your exceptional loyalty. Six weeks? The web application that I interacted with probably can't talk to (is not integrated with) the application that updates the mileage credit. Ever land at an airport and the gate was not available for the plane to park? Happens to all of us. The Gate Scheduling System is not integrated with the Flight Arrival System.

I had been thinking about getting a cappuccino maker and a friend had one not in use that he offered to loan to me for a trial. The machine is called a Nespresso and is made by Nestle. It uses pre-packaged "capsule" of coffee. I stopped in a local gourmet cooking store that carries the Nespresso line and asked if I could buy some of the capsules of coffee. "Oh no", said the proprietor. "They can only be bought directly from the company. Didn't you fill out the form to register for the buying service?" I explained my situation and said I had no form. I was told to call the 800 number. I went home empty handed and rather than call, I decided to visit the website. I was in luck, or so I thought, because I quickly found a "click here to buy" area of the site. Upon landing at the buying page I was asked to enter my customer number. I have no customer number and could find no place on the site to get one. I was really determined to get these "capsules" so I broke down and called. The good news was that it was not 9-5 M-F and a real person answered and I didn't have to wade through a complex call center menu. The person was very cordial and explained that the only way I could get a customer number was to buy something from them by phone and then I would be sent a customer number in the mail!

Attitude problem: These problems are viewed as very complex with fixes that take a lot of time.

Net attitude: The long-term fix will take time but in the meantime applications can be enabled to send messages to each other behind the scenes and give the customer the effect of a completely integrated solution. Some technology investments will be involved but it is mostly an attitude of wanting to make systems talk to each other. Chapter 12 will describe how this is done.

Click Here To Send A Fax, Fill Out A Form, Or Get Our Phone Number And Hours

I went to the website of a California software company one Sunday afternoon and I was ready to buy some software they had for sale. In fact, I wanted it really badly and was ready to pay nearly any price. I clicked to buy and up came a form. No problem, Mr. Patrick. Step one; print this form. Step two; fill it out and fax it to us! This doesn't sound like e-business. Unfortunately, there are a large number of websites that say click here to buy and then present us with a screen of where to call or a form to be printed out and faxed. More recently I was looking for a very unique light bulb for an outdoor lamppost. I search around the web and discovered that I was not alone in having trouble finding unique light bulbs. My search turned up quite a few postings in the Philips Lighting Forum for Home Lighting. In reply to a customer asking for the same bulb I was looking for, the folks at Philips posted a reply which said "Please call 800 555 0050 for the nearest distributor in your area."

Many websites say they have information about their products and services available but when you click to see it, up comes a webpage form which you are asked to fill out and send to the company so they can mail you a copy of the instruction manual or other information that you are requesting. In other cases you can't even get the information through the website at all. I bought a new Motorola mobile phone in Australia during the Sydney Games. I was really pleased with it but had a question about how some particular feature worked. I went to the Motorola site and looked around. I found a link to exactly what I wanted to know. When I clicked it I got, "Motorola can assist you in matching one of its newer phones with your existing service plan. Please follow these easy steps: have the name of your service provider handy; call 1-888-647-9988 (Mon.-Fri., 7:00a.m. – 7:00p.m. CST). Motorola's customer service representative can help you select a phone that is supported by your service provider and discuss the options available to you."

Contrast this with a visit to the State of Connecticut Department of Motor Vehicles. I was looking for a particular manual and to my delight I found the following on the webpage: "The DMV provides driver's manuals with all the graphics and illustrations featured in the print edition. These versions are in portable document format (pdf) and must be viewed and printed through Adobe Acrobat. The software is available free from Adobe. To get a free copy of the software, click the "Get Acrobat" image below." Adobe's portable document format (pdf) is a de facto publishing standard that can be used to create any kind of printed materials. Adobe Acrobat is free software program that enables a person to read the pdf file. A pdf file can be printed out and it looks exactly like the "real" thing; complete with all the graphics, formatting, and fonts that you would see in printed materials. The United States Internal Revenue Service was one of the first to use pdf files on the Internet. They offer virtually all IRS forms and booklets that way. Radio Shack offers owner's manuals for nearly all their products as pdf files. Unfortunately, The Connecticut DMV, IRS, and Radio Shack examples are in the minority.

Fax machines arose to ubiquity for two reasons: the information technology industry had no standard for the exchange of documents and the Internet had not yet become ubiquitous. Much of the use of fax machines today is due to habits. Document formats such as Adobe pdf files can enable the sharing of sophisticated graphical information without paper. Webpages can be used for business forms of all kinds. For those who would like to make the plunge and get rid of their fax machine (like I have) but have friends and colleagues who still have them (as I do), there is a good answer. eFax (http://www.eFax.com) offers a fast, free, and easy way to receive faxes — whether you're on the road, at the office, or working from home. With eFax you receive your faxes and voice mail as attachments in your email account. No more standing around the fax machine waiting for your fax to arrive. No more wandering eyes looking at your confidential documents. For a monthly charge of $9.95 you can also have a convenient way to send faxes. No need to print and manually fax a document anymore. No need to be tied to the location of your fax machine. With eFax you can fax documents right from your computer. The fax machine has served us well. Let it rest in peace.

I was having a problem getting my Hewlett Packard ScanJet scanner working and visited their website to look for a fix. I found a very sophisticated support structure and searched for my particular problem. I was successful in finding the exact problem and I clicked to get the fix. Up came a webpage that said to call during their normal business hours and give them my address so they could ship me a CD. Why not a download I asked? I was told that too many users were downloading the file for the wrong reason and then the users were complaining that the download didn't fix their problem. Rather than work on a better way of explaining who should download the file and for what purpose, HP decided to take the file off of their site and offer a CD solution instead.

The next example illustrates that email is not yet accepted as an equal in terms of communications. I was in Europe on a business trip and realized that there was a small matter that I needed to take care of with a major financial services company with whom I do business. It was a small but important administrative matter that had a deadline for completion that day. It did not involve any securities trading or movement of money. It was early morning in Europe and very early in America – customer service would not be open. Since I would be busy all day and would not be able to call when the American offices opened I decided to send them an email. I was pleased to find a "mailto" link on their website and I sent my simple request. I got back to the hotel late that night and found an email reply from the firm. I have edited the reply slightly to protect the guilty.

"Dear Mr. Patrick thanks for your recent inquiry. Unfortunately, we can't do that by e-mail, you have to speak to a customer service representative at our customer service department. Call us Monday to Friday, nine to five at 800-999-1234 during our normal business hours. Of course if you have any other questions, send us an e-mail." Duh. By the way, this response is more insensitive than it may seem on the surface. Call our 800 number? You can't call 800 numbers from Europe. I later called a manager of the firm and asked why they couldn't handle my request by email. He explained to me that email is considered correspondence by their legal department and any correspondence has to be reviewed and approved by a manager before it can be sent. Therefore they prefer the telephone where this extra step is not required. In other words, a representative on the phone can tell me anything but if they have to send me an email then it has to be reviewed and approved. This doesn't make much in a world of converging media where more and more people would say that email is their preferred way of communicating.

I sold my five-year-old car on eBay. The buyer was a gentleman in Kentucky. He had a personal problem and was not able to come get the car in a timely way so he offered to put the money in an escrow account at my bank as a show of good faith that he would definitely be taking the car. I said I would check with them on how this might be done (this was before I knew about escrow.com). My "relationship manager" said he would have to check with the legal department. He called back a few hours later and said it would be "very difficult". "Things are tough in a big hierarchy like this". It could possibly be done but the "bank has to protect itself". "You would have to fill out a lot of paperwork and the bank will take no responsibility for the money or to make sure the escrow would actually work". This was my own bank!

He said it may not seem very user friendly but they are a very big bank. The two options he said would be possible were to either use a "Letter of Credit" or get a "Court Order". He had no idea how either would work or how much they might cost. It was obvious that neither of these were appropriate to sell my car to the gentleman in Kentucky. (I later visited escrow.com and they said "No problem". Just go to the website. Either party can fill out the online form. The other party will be notified by email. When both agree to the terms, the money is deposited. When both have been to the website to agree the terms were actually met, the money is released. Fee: $100. No problem. Expectations met.)

Are these examples of e-business? I don't think so. I am sure that Motorola's customer service representative can help me select a phone that is supported by my service provider and tell me about the options available to me but I would think their website could do this too – and do so whenever I want to not just during some selected Central Standard Time hours. I know the financial services firm can help me by phone but why can't they help me by email? And on and on.

Attitude problem: Many organizations are clinging to the communications methods of the past and not capitalizing on the tremendous power of the Internet.

Net attitude: The technology is here to give people the information and services that they want on the Internet whenever they want it. Information doesn't need to be free but it does need to be readily available and 24 x 7. Any artificial inhibitors that are created will drive customers to a competitor. Expectations are rising fast and when the Next Generation of the Internet arrives expectations will be even higher.

Down For Maintenance

One of the most significant problems causing user expectations to not be met is site availability. "Site down for maintenance" at midnight seems reasonable for an American hosted website except that it is lunch hour for their Asian customers. One late night, between midnight and 1 AM I visited American Airlines to check on a flight. The homepage said, "Due to scheduled maintenance, AA.com is currently not available". This was the homepage of one of the largest airlines in the world that in fact is an "international" leader. Websites need to be available all the time. Traditional thinking would tell one that 1 AM is a great time to do maintenance of a website. Nobody is using the site. In fact, a lot of people use the web on their lunch break. It is always lunchtime somewhere in the world. Two in the morning in New York is three in the afternoon in Tokyo. The old model doesn't work anymore.

I received an email one day which said "Dear JOHN R PATRICK, your American Express Statement of Account for December, 2000 is now available for viewing at the following secure site. Please review this statement at your earliest convenience as your payment due date is December 19, 2000." A URL was provided in the email and I clicked on it. I got a message that said "We're Sorry... we are currently upgrading our site to improve American Express Online Services. During this time, you may experience intermittent system delays. If you wish to review your account, please call 1-800-528-4800 and a Customer Service Representative will be available to assist you. If you wish to make a payment, you can pay via telephone by calling 1-800-472-9297". I know American Express has great customer service by phone, with no recordings saying they are only open 9 to 5 Monday to Friday, and I know I could have paid the bill by phone but I was anxious to use the new capability of paying it online. I waited and tried the URL again the next day. Same message. After it persisted for more than a week I called American Express technical support. They said the problem was that my browser had too much history saved and that to use their site I would have to delete all the saved locations from my recent browsing. The support technician was able to step me through correcting the problem but from my point of view he was asking me to give up something to make the site work for me.

Attitude problem: Some organizations are managing their e-business websites the same way they have managed their traditional systems.

Net attitude: Many people tend to do their shopping, banking, and other web transactions at "unusual" times; certainly not all during the hours of nine to five, Monday to Friday. Websites need to be up and running around the clock.

Guitars And Chickens

Another dimension of the dissatisfaction is the difficulty in simply finding something on the web. My mother was anxious to get an 8-inch electric frying pan. My wife looked everywhere and couldn't fine one. "No problem", I said, "I'll find one on the Internet in no time". I did some looking around and found a site that claimed to be all about electric frying pans. There were four featured links. None of them had anything to do with electric frying pans. There were twelve featured manufacturers of frying pans. Eight of them were dead links. Four were good links to great looking frying pans but none were the small size I wanted. Undaunted I decided to use a more sophisticated search. Search = "Small electric frying pan". I got two matches.

Match #1
Lemelson Center Invention Features: Electric Guitars
This exhibit, presented by The National Museum of American History features instruments that illustrate how innovative makers and players combined the guitar with a pickup (sensor) and amplifier to...

Match #2
FRIED CHICKEN
Start with a whole fryer wash with water cut breasts and wings in two shake chicken and flour in paper or plastic bag in electric frying pan, brown chicken at high heat

Attitude problem: The web is a great new way to publish information. It is easy to put very large amounts of information on your website.

Net attitude: Having more information on a website doesn't mean that it is easier for people to find that information. Information needs to be carefully organized and structured so that it can be maintained and so it can be easily searched and retrieved.

Listen Carefully; Our Menus Have Changed

"Surfing" the web has become a very natural thing to do for millions of people. They have also mastered "click here" to buy something or to make a choice. The simplicity of this has raised expectations, and frustrations, with the Call Center. There are many fancy technical terms that are used to describe Call Center technology but the bottom line is that they provide an automated way to interact with people. Seems like every organization of any kind has one. The reduction in staff made possible by substituting a recorded voice response for real people is compelling to the organization. To people, well that is a different story. Simple menus didn't seem so bad and in fact reduced your time on the phone. Press one for sales; press two for service; press three for parts. Nice. Gets you to the right place in a hurry. But then the success of these simple menus motivated organizations to get more sophisticated. Do they still save us time and increase our satisfaction? Let's listen in on a typical "dialogue".

I want to change my mailing address on a service contract I have on my home vacuum system. I call the company's 800 number. "Welcome to Ajax. Ajax is the world's leading provider of home vacuum cleaning systems. Press 1 if you are using a touch-tone phone. I press 1. Press 1 for English, 2 for Spanish. Presione 1 para el Inglés, 2 para Española." I pressed 1. "Please listen carefully because our menus have changed". Do I really need to hear about the status of their menus? I care about what it is I am calling about. When do we get to something relevant to my problem? "Press 1 to learn more about our exciting new home vacuum system that is currently being offered at a special introductory price. Press 2 to order one of our products. Press 3 to learn how to use one of our products. Press 4 for detailed instructions on how to return one of our products". All I want to do is change my address! "Press 5 to request shipping materials to return one of our products. "Press 6 for the locations of our nearest retail centers." I am ready to scream. "Press 7 for the locations of our nearest repair centers". I wonder if customer service is going to be 8, 9, or zero? I'll try 0. "Sorry, that option is not available". "Press 8 to repeat the menu options." 8. "Press 1 to learn about our exciting new home vacuum system that is currently being offered at a special introductory price. "Press 2 to order one of our products". "Press 3 to learn how use one of our products". "Press 4 for detailed instructions on how to return one of our products". "Press 5 to request shipping materials to return one of our products". "Press 6 for the locations of our nearest retail centers." "Press 7 for the locations of our nearest repair centers". I'm getting close. I don't dare press anything. "Press 8 to repeat the menu options". "Press 9 to speak to a customer service representative". At last. 9. "We are sorry but our customer service representatives are only available Monday to Friday from 9 AM to 5 PM during our normal business hours." I look at my watch. It is 5:01 PM. If only I hadn't pressed that 8 earlier!

The call center is controlling you via its menu structure. It was ok for the simple menu with three choices but the complex labyrinths of today are more than frustrating. In those instances when you finally get to a person you then discover that the computer has not only controlled you, it is also controlling the person you are talking to! "Press 0 to speak to a customer service representative." "Enter your eighteen digit customer number followed by the pound sign." A representative comes on the line. "May I have your account number please?" You tell the person you just entered it and the person tells you, "I am sorry but it didn't show up on my screen." You give them the eighteen-digit customer number and then the person says, "Thank you sir, now, may I help you?" "Yes, thank you. My name is John Patrick and I would like to change my zip code". "Ok, sir, I would be glad to help you. What is your name?" The customer service representative probably selected an application for "Change zip code" and a screen came up to "guide" him or her through the steps. Step 1 – what is your name? As soon as a competitor a simple webpage for "add/change/check status" kinds of things, perhaps integrated with the call center, customers will switch to that vendor as fast as possible.

Attitude problem: The web is a great new way to offer "click here to buy" and that is the priority, in some cases the sole priority, of many e-businesses. "Click here" satisfies many people but when they later have to call customer service and talk to a call center their satisfaction goes away.

Net attitude: Call centers and the Internet can be integrated. "Click here" to get your problem solved and if that doesn't solve the problem, "click here" to talk to someone.

For Your Own Protection

Does that stream of wet ink we call a signature really make things better? Our financial and legal system in most of the world is based on paper and ink. It hasn't changed for hundreds of years. It doesn't matter that we can buy things with a mouse click. If we want to transfer securities, open a new account, set up a trust, establish a life insurance policy, or countless other transactions, then a piece of paper with our signature in ink is required. We are told it is a requirement, that is the company policy or, that is "for your protection". Is it really?

Recently I owed a contractor some money for a project he had completed for me. I accidentally forgot to make the payment when I said I would and as soon as I realized my oversight I decided to write a check and take it to the bank and deposit it directly to the contractor's account. I knew which bank the builder used and I had his bank account number from a prior transaction with him. I pulled up to the teller window in my car and gave the teller my check made out to the builder and with his account number on it. After she processed the check I started to put my car window up and then I heard the teller say, "Here is your receipt". When I got home and took a look at the receipt I could see the amount of the deposit and also the builder's new account balance! By simply knowing the bank account number of the builder I was able to (unintentionally) invade his privacy and see his bank balance. If I want to check his balance again in the future I can just deposit $1 at the drive up window! Maybe the brick, mortar, and paper world isn't so secure after all. It could have been much more secure and private if I could have wired the money to the builder using the Internet.

Digital ID's are now legal in America and other parts of the world. They provide authentication, authorization, confidentiality, integrity, and non-repudiation. In fact they are far more durable and powerful than signatures with ink. Digital ID's will empower us and simplify our lives. Much more about what they are and how they work coming up later.

Attitude problem: Commerce in most of the world has been based on paper and ink. Nothing much has changed for hundreds of years.

Net attitude: The technology exists to make Internet-based digital signatures not only work but make them more secure than paper and ink.

Yes, there are many uses and instances of paper that are just not needed -- because they add no value. But paper is not going to go away and it shouldn't. Just like in all introductions of new media types, the electronic media is a supplement to paper not a wholesale replacement. Sometimes the uses change though. Newspapers actually serve many purposes. Some people use them to keep the rain off of their head, others swat flies with them, and some wrap fish in them. And then there is just plain old writing paper. When you put a fountain pen to it magical things happen. You have this special feeling when using a fountain pen. And if your heart is in the right place you can inspire or uplift the hearts of others with the words you write. Nothing digital has quite the same impact.

Peanuts And Potato Chips

Increasingly people expect to have their providers of goods and services think about customer satisfaction from an end-to-end point of view. Click here to buy is one small piece of this. The end-to-end concept starts from the moment we perceive that we have a need or a want for a good or service up to and including after the sale service and support. There are many aspects to this. Long before a person is ready to buy something they may want to learn about what is available and gain assistance in determining exactly what they need. Carpenter Technology Corporation a leading manufacturer and distributor of specialty alloys has a website called carpenterdirect.com where industrial buyers can purchase stainless steel, aluminum, brass and many other kinds of alloys. The website has an online e-commerce catalog but, more important to their business customers, is a vast amount of technical data to help an engineer determine what is needed for a particular project. A section of their site, called MyMetallurgist, provides descriptions of alloys and detailed technical properties so that engineers can make selections based on corrosion, magnetic, or tooling requirements. Services such as this can become a technical information resource for Carpenter customers and if it is valuable enough the customers will become hooked on it and will find it a very natural step to "click here to buy".

An example of a step in the cycle after "click here to buy" is packaging. It has to do with problems in the "last analog mile"; referring to the physical delivery of things we buy on the Internet. The issue initially struck me when I had received my very first order from net.grocer (www.netgrocer.com). I ordered an assortment of salsa, condiments, Tabasco, paper towels, potato chips, pickles, and other essentials. I was quite pleased and proud of my e-commerce prowess (e-business hadn't been invented yet) in walking the talk and acquiring all of my favorite goodies online. I was reveling in my predictions about how everybody would buy everything on the Net. Then I got a lump in my stomach as I looked at these two large cardboard boxes on my kitchen floor. And, the piles of white poly-whatever "peanuts" were all over the place. Some stuck to my hands, arms, and clothing. What was I to do? My wife would be home soon and she would have a lot of questions about my plans to clean up the mess I had created in the kitchen. All the glory I felt about acquiring Tabasco and potato chips would be nothing compared to the wrath she would unleash about the mess if I didn't get busy. No problem. I'll just clean it up. All I have to do is separate all the various packaging materials into their respective categories, burst the cardboard boxes, put the "peanuts" into a bag so they don't end up decorating our lawn, and then stow everything away in our recycling center. Shouldn't take me more than a half hour. Let's see -- how much time did I save with my Net purchase anyway? Even with the purchase of something really simple, say a small cell phone, the ratio of the packaging material to the cell phone (on a volume basis) must be 100 to 1 or more.

Even later in the cycle than packaging is fulfillment. Some websites remember your prior purchases but soon purchasing agents and consumers will expect fulfillment models where they can set up a list of things they just want to show up on a scheduled basis. Industrial chemicals and supplies for the business and paper towels, printer paper, stockings, and potato chips for the home. More sophisticated e-businesses will monitor purchases and advise their customers of ordering levels that will minimize shipping cost. Really sophisticated e-businesses will provide complete inventory management systems for their customers. When the customer wants to check what is on hand of a particular item they won't go to their inventory system, they will go their e-business supplier's website. This is a great way to tie the customer into a long-term relationship.

By paying attention to the end-to-end process, looking at possible annoyances anywhere along the process, successful e-businesses will uncover more and more ways to satisfy their customers. There is room for leadership here and breakthroughs are possible. I used to be so frustrated with opening the half-gallon orange juice cartons. Did I say opening? I meant mutilating. Then along came International Paper Corporation with a breakthrough idea -- the screw cap on the carton.

In fact, there are a number of creative and constructive developments going on in the packaging industry. For example, ECO-FOAM (http://www.eco-foam. com/) offers packaging material made from a renewable resource – corn. The product is completely biodegradable and dissolves in water - makes great compost. Another company, Metabolix (http://www.metabolix.com), is developing dissolvable plastics made from two of our most easily attainable and renewable sources: carbon dioxide and water!

> Attitude problem: E-commerce for businesses and consumers is here to stay. In the rush to get catalogs of products on line, many businesses overlook the complete end-to-end experience.

> Net attitude: Customers are going to expect much more than "click here to buy". It isn't a technology problem.

I began thinking about packaging as something important some years ago when trying to open a cereal box without destroying it and its subsequent ability to keep the cereal fresh. It is a nontrivial challenge - maybe an art. If it is a science then I haven't found the instructions anywhere. One starts by using a sharp knife with a long blade. You carefully slide the knife under the tab in the center of the top of the cereal box. Then you slice the material to one side while applying a slight upward pressure via the tab. Repeat for the other side. I give being able to do this without damaging the box top about 75% odds. You are now almost a third of the way through the task at hand. Now that you have freed up one of the flaps you have to free the other flap by tearing it from the side flaps. Completing this without damage is also about 75% odds if you are quite careful. You are now two thirds of the way to the cereal. Last comes opening the bag inside the box that actually contains the cereal. This is often the hardest part. If you grasp the two sides of the bag and pull very carefully you have about a 50% chance of opening the bag without tearing it. After opening the main part of the bag you need to open the corners of the bag so the cereal can flow smoothly into your cereal bowl instead of bubbling out onto the floor and between the bag and the cereal box. Putting the collective probabilities together gives you a 50-50 chance at best of having an open cereal box that pours the contents smoothly and can be closed to protect freshness. Some packaging! I could go on about jars that require a hammer to open, pill bottles that can only be opened by children, fresh fruit containers that have to be squeezed until they break to open, soap in hotel rooms that is hermetically sealed in thick saran wrap that defies being opened, etc. etc. etc. I suspect those who suffer from arthritis of the fingers could make my examples seem trivial.

It Is Not All Gloom And Doom

There are some e-businesses that are doing a great job with end-to-end satisfaction. Stamps.com is a good example. Stamps.com is the leading provider of Internet mailing and shipping services. The company was started in 1999 and has Marvin Runyon, former U.S. Postmaster General, on its board of directors. The company provides valuable e-services to businesses of all sizes, allowing companies to control costs and efficiently manage their mailing, shipping and returns operations. Its business is anchored in key relationships with the U.S. Postal Service and United Parcel Service (UPS) and other carriers. For consumers and small businesses stamps.com has eliminated hours of waiting time at the local post office. They insert a link in your word processor so that after writing a letter you can select to have an address label printed along with the postage. They actually have a three-part label that prints the return address, the addressee address, and the postage. You can even connect your label printer to a postal scale and weigh a package and automatically print the proper postage. They have integrated their Internet service with the postal service so that each address is checked against a national database over the Internet to ensure that you can't print an address unless it is deliverable. The nine-digit zip code is automatically inserted if you don't know it. USPS packaging materials (no "peanuts" included) are integrated with the printing choices. When your packages and letters are ready to go you just put them outside by your mailbox and the USPS mail carrier picks them up and there are no added charges. The fee to stamps.com is ten percent of the postage printed with a minimum of $1.99 per month. This is a bargain considering the convenience it enables. The local newspaper where I live ran a story recently with a headline that read, "Parking, lines giving postal patrons a pain". This is understandable. What is not understandable is the local cry to build a larger post office to handle the demand. If people were aware of the great service provided by stamps.com they could avoid the lines and gridlock parking and print their postage in the comfort of their homes.

One of the most empowering places on the web has got to be eBay. Buying and selling on eBay is a great experience. They are constantly adding new services to make the process – from end to end -- easier for both the buyer and the seller. They create a community around the auction process and people trust it. In the beginning making or receiving payment for your basement artifacts or favorite baseball cards was a real hassle; going to the bank to get a cashier's check or to the long line at the Post Office to get a money order. eBay has addressed the problem through BillPoint, a credit card based approach, that allows a buyer to pay a seller electronically. It is basically a special purpose electronic funds transfer. The purchase price gets charged to the buyer's credit card and then the money gets deposited directly into the seller's bank account. It works very well and charges a modest fee to the seller. EBay empowers people and meets people's expectations. They keep getting better and better. As a result it is making a profit and growing rapidly. In the first quarter of 2001 the market capitalization of eBay, a relatively brand new company, was identical to that of Sears Roebuck & Company.

All kinds of web-based services are springing up that do meet people's needs. PayPal allows a person to send money to any other person by simply entering the recipient's email address at http://www.paypal.com and specifying the amount of payment. The recipient gets an email asking him or her to enroll in PayPal, if they are not already a member, and then they get the payment credited to their PayPal account. Balances earn interest. If they don't want to use their credit balance to buy things at eBay or elsewhere they can request a check or even a direct deposit to their bank account. People use PayPal for auctions, paying their share of a meal, and sending money to the kids at college. Another payment option for auctions is BidPay (http://www.bidpay.com), which allows a buyer to go to a webpage and enter the physical name and address of the seller and for a modest fee BidPay then sends a money order to the seller. An email is automatically sent to the seller so he or she will know that the money is on the way. Both of these payment methods are simple and effective. They are not banks or credit card companies. Perhaps they don't have the various protections that those entities have. Who knows if they will be successful? They do work, however, and large numbers of people are using them. Traditional financial services companies should pay very close attention to them.

And Now To The Future

While there are some notable positive exceptions, the bottom line is that most e-businesses, whether they are serving businesses or consumers, are not meeting expectations. The Internet has transferred power to people, both those working inside of businesses and those at home, and each day those expectations are higher than the day before. We saw an initial burst of excitement about surfing the web in 1995. Over the next five years the Internet became faster, more reliable, and reached much larger numbers of people. New Internet startups or "dot coms" emerged with some great ideas (but not always great business models) and existing companies "web enabled" many processes. E-commerce flourished. However, by the end of the millennium many users of the Internet began to become disillusioned and at times frustrated. They couldn't find what they wanted or e-businesses in some way let them down at a time when their expectations were rising. How does an organization address this widening gap? The first part of the answer lies in anticipating and exploiting the Next Generation of the Internet – the NGi. The second part is about Attitude.

Part Two

The Next Generation of the Internet

Part two of Net Attitude *was about the Internet itself: what it is, how it works, and how its capabilities are evolving. I described the evolution as the Next Generation of the Internet. The projections I featured came to pass and were largely accurate. What I would say differently today is the Internet is continuously evolving. Improvements are continuous. I see no end in sight. There is no "next generation" to the Internet.*

I described seven characteristics of the Internet: Fast, Always on, Everywhere, Natural, Intelligent, Easy, and Trusted. There are no precise definitions for these characteristics. They served as a somewhat arbitrary way of parsing the many aspects of the Internet and providing examples showing their implications. I believe the same seven evolutionary characteristics are a valid method to describe what is happening with the Internet today.

The specific examples have changed but the principles behind them have not. Some Internet transactions which are easy today, such as making an online purchase, were difficult in 2001. What was fast then would be considered very slow today. Although there were no iPhones or Android phones, the principle I described for Everywhere was right on. I said that the Internet was where your desktop was, but in the near future, the Internet will be where you are.

T he Internet has been around for decades. Until the middle of the 1990s it was a communications network used mostly by scientific, academic, and government students and researchers. With the advent of the browser, the spread of Microsoft Windows, and improved reliability of telephone circuits, using the Internet became something the rest of us could do. Then with the development of security technology to protect credit card numbers, things really took off. The number of users has grown and continues to grow rapidly. Five years from now there will be three quarters of a billion people using the Net and during that same time the nature of the Internet, the things it can do and how it does them, is going to undergo a rapid evolution. In fact the Next Generation of the Internet is already unfolding and this part of *Net Attitude* will explore it in depth.

CHAPTER 4

Fast

Internet speed is dramatically faster than it was when I wrote Net Attitude. *In 2001, the speed depended on where you lived. I offered an optimistic view that technology advances and competition would improve and make things better. The technology has evolved rapidly as forecasted. Competition between Telco's and cable operators has provided some improvement, but there are still many rural areas where you have only one choice for a service provider.. I continue to believe we need more competition. Comcast and AT&T customer service has improved over the past ten years but surveys and ratings still rank them well below many online retailers and technology companies. Unfortunately, the criticisms of cable companies I described in 2001 in a large part are still valid.*

This chapter starts with some background on what the Internet was and how it worked. I wrote it without technical jargon to make it easy to understand. The most common feedback I received about Net Attitude *was it helped people understand how the Internet worked. I hope you also will find this to be true. In 2001, Internet speeds were asynchronous, meaning the upload speed was much slower than the download speed. Although speeds have increased dramatically, the asynchronous characteristic remains. My connection as I wrote these words was 60 million bits per second for downloads and 3 million for uploads. This needs to change so that video conferencing, telemedicine, and interactive games can continue to evolve into more natural experiences. Hopefully, competition will bring the needed change.*

The Packets Don't Care

T he Next Generation of the Internet (NGi) is about new characteristics of the Internet that we will gradually begin to experience. The obvious one is *Fast* – more speed.

Bandwidth is a technical term but in essence it means the capacity to transfer data using an electronic communications system. The term bandwidth has become the common way to refer to the speed, or responsiveness, we experience when we are connected to the Internet. Higher bandwidth means higher speed. Soon we will be awash in bandwidth! If, like me, you have been in a hotel room recently and got connected at 19,200 bits per second or less and were relieved to get even that much speed you may wonder how I could make such an assertion. Bandwidth galore? At times it seems like we are starving for bandwidth; however, these are short-term limitations that we are experiencing and that will soon seem like history.

> We often hear the term "twenty-eight-eight" or "fifty-six-K". These terms refer to the bandwidth or speed. For example, "fifty six K" means 56,000 bits per second. A bit is a one or a zero. Nine bits make up a "byte". A single alphabetic character (e.g. "a") is represented by a "byte". The banner across the top of the Yahoo homepage is represented by 8,000 bytes. So "fifty six K" or 56,000 bits per second really means approximately 6,222 bytes per second can be sent from or delivered to your PC. That means it would take a little more than 1 second to transmit a 1,200 word email or the banner at the top of Yahoo's homepage. Pictures and colors and fancy fonts can actually require many thousands of bytes and that is one of the reasons why it sometimes takes so long for a webpage to fully appear in your browser.

You are probably thinking that maybe where "you" live it is fast or going to get fast but where I live it doesn't seem to be in my future to have fast Internet access. The reasons to be optimistic are two; technology and competition.

First, just a bit of background on how the Internet works. All information that travels across the Internet is broken into packets. Every email, webpage, instant message, or Internet Protocol (IP) telephony call is broken up into packets that then traverse the Internet. An average packet contains between five and ten thousand zeroes and ones. Each packet has a source and destination address and they traverse the Internet by traveling between specialized computers called routers. The routers look at each packet and determine where it should go next. Typically a packet may take ten to fifteen "hops" before it gets to its destination. Then the packets get reassembled into an email, webpage, instant message, or IP telephony call. The nice thing about the packets is that they don't care what media they travel through. They are agnostic. Copper wires of the telephone network, fiber optic cables under the ocean, coaxial cable of cable companies, in radio waves through the air from antennas, or from satellites, or even through the power grid of the electrical system. All of these media — telephone, cable, radio, and satellite — are competing to become the primary conduit of the Internet. Given what we know about competition — how it encourages innovation in the mad scramble to grab market share — this is nothing but good news for consumers. In some ways each of the medias threaten the others and the result is that we have Adam Smith's "invisible hand" at work on bandwidth.

> The origin of "packet switching" goes back to the "cold war" during the 1950's. American policy and technology thinkers were concerned about the possibility of an attack that might wipe out American communications systems and negatively impact the country's ability to defend itself. The concept of breaking messages into packets was devised to protect against communications loss. For example a message from New York to San Francisco could be broken into multiple packets. The packets then might take a path from New York to San Francisco but rather than go directly they might go from New York to Kansas City to Dallas to San Francisco. If that "route" became disabled because Kansas City got wiped out the packets could be rerouted to flow from say New York to Chicago to Dallas to San Francisco. Also, if some packets got lost in the process at least the whole message would not be lost.

Adam Smith's Invisible Hand

Dozens of players are already placing their bets and investing in the delivery infrastructure and this will accelerate the role-out of bandwidth galore. Telephone companies in many parts of the world have now mastered a technology called digital subscriber line (DSL). It comes in about a dozen different "flavors": ADSL, XDSL, HDSL, etc. Most communities in America have a small red brick building near the center of the town that has no windows in it. This is the Central Office or CO. If you live within roughly two miles of a CO then the telephone company can offer you this "digital subscriber line" that in effect provides a local area network between you and the CO. It can operate at a speed of up to 1.5 million bits per second. That is today. In the future DSL has the potential to not only operate at tens of millions of bits per second but also to reach beyond the two mile or so limit to a range of perhaps five miles or maybe more. Even the speed offered by DSL today is more than fifty times faster than the "twenty-eight-eight" (28.8 thousand bits per second which most people still have). It is being rolled out in communities around the world. A significant percentage of people live within two miles of a CO in many parts of the world. As of year-end 2000, 100% of the population in Taiwan is in sufficient proximity to have DSL service.

DSL enables broadband, a fancy word that means *Fast*. And once you have fast, that means you can have video and when telephone companies can deliver video that provides a threat to cable companies. Cable companies meanwhile can also deliver fast Internet access through their cable system. Today the cable companies primarily offer a "one way" system. They broadcast their content from their "head end" through the cable infrastructure to your home. The "head ends" can do much more than broadcast though. First of all the "head ends" are being upgraded to make the cable two way so that Internet access is possible. The "head ends" can also be connected to the PSTN (public switched telephone network) and thereby they can deliver telephony over the cable. In fact by using only a small percentage of the bandwidth available over the cable, they can offer multiple lines of telephone service to a home or small business. How many lines would you like one, two, six? With no noticeable degradation to your web access speed it is possible to have crystal clear digital telephony. This, of course, is a threat to telephone companies.

And then there are companies like Winstar, Terrabeam, Teligent and others who are delivering high-speed Internet access through wireless and optical technologies. A technology called Local Multipoint Distribution Service (LMDS) can provide two-way Internet access at very high speed using radio waves. Using LMDS, transmission speeds of several billion bits per second (gigabits) is possible along line of sight distances of several miles. That means that a wireless antenna in the parking lot of an apartment complex or a campus will be able to deliver very high speed Internet access to thousands of users within a radius of several miles.

Meanwhile there are satellite companies such as DirectPC, Tachyon and Gilat-To-Home that are aggressively entering the market for high speed Internet service. I first got Hughes PC Direct in March of 1995. It was what we call asynchronous. That meant that it was very fast at downloading information from the Internet but very slow in sending information back through the Internet. This is ok for many things like "click-here-to-send-a-short-request" to download a movie or a new software program. But if you want to have an interactive videoconference with a colleague you need high speed in both directions and satellite service was ineffective. Worse yet the early satellite Internet services required that in addition to the satellite dish you still needed to have a "dial-up" telephone connection for the outbound link. Things have come al long way recently. Current satellite systems are still asynchronous (not the same speed in each direction) but the slow speed is hundreds of thousands of bits per second. This will be a threat to telephone companies, cable companies, and wireless companies.

So Who Is The Winner?

Many questions involving the Internet beg a binary yes/no answer. Who will be the winner, cable or DSL? The answer is Yes. Will it be wired or wireless? The answer is Yes. Ground based wireless or satellite? You guessed it, Yes. We are at the very beginning and things are going to heat up. At the moment DSL and cable modems have an edge. But telephone and cable companies are learning how to quickly replicate the installation process with good customer satisfaction. The speed that you get is somewhat a function of how fast the local rollout of service is. If you are the first in your neighborhood to get a cable modem you will enjoy a higher speed than DSL. As your neighbors join you the total bandwidth available is shared. As the neighborhood gets more and more users the cable company will need to upgrade the bulk capacity available to the neighborhood. Telephone companies seem to be better prepared to rollout even levels of service. Speaking of service the telephone companies are used to responsiveness when you have a problem. At least compared to cable companies. My experience has been that when I call the cable company with a problem and have to schedule a service call I get asked, "will someone be home from one to five in the afternoon a week from Tuesday?" Wireless and satellite companies are even less mature in their service capability. On the other hand the wireless companies can offer an un-tethered environment and satellite companies have a significant advantage in the many rural communities where DSL, cable modems and wireless services are unlikely to be available for quite some time.

In summary we have Adam Smith's invisible hand at work on bandwidth. The battle is just about to heat up. This is a very good thing for consumers and for businesses. And it is happening now. If you are lucky enough to live in an area that offers more than one of the competing services you will likely see speeds go up and cost go down. If you think of a "twenty-eight-eight" connection as a one inch in diameter garden hose delivering a "stream" of content to your PC, a 1.5 million bits per second (megabit) DSL connection is like a pipe three feet in diameter! Imagine what that will mean to the content you will be able to receive. Full screen video for example. More on that later. So, when will broadband be here? It is here now. Everyone doesn't have it but each day more and more do. There are many implications.

I was in the Holiday Inn in Beijing a couple of years ago. There was no jack to plug into. Everything was "hard wired". A maintenance man was nice enough to come to my room with his tool bag (I used to carry my own). He opened up the wall module, exposed the wires, and installed a temporary jack that I could plug into. After many attempts I finally connected at 2,400 bits per second. It was so slooooooow! But at least I could send and receive my email even if it took a very long time to do so. (There was no way to effectively surf the web at such a slow speed). It was such a good feeling to be connected from so far away. In this case the speed didn't really matter. It was the ability to send and receive my email that made my day. And while we all complain that even "fifty-six K" is not enough, the Sojourner rover sat on the planet Mars communicating with the Pathfinder robot at just 2.4K!

From Wired To Wireless To Optical

The first implication is that now that we have fast access at our home or small business (large businesses can already have fast access) where will the next bottleneck be? The current bottleneck is called the "last mile". This is a term that originated at telephone companies because your home is part of the "last mile" from their infrastructure. As more and more people and businesses get DSL, cable modems, high speed wireless, and satellite service some predict that the bottleneck will move to the backbones, the arteries or "Super highways" or "Autobahns" that connect all the various nodes and network access points of the Internet. The backbones have to carry the aggregate traffic of all the consumer and business traffic of the Internet.

> Why do we call that stretch from the telephone company to our home the "last mile"? It is a matter of perspective. Many companies think "inside out". From them to us. The Internet has transferred the power to us. Why shouldn't it be the "first mile"; from us to the Internet?

IBM, MCI, and the Merit System of Michigan built the first transcontinental transit network for the Internet in 1988 under a contract from the National Science Foundation. The NSFNet as it was called was able to interconnect the many regional educational networks and create one large "Internet" in America. It had a speed of 56,000 bits per second. Amazing that the entire backbone at that time was only as fast as a single person's average connection to the Internet is today. A few years after that It was upgraded to "T1" which was a speed of approximately one and a half million bits per second. A transoceanic link was added under a technology grant from IBM. It was the first high-speed data network to cross the ocean. A few years later It was upgraded to "T3" which is a speed of 45.3 million bits per second. Subsequent to that major portions of the backbone have been upgraded to 633 million bits per second and a non-profit called the University Corporation for Advanced Internet Development (UCAID) implemented a project called Internet2 which is an academic and research backbone operating at a speed of 2.5 billion bits per second. That is just the beginning.

What is enabling the dramatic increase in speed of the backbones is fiber optic technology. Think of a glass fiber smaller than a human hair and imagine shining a light through the fiber. Turn it on and you get a "1". Turn it off and you get a "0". In the near term the limit of this will be 10 billion "ons" and "offs" (bits) per second through a single fiber. That limit will soon be 40 billion bits per second. In addition to this incredible speed through a fiber, a technology called Dense Wavelength Division Multiplexing (DWDM) can enable more than one light to be passed through a fiber at the same time. This is done by using multiple colors of light called "windows" or Lambdas. Current fiber optic cables are utilizing 160 "windows" but work is underway to upgrade that to 320 "windows". The state of the art in research laboratories is currently approximately 1,000 windows and some startup companies like Avanex are now talking about the possibility of having 100,000 "windows" per fiber.

Lucent is currently building cables that contain nearly 1,000 fibers. The numbers are staggering when you add it up. The aggregate capacity of a fiber optic cable may be 40 billion bits per second per "window" times 100,000 "windows" times 1,000 fibers per cable. That comes out to 4 million terabits per second per cable! There are hundreds of companies putting fiber in the street alongside water pipes, in the ground alongside railroad tracks, and under the oceans. There are already tens of millions of miles of fiber in place. New fiber optics companies like Qwest, Level 3, Global Crossing, and Williams already have an aggregate capacity that exceeds what AT&T, MCI, Sprint, and WorldCom combined currently have in service.

An entire optical infrastructure is emerging causing the Internet to morph itself from a wired world to an optical world. While the "last mile" is expanding from a one inch garden hose to a 3 foot in diameter pipe, the backbones are moving from six foot in diameter pipes to ones which are hundreds of feet in diameter. Bill Alpert, in a December 2000 story in Barron's called "Optical switches will be the next big thing in data transmission" said "The optical Internet is a modern wonder." The backbones will not be the bottleneck.

Where Does The Bottleneck Move To?

The bottleneck is going to move away from the "last mile" and away from the backbones. So where does the bottleneck move to? Part of the bottleneck will move to getting the bits from the backbone through the last mile to the end user or business. Part of the bottleneck will be at the server. Servers are specialized computers that deliver the webpages and video streams and music and e-commerce applications to millions of users on the Internet through their browsers. If you have moved to a cable modem or DSL from your former slower speed Internet service you may not have actually noticed as dramatic an increase in speed as you had hoped. This is partly because there are servers that are too busy and don't have the capacity to deliver more bits. Websites are going to need really, really powerful servers. This is a good problem to have for companies like IBM, Sun, HP, Compaq and others. A lot of progress is being made to customize the server hardware and software to enable them to serve webpages more efficiently. (At times a contributing factor is that there may be delays in the Internet topography between you and the server.)

The other that is going to change is that content will be closer than you think. Content today is highly centralized in servers. Lets say that 1,000 people in a large office building all go to cnn.com or yahoo!.com or any popular site today. In this scenario those 1,000 people actually do go to those websites and they all get (download) the same homepage. A page that likely has not changed in the past day or so. When you think about it, much of the content of the Internet doesn't change that often. So why isn't that "static" content broadcasted from satellites down into Internet service providers, who in turn move it out to servers in the basements of large office buildings and to "set top servers" in our homes, or perhaps even into those little green boxes on telephone poles that in the future may contain smart disc drives? Already companies like Akamai, Sandpiper, Inktomi, CachFlow and others are deploying "caches" for content. A cache is a temporary storage area for content that is frequently accessed. The storage areas are connected to PC's that are placed in widely distributed locations at Internet Service Provider locations. Thousands of them. So when you go to retrieve a news story that is very much in demand you will likely be retrieving it from a "cache" in a PC or server somewhere nearby. The content will be much closer than we think. The result will be that we will receive it with much less delay.

So What Do We Do With The Speed?

So what's the big deal with speed? Video. Video on the Internet today appears in a tiny one-inch or so window. It is often grainy looking and appearing in fits and starts. It is a novelty the first time you see video on the Internet but then it becomes not particularly interesting to look at. When you get a million bits per second bandwidth with a cable modem or DSL, things change. That same video window becomes larger and much less jittery. When you get to two million or so bits per second it will begin to look like television. What does it mean when we get to have high-quality, jitter-free, full-screen video over the Internet?

First it introduces geo-independence. This in turn will have a big impact on experts and people who use experts. Experts are people who live on airplanes, traveling the world sharing their expertise. They go to where the problem is. With geo-independence experts are wherever they are and the problems are wherever they are. Video over the Internet will be what connects them. Wall size video screens will make people appear very close. A doctor may be on that video wall while you are at a local hospital. You get inside of a functional MRI machine and the doctor, who is an expert in your particular condition, is 5,000 miles away but on the video wall talking to you, and the doctor says, "please bend your knee". You bend your knee and the doctor sees what's happening in your brain! Geo-independence.

Dr. William Magee is co-founder and chairman of Operation Smile (http://www.operationsmile.org) in Norfolk, Virginia. Bill and a team of other plastic surgeons make trips to under developed countries of the world to repair cleft pallets of children. These incredibly deformed children are often ridiculed and sometimes even hidden away from society. They have no life. No smiles. Until Bill and the team arrive. Lives are changed. The impact is amazing. Unfortunately, most of children who need the assistance are turned away. There are not enough days, supplies, and surgeons to meet the needs. Bill told me that one of the reasons that local plastic surgeons can not handle the needs is training. Lack of modern text books. Lack of knowledge of the latest techniques. Imagine if a doctor in Thailand could not only receive training from Bill over the Internet but if Bill could remotely participate in a surgical procedure real time over the Internet. It will happen and lives will be changed.

College professors will give lectures to students on different continents. Engineering experts will "arrive" on the scene of complex situations via video walls. Their time will be leveraged. How many additional situations could experts handle if they didn't have to spend so many hours on airplanes?

The next implication has to do with Expectations. Everyone will not have high bandwidth immediately; it is going to roll out at different rates and paces in different parts of the world. However, there already are millions who have it and those who do expect to see very creative content. I remember back in the early 1980's when color displays were first introduced. This was before the IBM PC. Displays were used mostly in large companies attached to mainframe computers. The screens were either green or gray and text appeared as either white or dark green. There were no pictures or graphics. Just letters and numbers. Then new displays were introduced which could show up to sixteen colors! Still no pictures or graphics but you could see negative numbers in red for the first time. They cost about 20% more than the monochrome displays and many people said, "who needs it?" It took quite awhile for them to catch on. Can you imagine a display on your PC not having color today? Of course not; and, soon you will not be able to imagine a website that doesn't have a lot of full screen video. You will expect to be able to say the word "Help" to a microphone embedded in your keyboard or display and to have a live person appear full screen with a smile saying, "Hi, how can I help you?".

We will also expect to see very creative content. Not just more webpages with bigger brighter banner advertisements on them. Video will be a norm but we will also expect to see very high quality graphics. The displays on our PC's today typically have 480,000 pixels. Each pixel contains some combination of red, green, and blue and collectively the pixels make up a "display" that looks like a single picture or page of text or movie. In late 2000 IBM shipped for the first time a high resolution computer display that has 200 pixels per inch and more than 9 million pixels in total on a 22-inch screen. The new display is as clear as an original photograph and 4.5-times sharper than top-of-the-line high-definition television screens and it will make the viewing of video and digital photos a completely new kind of experience. It will also significantly reduce eyestrain and the need for printing hard copies as we all often do.

Displays of this type will make it possible to replace conventional film X-rays. Physicians will be able to view digitally photographed X-rays immediately on the display. The X-ray images could also be sent online to specialists around the world for instant feedback and counsel. Large printed satellite maps and photographs will be replaced with photo-quality digital images, allowing meteorologists to quickly interpret weather patterns and instantly share them with colleagues around the world. Such applications as these will require bandwidth to be able to deliver all the bits that will be needed to light up all those millions of pixels on a nearly instant basis. So it is not speed for speed's sake but rather speed to enhance our Internet experience and enable us to interact with high quality media. The Fast Internet represents the evolution of not *a* new medium but *the* new medium. It presents a tremendous opportunity like nothing we've seen in many decades, maybe ever. It will have a profound impact on our business and personal lives.

CHAPTER 5

Always On

The prior chapter described the origins of the Internet and how it worked.. This chapter described the World Wide Web and how it worked. To many people, the Internet and the web were the same thing, but they are actually quite different. The Internet is the underlying communications infrastructure which moves packets of ones and zeroes from one router to another. The web is an application which uses the Internet to enable users to find and download webpages and use applications for learning, e-commerce, entertainment, and much more.

This chapter described examples of applications which use the Internet without the web. One example I wrote about was controlling devices in the home. I was quite a bit ahead of the market in this area. Home automation just now is beginning to emerge into the mainstream. One of my primary interests currently is home automation. I will be writing about the subject in the future.

The second characteristic of the Next Generation of the Internet is that it will be Always On. Today, for most people, the Internet is not always on. When we are ready to use the Internet we go to our PC. We "boot" it up if it is not already running and then we startup a program called a "dialer" which is used to "log on" to our Internet Service Provider who in turn establishes a connection for us to the Internet.

The dialer is a program we have all come to love at times and hate at others. When we click on the "connect" button the dialer places a call to the ISP.

There is a pause and then, unless we have selected the mute option, we hear this cacophony of screeching, whirring, and then hissing sounds of our modem "talking" to the ISP's modem. Sometimes in a matter of fifteen seconds or so we get some indication that the connection has been established. The modems, screeching at each other, were music to our ears. We are now ready to get our email, engage in some Instant Messaging, or surf the web. On other occasions the process takes a minute or more. The connection is made and then in a matter of seconds it disconnects and we start over again. Sometimes it doesn't connect on the first attempt at all. Sometimes it takes many attempts. Sometimes we give up.

If you visit an Admiral's Club or Crown Room at an airport you can go to the "workstation" area where you will see businessmen and businesswomen dialing, re-dialing and sometimes cursing. These are men and women who are desperate to get connected. The quality of the phone lines from the Admiral's Club in San Francisco used to be so bad that I have spent entire layover periods trying to connect and leaving unfulfilled. Some "road warriors" have mastered the skill of getting connected. They carry toolkits, adaptors, cables, power converters –and a lot of experience-- to hook up their PC to electrical power and a telephone jack. They have to remove a plastic cover from the wall and pull out the wires and then use "alligator clips" to connect to their PC modem.

When visiting a customer office or conference center I have often looked high and low for a place to connect my ThinkPad to get my email. Over time I have learned that the simplest way is to just say to someone, "excuse me, could I borrow your fax machine?" You can be certain that somewhere in nearly every building on earth there is a fax machine. Fax machines are all the same in that they have RJ-11 jacks. RJ-11 is short for "Registered jack". RJ-11 is a particular standard for a six-conductor plastic jack that typically contains four wires (two for each phone line). The RJ-11 jack is the most common telephone jack in use worldwide. Typically a wire from the wall plugs into a jack on the fax machine that is labeled "line". Almost always the fax machine has an additional jack that is vacant. It is labeled "phone". That is where you plug your PC modem. Then you just have to find out if it is necessary to dial a "9" to get an outside line and you are on your way. Ready to get connected and then stand there by the fax machine like a lurker. It is embarrassing when people come by to fax something or to pick up an urgent incoming fax they were expecting and there you are, a complete stranger, hoarding their fax machine. "I'll be finished in a minute", you say hoping that your email program isn't downloading a huge multimedia file that will take the next hour. Sometimes it is anything but easy to get connected to the Internet.

Although we all look forward to more Internet speed, being Always On will soon be perceived as being even more valuable and important. If you are lucky enough to be using a cable modem or DSL or even better yet, being a student at a college or university having an always-on local area network in the dormitory, you know what I mean. You are Always On. You don't "log on". You just "are on". Soon the concept of logging on will be as old fashioned as "ring me up an operator" to make a telephone call like people did in the 1950s'. You don't "log on" to the power grid so you can use your toaster. You won't "log on" to an ISP in order to use the Internet. When we are Always On things change. It is a different experience than what most people face today.

By being Always On, not only does the frustration go away but, some very subtle yet profound things happen. When you don't have to log on -- you just are on -- your propensities to do things on the Internet change dramatically. If you are leaving the house in the morning to fly to a city 1,000 miles or so away you don't go to your PC, boot up Windows, dial your ISP to get connected, start a browser and surf to a weather site to check the weather at your destination. In fact the overhead associated with getting connected is so high that people don't normally connect to the Net unless they are planning to make a session of it, perhaps a half hour at a minimum so you can do other things on line too. The overhead to connect for a simple weather check is just not worth it. You wait until you get in the car and hope you hear a forecast for your destination or get a newspaper.

If you are Always On, on the other hand, you just go over to your PC and touch the mouse. Your energy saving monitor springs to life and you click on the weather icon. In fact your proclivity to go check the weather, the news, the sports, the stocks, to shop, to learn, to be entertained, becomes quite different than today because now you are Always On. We begin to think of the Internet not as a new medium but as *the* new medium. Like electricity it is just there when you need it. And increasingly, it will be.

The other change will be that when we are always on, we will begin to think of the Internet differently. It is easy to think of the Internet and the web as the same thing. For millions of people they are in fact synonymous. The browser is their sole Internet application. They use it for surfing websites, email, banking, shopping, and participating in discussion groups. All with their browser. Actually, the Internet and the web are two different things. The Internet is a global communications network. It delivers packets of zeroes and ones from origin to destination. The web is an application that utilizes the Internet.

The web was born in Europe at CERN, which is the European Organization for Nuclear Research based in Geneva, Switzerland. Thousands of scientists and researchers there are engaged in advanced work in physics; specifically, the area of particle research. In the late 1980's a systems programmer by the name of Tim Berners-Lee was working at CERN on software for real time data acquisition from physics experiments. That was his day job. At the same time he had a skunk works project going on to find a way to cope with the huge growth of documents from the many research projects. There was great interest in CERN's work not only by the thousands of staff and researchers in Geneva but also by colleagues all over the world. The problem was that everyone had different kinds of computers; Unix, Apple, IBM, DOS, Windows, Linux, and many others. A highly centralized hier-archical approach was not meeting the needs of those who wanted to get con-nected with all the research that was going on. It would have been nice to find some way to make all the computers compatible but Tim had a much better idea; make the data compatible.

Two basic ideas make it work. First is a "protocol" called HTTP or hypertext transfer protocol. HTTP defines a series of exchanges between a browser and a server. Using HTTP the browser enables you to request a page of information from the server. The protocol specifies the address of a server somewhere on the Internet and a document name. The request goes to www.amazon.com, for exam-ple, and you receive the homepage from their server downloaded to your PC. The second key part of the web is HTML or hypertext markup language. HTML utilizes "tags" that define how the content of a document is formatted. For example, a <b> tag means that the text associated with it should be highlighted in **Bold**. Other tags are used to underline, center or enlarge text. The tags themselves are not visible but they control what a webpage looks like. Most importantly there are tags that specify that certain text is a hyperlink; i.e. a link to another document in another server. Click on it and the HTTP protocol results in you "surfing" to the desired page. This all works so smoothly and intuitively that in a remarkably short period of time more than a hundred million people had mastered it. Hence, the result that many people think the Internet is the web and the web is the Internet.

Using a browser to visit websites, however, is just one of the things that the Internet makes possible. In addition to delivering webpages the Internet can deliv-er other things. For example, a colleague of mine, Andy Stanford-Clark, purchased roughly $300 of weather monitoring equipment at Radio Shack and installed it on the roof of his house on the Isle of Wight, which is off the coast of England. The weather equipment monitors temperature, humidity, barometric pressure and trend, rainfall, wind direction, and wind speed. The data is sent to the PC in his house, which in turn delivers it to a server at another location. Andy (or his friends and family) can utilize a simple application program on the desktop of his PC called the WeatherBox and can see what the weather is doing at his house over the Internet from wherever in the world he happens to be. The data is delivered directly to the WeatherBox not to a browser.

The WeatherBox is an example of a class of applications called SCADA (supervisory control and data acquisition). SCADA is used for delivering real time data for monitoring a city water supply, an oil pipeline, or a plant floor automation system in a factory. With an Always On Internet, data from these applications and others can be delivered to remote engineers and others who have a need for the information. No longer will it be necessary for a person to be at the site in order to monitor what is going on at the site. A practical application of the technology is Automated Meter Reading. This will mean that no longer will people have to come to read your electricity/gas/water meter. They will be able to query it remotely across your Always On home connection!

And the applications are not limited to the industrial arena. Imagine that you are on the train commuting to work. All of a sudden you realize, oh gee, did I close the garage door? Did I remember to put down the blinds in the sunroom? I was supposed to put down the blinds so that the sun doesn't bleach the fabric of our furniture. You grab your mobile phone which has a built in Internet capability. Since your home is Always On you are able to connect to a server on the home LAN. An application on the server sends status information to your phone that confirms what you suspected; the blinds are still up. You move the cursor on the display of the phone to "blinds down" and click. Down go the blinds. While you are at it you confirm that the garage doors are down. Later that day while en route to your weekend retreat you connect to its LAN and turn on the heat so things will be cozy when you arrive. Always on.

My father has a pacemaker installed in his chest. It is a great technology that regulates the rhythm of his heart. Periodically, my mother helps him place some sensors on his chest, which are connected to electrical leads, which in turn connect to a modem. They dial the hospital and the modem transfers data about how Dad's pacemaker is working. If there is an irregularity of some kind, a visit to the hospital may be needed. I look forward to the day when Dad's pacemaker will emit an RF signal that can be picked up by a device in the house, which in turn is connected to the home Local Area Network. If there is any irregularity going on a message gets sent to my brother and me and to the doctor. No need to wait for the next scheduled test. Real time. Always on.

Most Internet access today is via telephone companies. The telephone was not designed for the usage requirements of the Internet but the telephone companies have adapted well. Generally speaking the telephone network is extremely reliable in most parts of the world. However, much of the wired infrastructure of the world has been in place for a very long time. In some hotels you get connected but then the bits have to go from your room to the network closet of the hotel and then under the streets via some ancient wiring that has been in place for decades. Some hotel telephone systems can only accommodate a fraction of their guests being connected to the Internet simultaneously. The result is often slow connections, broken connections, and sometimes no connection. Many parts of the wired world are just not prepared to handle the Always On environment that more and more people are coming to expect.

A new standard introduced by the Institute for Electric and Electronic Engineers (IEEE) called 802.11b is gaining a lot of momentum and is about to change the game for Always On. 802.11b utilizes a PCMCIA card that you plug into the side or back of your notebook computer. A tiny antenna on the end of the card can then communicate with another antenna that may be in the ceiling or in a closet. The antennas can communicate with each other within a range of roughly three hundred feet. For most homes this will cover the entire home plus the patio!

Although the priority for this new wireless capability has been notebook computers there are now devices being introduced to outfit desktop PC's as well. This is going to become extraordinarily popular for use in homes where putting Local Area Network cable in the walls is often difficult and expensive. The biggest impact of 802.11b is for the "road warriors". Having a Notebook computer with an 802.11b wireless capability means being able to connect to the Internet while in airports, train stations, hotels, hospitals, building lobbies, and other public places. Starbucks coffee is starting to install this wireless technology in all of their locations. Your next coffee order may not be a "to-go" order, especially when you can relax with your coffee and be connected to the Internet.

No longer will people have to look for the fax machine to get connected. Companies such as Wayport and MobileStar are rolling out services now. Not only does this new wireless standard allow you to connect your PC to the Internet at a speed of up to eleven million bits per second but also does so with no wires. American Airlines has installed the MobileStar service in their Admirals Club lounges. For a modest fee you can have high-speed access, no hassles with dialing, and sit anywhere in the lounge that you want. The multi-megabit speed is between your Notebook and the "gateway" in the hotel or airport lounge. The actual speed you experience will depend on how many users you are sharing with and the speed of the connection between the hotel or lounge and their Internet Service Provider. But it is almost always far better than the old way of using a dial-up connection. It also eliminates the wires and provides encryption so that another user or hacker is not able to eavesdrop on your activity. A new version of the wireless technology, called 802.11a, will be launched in 2001 that will be approximately 1,000 times faster than the 56K speed that comes with PC's today. This will put wireless in clear contention to be an alternative to the high speed networking cables that are being put into virtually all new office buildings and upscale new homes.

> But then there is the power receptacle. Battery life is going to improve for our Notebook computers and cell phones, but until it does we still need to charge our batteries when we stop by the airport lounge between flights. It is great that we can connect to the Internet in a simple wireless manner and enjoy the high speed but where is the power receptacle to plug in and charge the battery? Sometimes I think that hotel and airline executives don't travel. I have been in lounges in the workstation area, the place for PC users, which have *no* power receptacles. Some hotels have gotten more with the program and now have an RJ-11 and a power receptacle right on the desk in the room. That is progress but now that I have my PC plugged in where do I plug my cell phone charger?

There is another wireless technology, called Bluetooth™, which will also have a big impact and potentially revolutionize our personal connectivity beyond just our PC and provide wireless operation for virtually any kind of device. Bluetooth is a technical specification for small form factor, low-cost communication between mobile computers, mobile phones, telephone headsets and other portable hand-held devices, plus connectivity to the Internet, all using radio waves. The initial version of Bluetooth will have a range of operation is approximately 30 feet but a later version will take it to 300 feet. Bluetooth is being driven by leaders in the tele-communications, computing, and network industries, including 3Com, Ericsson, IBM, Intel, Lucent, Microsoft, Motorola, Nokia, Toshiba, and over 2000 associate and adopter companies.

Bluetooth will eventually help us all perform everyday tasks in extraordinary ways using wireless technology. You will be able to walk into a room where your PC is and your Palm Pilot or other PDA in your pocket will detect the PC and then automatically unlock the PC, log you in with your password, decrypt your files, open up your applications, and automatically synchronize data between the PC and the PDA. When you step away from the PC it will automatically be secured, preventing unauthorized access.

Imagine that it is Monday morning at home and you are headed out to the airport to attend an important customer meeting. You come down to breakfast in the kitchen. While eating your cereal, you use your "InfoPad", an 8.5" x 11" paper-sized wireless information appliance, to log on to the Internet (using Bluetooth to dial out through the PC in your basement home office). You check on your flight schedule and the weather at the destination city, so you know if you have to bring a jacket or a raincoat. While online you quickly check some stock prices and put in an order to buy one that you have been following.

Your mobile phone, which utilizes Bluetooth wireless technology, will enable you to purchase gas and coffee at the gas station. While the gas is pumping, a Bluetooth server in the pump sends ads to your mobile phone and allows you to browse gifts from the gas vendor's Intranet. Your mobile phone may also allow you to control various devices in your home environment such as turning lamps or appliances on and off. Some research analysts claim the Bluetooth Headset will become the most popular product that utilizes Bluetooth wireless technology. The Bluetooth Headset will be connected to a compatible mobile phone and then the user can either receive or make phone calls. Voice dialing will also possible.

Another idea that is likely to become quite popular with Bluetooth will be to control home entertainment units such as CD-players, MP3 players, televisions, and home theatre systems. Instead of today's remote control units we will be using our Palm Pilot or Handspring PDA. Having a single interface will be quite desirable.

We will also be able to download programs from the Internet that will enable us to personalize our PDA to handle new devices and also to tailor the way in which we want our entertainment to work. At 6 PM turn on the news from a satellite station and then at 8 PM capture a movie and store it on the home music and video server in the basement. At the touch of a button on the PDA bring the news to the kitchen on a wall mounted flat panel monitor. With another touch of a button the monitor becomes a PC monitor and the PDA becomes our keyboard and mouse for surfing the web.

Being Always On will change our lives. It will enable us to have access to information when we need it not just when we happen to be at a place that is "wired". It will allow us to receive real time data from a variety of sources and even use the Internet more like an intercom to reach colleagues or family members on a timely basis. Even though we can be Always On that doesn't mean we will have to be Always On all the time; just when we want to be.

CHAPTER 6

Everywhere

In 2001, I believed the Internet was going to be everywhere. I was direction-ally correct, but perhaps a bit optimistic WiFi would become pervasive. An increasing number of places offer WiFi, but too many hotels still charge high fees. Although almost all public libraries offer free WiFi, too many physician office waiting lounges and small restaurants do not. The majority of medi-cal waiting areas I have visited have no WiFi; clearly a net attitude problem.

Gigabit WiFi arrived in 2012, but it has a long way to go before becoming ubiquitous. My view was and still is WiFi should be free to the consumer. I understand just as there is "no free lunch", hotels, airlines, and medical prac-tices must recover the cost of installing and maintaining WiFi. However, they all provide electricity, lighting, heat, air conditioning, and running water for free. Why not free WiFi? The cost for these necessities is recovered through the price of products and services. They are a cost of doing business. WiFi should be the same way. Many hotels have seen WiFi as a way to boost profit from a guest's stay, but they are beginning to get the word loud and clear from customers who resent the additional charges. Hyatt Hotels re-vised their policy in this regard in 2015.

In 2001, I predicted many people would have multiple devices, depending on who they were and where they were and when they were ready to engage in certain Internet activities. Although there were no iPhones or Android phones at the time, I could see the shift coming. I suggested some people would choose to have no devices or just a PC. I saw the Internet kiosk filling *the gap. Although Internet kiosks are in use, the ubiquity of cell phones has mostly obviated the need for them. I wrote about location based services, something we now take for granted, but the examples I wrote about have still not appeared. I still believe they will.*

The third characteristic of the NGi is that the Internet is going to be everywhere. Today the Internet is not everywhere. The Internet is where our PC is. If you are out for a ride in the car, walking down the street, visiting some friends, or wherever, and you get the idea that you want to do something simple on the Internet like check the weather or a sports score, your first step is to go to where your PC is. It would be great if the Internet was everywhere when we need it. In fact we are already seeing dramatic changes along these lines – a huge shift is underway.

The evolution of the universal browser has had a huge impact on making Internet content available Everywhere. Before Mosaic, the first widely used browser; there was no expectation of a uniform interface and way to interact. Today we take it for granted that we can walk up to any computer connected to the Internet and expect to find a browser there. Not only that but we automatically know how to use it! The world went from zero to tens of millions of users in a very short time. In effect, the largest focus group ever validated that "browsing" was a fundamental human trait. No training required.

The vast majority of webpages are viewed through a browser on a PC. Two years from now it may be less than 50%. Might be a lot less. Is the PC going away? No. It is not a decline in PC's causing this drop in the percentage of web accesses. In fact PC's are growing. I cannot imagine giving up my PC. However, the era of the PC as the center of innovation and activity on the Internet is over. It has shifted from personal computing to pervasive computing. Pervasive computing, as it's name implies, refers to computing devices which are Everywhere. This would include personal digital assistants (PDA's), mobile phones, pagers, public kiosks, and a new generation of devices we haven't heard of yet. A vast assortment of devices that fit our every need or whim and they will all be connected to the Internet.

When people go to weather.com to check out the conditions for the weekend the vast majority go to their PC and view the weather forecast through their browser. But some people may want to see that same information using an Internet connected television. For those people their television is a television 85% of the time, but 15% of the time the television serves as their browser. Other people would like to see that same weather.com information on their pager. According to Richard Shim at Ziff-Davis, "The once-ubiquitous pager is fast being squeezed out of the market by ever-cheaper cell phones and more-capable handheld devices". True enough, but many people swear by their pager. They wear it on their belt morning, noon, and night. Pager users will expect to be able to view the weather information on their pager screen. They won't need to see the different sun and cloud icons, the banner advertisements, or the various graphic "trim" from the webpage. They primarily want to know if it is going to rain and what the temperature is or is going to be. Transcoding technology – see below -- will be utilized to look at a page, figure out what the real content is, what makes sense, what's important on this page and to deliver that particular content in a clever compact way to for the small screen size of the pager.

Internet Transcoding for Universal Access

More and more pervasive devices, such as personal digital assistants (PDAs), hand-held computers, smart phones, TV browsers, wearable computers, and other mobile devices are gaining access to the Internet and other multimedia-rich information sources. However, the capabilities of these devices to receive, process, store and display Internet content vary widely. Given the large variety of devices that people will be using, it will be difficult for Internet content publishers to tailor the content to individual devices.

Enabling universal access of multimedia content has become increasingly important. Universal access describes the mechanism for adapting multimedia content to the constraints of the client devices. As an example, a smart phone can access a text document through the use of text-to-speech synthesis.

To enable universal access in the coming age of pervasive computing, IBM has developed a system that tailors the content of webpages for pervasive computing devices. This tailoring process is called *transcoding*. The transcoding system adapts video, images, audio and text to the individual pervasive devices using a framework that allows the content to be *summarized, translated* and *converted,* on the fly. It isn't perfect by any means but until the world's content developers produce device independent content it is a often a good alternative.

Other people will choose to get their weather.com page on their wireless personal digital assistant. For many people, perhaps for quite a few million people, the PDA will be their only computer. For them it has everything they could want. PDA's such as the Palm Pilot, Handspring Visor and the RIM BlackBerry are gaining capability and popularity. Already they are available with a color display, more than enough capacity to store your address book, calendar, to do list, memo pad, a portfolio of useful software applications, and of course a wireless connection to the Internet. What more could you want? For millions, nothing. For others, plenty. I love my IBM WorkPad PDA but I still want my ThinkPad and desktop PC.

And yet millions of other people are beginning to prefer the cell phone (mobile phone) as their web access device. Although the growth is significant in America it is not as dramatic as in other parts of the world. People in Europe are using their Internet enabled mobile phones on trains, checking the weather and also paying their bills, trading stocks, and shopping. We will be hearing a lot about WAP phones. This refers to the wireless application protocol, which is catching on strongly in Europe. WAP includes a wireless markup language (WML), which is well suited for building Internet applications for use on mobile telephones. Handelsbanken, one of the largest banks in Sweden, is working with IBM to use WAP to enable its mainframe banking applications to become available on their customers cell phones.

The popularity of cell phones in Europe is in part due to the fact that there is a single standard called GSM. During the early 1980s, cellular telephone systems began to become popular in Scandinavia, the United Kingdom, France and Germany. Unfortunately, each country developed its own system and none of them were compatible. People could not use their phones across national boundaries at a time when Europe was beginning to unify. A related problem was that each country's system was limited in scale and therefore expensive. In 1982 the Conference of European Posts and Telegraphs (CEPT) formed a study group called the Groupe Spécial Mobile (GSM) to recommend a system that could provide attractive cost and quality and also support international roaming. By 1993 there were 36 GSM networks in 22 countries and it has since spread to hundreds of networks in over a hundred countries around the world. The acronym GSM now stands for Global System for Mobile communications. Deutsche Telekom acquired an American GSM company called Voicestream in 2000 further building momentum toward enabling a person to buy one cell phone and have one cell phone number that can work anywhere in the world.

Profound things are likely to happen with the use of mobile phones in Europe. The GSM standard used throughout Europe includes a computer chip called the Subscriber Identity Module (SIM). The SIM chip is about half the size of a postage stamp and it fits inside the phone. If you take your SIM chip out of the phone and put it into another phone you can then use that phone because the chip contains information about your identity and even your phone number list. Access to the chip (and operation of the phone) is password protected. I am sure it was not planned back when GSM was first devised but by having this password-protected chip it becomes feasible to put a digital ID in it for use in e-commerce applications. This opens up a lot of interesting possibilities.

For example at some point you may be able to walk up to a vending machine, grab your cell phone and press a button that prompts you for your name. You say "this is John" and the phone recognizes that it is you because your voiceprint is stored in the chip. You then press another button and the vending machine gives you a soda with the charge being sent to your credit card or bank account. Another exciting possibility is to walk into a hotel and dial a number that is on the marquis. You say "this is John" and you get a reply that says, "Room number 1045 is ready for you". You go to the tenth floor and point your infrared enabled phone at the door lock. A light flashes. You say to your phone "this is John" and the door unlocks.

Meanwhile the idea of Everywhere in Japan is taking an additional approach and the result is explosive. In early 2000 the Asian edition of BusinessWeek ran a cover story called DoCoMo. It refers to the subsidiary of NTT, Japan's former telephone monopoly. Since the company was partly spun off from NTT in 1992, DoCoMo has become the world's most valuable cell-phone company -- with a market value of over $300 billion as of early 2000. DoCoMo is the largest single-country cell-phone operator in the world, with more than 25 million Japanese subscribers.

According to BusinessWeek, "There are a few things a Japanese teenage girl doesn't leave home without: her six-inch platform shoes, some touch-up toner for her hair color of the day, and her i-mode phone. Teenagers in Japan are sending black and white pictures of themselves back and forth to each other using their I-mode Internet phones. The pictures are stored on servers at DoCoMo. There are also thousands of websites that have custom content to fit nicely on the I-mode's small display.

When the next generation of wireless Internet service, called 3G, arrives for cell phones over the next few years the teenagers will be playing music and watching video on their phones. Many DoCoMo users probably don't own a PC. For them the phone has become the way they get the Internet Everywhere. We may find the DoCoMo phenomenon in America soon. In late 2000 an alliance was struck between NTT DoCoMo and AT&T Wireless whereby DoCoMo has taken a sixteen percent equity stake in the AT&T Wireless tracking stock. The partners believe that the alliance will facilitate the rapid development of next-generation mobile communications system and related mobile services in the U.S. market. DoCoMo has set up an advisory board of top American thought leaders to get advice on how to best integrate DoCoMo into the American market. The impact could be significant. In May of 2000 Japan became the first country in the world where more than half of the webpage accesses were not from a PC browser.

The application possibilities are endless. News, weather, sports, stocks and email are the obvious ones. Transaction oriented applications will ultimately prove more useful however. Have you ever risked your life speeding to an airport to catch a flight only to find out when you arrive exhausted at the gate that the flight has been delayed by an hour? Worse yet, it is on time but had a last minute gate change and the new gate is a mile away! Using a mobile phone to check the very latest status, or better yet, having your phone ring with a message about the schedule or gate change is a valuable service.

Location based services are already emerging and they will get very sophisticated. Suppose you are walking down the street in Winchester, England at 4 PM in the afternoon. Your phone vibrates or rings and you observe that a message has arrived for you. The message says, "Please stop at the King James Pub for an early bird special. Corner of Chestnut and Main. Less than two blocks." An application service provider has worked with the wireless provider and various merchants to make offerings like this possible. The service, of course, knows what time it is, and based on either a Global Positioning System chip in your phone or triangulation to your phone from nearby cellular towers, it is able to determine where you are. Anyone within so many blocks during a certain timeframe will receive the special offer.

The good news is that mobile phones are becoming ubiquitous and using them for Internet access, while still nascent, is beginning to take off. Service providers are moving from just putting the same content that is on a webpage on the wireless device, to more sophisticated approaches that will reduce the size of messages or email by more than half through the use of clever abbreviations. They are also customizing tailored to make them more modular so that screen menus can be based specifically on the nature of the applications. The bad news is that there are multiple cell phone standards around the world and Internet standards are not being consistently used for Internet applications on cell phones. WAP phones are being deployed in Europe. In Japan DoCoMo is using a different approach and the American market is taking yet a different approach. Actually, in America there are multiple standards and multiple Internet application approaches. In total, things could be described as a mess but there is hope on the horizon. The World Wide Web Consortium (W3C) at MIT has recommended a new standard called xHTML. It is device independent. That means it will be possible to create Internet applications and publish content in such a way that deployment can be on a PC or a cell phone or a PDA or other devices.

As Internet standards become integral to cell phones we will see deeper integration of the cell phone into all forms of Internet communication. One example is the integration of the cell phone, corporate directories, and Instant Messaging. IBM has made its entire employee directory accessible via cell phones over the Internet. An employee can login in to a website using any cell phone that has a micro-browser. Many cell phones now have these and soon most will. The employee enters a few characters of the person's name he or she is looking for and the person's phone number appears on the phone display. The number can then be called with the touch of a button. In addition, if (and only if) the person is currently connected to the company intranet, the employee doing the search will see an additional choice on the phone display. That choice says IM, which means instant messaging. If that choice is made another menu appears on the phone display giving the employee the choice to send an instant message that says "Call me ASAP" or "Call me in 5 minutes" or "I'll be there in 10minutes", etc. At the touch of the button the instant message is sent to the PC desktop of the person. The person can then send a reply from the PC and it will appear on the phone display of the "caller". On many occasions it is a waste of time to call a person. They are most likely on the phone or out or just busy. But, if they are connected and you know they are connected and have the ability to send them a quick message from your cell phone it opens up a whole new method of communication.

And then there's a whole new range of devices. Internet radio receivers are emerging that plug into a high speed Internet connection. The tuning knob won't be limited to radio stations within 30 or 40 miles like "normal" radios. More than 5,000 radio stations already broadcast over the Net. The Netpliance i-opener is a non-PC device that offers one-button web access and e-mail. The Handspring Visor uses a technology platform called Springboard that allows a myriad of devices to be plugged into the PDA-like device and change what it does. It can be a plain PDA like the Palm Pilot or it can turn into a cell phone, a TV remote, camera or virtually anything. The list of net appliances or Internet gadgets goes on and on.

AOL In Your Kitchen?

Online services giant AOL is partnering with PC maker Gateway on a family of Internet appliances -- including a wireless keyboard with flat-panel monitor that can be mounted under a kitchen cupboard like a microwave. The PC blends into the environment and becomes an "appliance"; download a recipe, check on inventories of food and supplies, or check food.com to see some cooking in action.

Becoming Mainstream?

Some people call them Internet appliances; some call them wireless gadgets. Whatever you all them they are small, inexpensive, lightweight, instant-on devices that connect to the Internet. It is still very early in the evolution of them and there are many variations on the theme. The early examples are a bit primitive and awkward to use but they will get better and better as consumers vote in the marketplace with their dollars. According to IDC Corporation 18.5 million Internet appliances will ship in the U.S. by 2001 compared to 15.7 home PCs. The numbers are expected to continue very rapid growth. Sega, Nintendo and Sony are adding modems, processors and memory chips to their game systems. Pervasive computing. Everywhere.

There are many implications to the onslaught of these many devices. Some people believe that there is going to be one device that will do everything; PDA, cell phone, pager, music player, global positioning system, and more. I don't believe it for one second. People are all different. Sure, in theory one device could do everything but people will want to optimize in different ways. Some people want the phone capability to be optimal. Others want the PDA to be optimal. Some people like a tiny keyboard and light weight. Other people will opt for more weigh but a more significant keyboard. And so on. The common element of all the devices is that they will all have either wired or wireless Internet connectivity and therefore mean that for each of us the Internet will in fact be Everywhere.

One additional characteristic about the many devices is that they offer the hope of making Internet connectivity much simpler. If you want to shut down your PC for the day, you have to go to the "start" button and select "shut down" but you have to be careful that you have first stopped all the applications you may have been using. Sometimes you get a message that says something like, "Do you really want to shut down?" At other times you may get an irreverent message that says something like, "Halt, you failed to properly shut down!" The implication is that you are an idiot. With a mobile phone or PDA, when you want to "shut down", you push the "off" button and you have completed the task. Turning things on presents an even bigger contrast. Consumer devices will increasingly come from consumer companies rather than computer or telecommunications companies and the result will be that they will be simpler to use.

Many people will have multiple devices, depending on who they are and where they are and when they are ready to do certain things. However, there are many people in the world who don't have access to a personal device no matter how small or inexpensive they may be. In some cases, it may be people who can't afford a device and in other cases it will be people who just don't want a device. No PC. No PDA. No cell phone.

Enter the public Internet kiosk. We are beginning to see these at airports. Public kiosks where you can get your email, check on your stocks, or buy something. The compelling low cost of communications will cause institutions of all kinds to drive their transactions to the Internet. The United States Social Security Administration requires a person to show a hardship case for why they can't afford to have a bank account where the SSA can deposit their monthly payment electronically. This approach will eventually spread to the Internet. The kiosk will be the way in which many people will gain access to the transactions; ordering something or paying a bill, doing some quick research, checking the status of a bank account or an insurance policy, or getting directions. When I was growing up, I remember going out to a vending machine to get a quart of milk. Some people will similarly go out to an Internet kiosk to run an "errand". The kiosk will address, in part, the question of the digital divide. They will be ubiquitous; on the street corner, in the jungle, churches, schools, government buildings, and on the plant floor. Manufacturing employees will be able to take a "web break" instead of a smoke break. The kiosks will play a key role in enabling the Internet to be Everywhere.

The large number of devices connecting to the Internet will place a lot of strain on the infrastructure. Today's Internet is not prepared to handle the billions of devices that will be connected over the next few years. The capacity has been steadily growing and the advent of pervasive optical fiber will likely meet the demand. However, we will soon run out of addresses for all the devices. When you connect to the Internet you are assigned a temporary Internet Protocol (IP) address. The Internet Protocol is the basic building block on which the Internet is built. The current version of the IP, called IP version 4, uses a four-part address for each device; 64.252.14.121 for example. Each part of the address can be between 0 and 256. 256 times 256 times 256 times yields more than 4 billion globally unique addresses. Sounds like a lot, but in practice, the number is considerably smaller because of the inefficient way in which the addresses are allocated. Even at four billion it is not enough. Cell phones alone are projected to in the billions. IPv4 has lasted twenty years but it is time to move on.

A new version of the IP standard has been approved called IPv6 or IP "Next generation". (No, there was never a version 5 – lots of engineers and committees. It is a long story.) IPv6 has 2 to the 128th power addresses. That means

340,282,366,920,938,463,463,374,607,431,768,211,456

different IP addresses can be assigned. Based on a world population of six billion, that means there would be more than

50,000,000,000,000,000,000,000,000,000

addresses per person! If you look at it by land mass it would be an average of slightly more than

200,000,000,000,000,000,000

addresses per square centimeter of the planet!

That should be enough!

IPv6 includes other benefits and simplifies end-to-end security. This will become very important for conducting e-commerce transactions via our many different devices. The initial deployment of IPv6 will take place in specialized markets such as in third generation wireless deployments in Europe and Asia during the next 2-3 years. Once IPv6 gains a foothold in new markets, pressure to upgrade other systems will begin to build. The transition to IPv6 will take many years, with a period of coexistence between IPv4 and IPv6 lasting a decade or longer.

CHAPTER 7
Natural

I had a vision the Internet would become much more natural to use. Most everything I forecasted about Internet use has happened and exceeded my expectations. In the mid to late 1990s, I managed an innovation group at IBM called WebAhead. Some very clever software engineers in the group deployed an instant messaging system developed by an Israeli company. The technology was called Virtual Places and the instant messaging program was called VP Buddy. (The technology was later acquired by IBM and renamed SameTime). Only our small group used VP Buddy initially. The CIO of IBM at the time asked me to stop promoting VP Buddy because it was not an officially supported system. It was run by our little group instead of the corporate IT function. I said it was growing because employees found it an easy and natural way to communicate. It grew from a few dozen users to hundreds of thousands across the company worldwide and became an indispensable tool. As the potential crisis of Year 2000 (Y2K) approached, the CIO asked our group to make sure instant messaging was up and available around the world. The innovation model followed by the WebAhead group offers many lessons applicable today.

I saw a bright future for online education because I believed it was a natural way to learn. I wrote about University of Phoenix and how they were growing. I had no idea nine years later I would embark on 3 ½ years of online study with the University leading to a Doctorate in Health Administration in 2014. The massive open online courses (MOOCS) are fulfilling the vision I described. There are many skeptics of MOOCS, just as there were of the

Internet in 2001. MOOC critics are concerned about low overall percentage of students who complete courses, but this ignores the huge growth of MOOCS with hundreds of universities, thousands of courses, and millions of students.[10] I remain optimistic about their future as an accepted learning tool.

The most natural form of use on the Internet today is social media. I did not foresee there would be more than 200 social media sites with billions of messages every day ranging from family pictures to tweets announcing corporate earnings. I did foresee and advocated the net attitude which underpins social media. It is all about "Power to the People".

I was optimistic about voice recognition, including the ability to translate languages. Adoption was slow for a decade, but is now accelerating with Amazon Alexa, Apple Siri, Google Now, Microsoft Cortana, and the Skype Translator.

The Internet needs to become more natural. Arguably it is not really that natural today. In fact, it is almost a contrived activity; you have to really want to be on the Net. As we move forward from a couple of hundred million people to a couple of billion people on the Net this has to change. One ingredient to things becoming more natural is instant messaging. Like so many things teenagers provide some clues to what things are going to be like. They get home from school, they get off the bus, they dash into the house to the PC, and they get on the Internet. Unlike a few years ago when using the browser was a big thing, they now focus on using instant messaging programs such as AOL instant messenger, ICQ, or Yahoo. Instead of surfing the web they send instant messages to their buddies – many of them the same ones with whom they were riding on the bus! To them this is just a natural way to communicate.

It Isn't Just For Kids Anymore

Instant messaging is much more than meets the eye and it is not a social phenomenon limited to kids. There are bigger things afoot here. Instant messaging is becoming the "back channel" in corporations around the world. In late 1997 a group of software engineers at IBM's Internet Technology Laboratory in Southbury, Connecticut met with Ehud Shapiro to discuss instant messaging.

Udi is a member of the Faculty of Mathematics and Computer Science at The Weizmann Institute of Science but at the time he was on leave of absence and had just formed a company called Ubique. Ubique had developed a technology called Virtual Places that enabled a user connected to the Internet to create a list of their "buddies". The program utilized a technology that could sense the "presence" of another user. This feature became known as "awareness". If any of their "buddies" were also connected to the Internet then his or her name would be highlighted in bold. By clicking on that name the user could then send an "instant message" to their "buddy". The program became known as VP Buddy.

The IBM engineers asked Udi for a copy of the software in order to experiment with it in a corporate environment and he happily complied. At first VP Buddy was a novelty among just a few of the engineers and myself. It rapidly evolved from being "cool" to becoming a useful tool to becoming a way of life. It became the "back channel" for communications.

I first realized how profound it was when I was in a hotel room somewhere working on my email. I was replicating email from the company server and while that was happening I was browsing some websites reading news. I was also connected to VP Buddy. When you installed VP Buddy it automatically became part of your PC. All of a sudden a message, an instant message, popped up on my PC screen. It was from Ronda, my assistant. Someone had called the office with an important matter and she wasn't sure what to tell the person so she thought she would try VP Buddy to reach me. I answered her question and went back to my email and news. I knew we were on to something big and important. If you were connected you could be reached and reach others who were connected. It didn't matter if you were at home, at the office, in a hotel with only a single phone line, at a customer's office, an airline lounge, or even on a train or plane with a wireless connection.

Email is great. We live and die by it. Some days we can't live without it. Other days we would rather die than open that inbox! It isn't going to go away but it needs to be supplemented. Email is asynchronous. You send an email to a person to ask them a question. They are traveling and don't get the email for a day or two. They answer you and meanwhile you are traveling for a day or two. By the time you get the answer the question has lost its relevance. In many cases the question you have is a simple one. You need to know right now. With instant messaging, you take a look at your buddy list to see if a colleague who likely has the answer is online. If they are you send them a quick instant message. They answer you and the communication is over. You are finished. You have what you need. This is called synchronous or "instant" messaging.

Assistants and secretaries at IBM found VP Buddy a very useful tool. Now they could reach their principal even if he or she was in a hotel room with a single phone line replicating their email. The engineers at IBM put the VP Buddy program on their intranet site so others could download and install it. It grew by leaps and bounds. There was no announcement of VP Buddy, no training program, no help desk, and no official support – just people helping each other with tips and techniques. By 1999 there were more than a quarter of a million users in the company! At any point in time there were tens of thousands of people connected at any one time and more than a million instant messages were being sent and received per day. The "back channel" was working.

A company attorney in New York and a company attorney in Chicago having a conference call with a vendor attorney found they could pass a note "under the table" to each other from thousands of miles away. Executives having press interviews over the telephone could receive instant messages from their media relations managers who were also on line. Questions and answers can be flying around in the background enabling the executive to be responsive to a reporter's line of questioning. Sales and services professionals could have chat sessions to solve problems for customers. At one point some middle managers in the CIO's office questioned whether allowing this unsupported application to continue to grow in such an experimental way was a good thing. Just before the end of 1999 the CIO himself declared the VP Buddy prototype application "mission critical" for the migration to Year 2000. At the stroke of midnight there were eighty software engineers in a single chat session discussing technical details of Y2K. If a customer disaster of some kind had arisen the experts from around the world were all connected and ready to solve the problem.

What about privacy when using instant messaging? Yes, there is a dark side of IM – it can be abused like any good tool can. Most instant messaging systems on the market have privacy options to help with this. For example, you can select who can see you when you are online. Options include anyone and everyone, only a specified list of people, everybody except a specified list of people, or nobody. You can also set modes of operation such as "I am away" or "Do not disturb". It is mostly self-regulating.

People are generally sensitive and follow the golden rule of instant messaging -- do unto others as you would have them do unto you.

Ubique was acquired by IBM in 1998 and was branded by its Lotus subsidiary as Sametime. Sametime evolved into a family of real-time collaboration products providing instant awareness, communication, and document sharing capabilities for the business world. Numerous other companies offer similar technology. Awareness is the cornerstone of these offerings. With the selected awareness of coworkers, partners, or customers online, users can communicate in a variety of ways -- from one-on-one instant messages to launching virtual meetings. Not only can instant messages be sent but live documents and applications can be shared. Whether presenting a new program to a field sales force or to offering live assistance to web customers, real-time collaboration is emerging as a major new area of Information Technology.

Once you see that your buddy is indeed online you may want to have a short e-meeting. Perhaps you have a spreadsheet with next year's budget that you want to review with her. You click on her name but instead of sending an instant message you select an option to "invite to an instant meeting". Your colleague gets the invitation instantly and then clicks on a button to accept the invitation. This opens her browser and takes her to the e-meeting page. The e-meeting page is a "virtual conference room" where the two of you (you could have multiple colleagues if you chose to) can review the spreadsheet. Suppose you use Microsoft Excel as your spreadsheet and your colleague uses Lotus 1-2-3. It doesn't matter. Whatever spreadsheet software you have appearing on your PC is what your colleague will see in the e-meeting "space" in the browser. This is called application sharing. Your colleague may say "what would happen to the budget if you change the growth rate assumption"? You change the percentage in your spreadsheet and your colleague sees the change in her view of the spreadsheet. You can even turn control of the e-meeting over to your colleague and she can make a change which you will then see. No longer do you have to say "fax me a copy of the budget". No longer do you have to ask, "Does anybody have the current version of the budget"?

The instant messaging buddy list typically includes your colleagues; people you work for and people you work with. The buddy list crosses organizational boundaries. People around the globe in different departments and even different companies, all of who are working on a project for a common customer can be part of the list. When the project is over the list may go away to be replaced by a new one. The buddy list doesn't have to be all business either. A good instant messaging system includes encryption so that the wrong people cannot read confidential information, but a more public part of the buddy list might include family members, the school nurse, and your stockbroker. Have you ever been interrupted in a conference room when a secretary brings you a phone message? You go to a private phone to call home to find out your spouse wants to know the name of a plumber to fix a leaky sink. Perhaps that ten-minute interruption could have been a ten second instant message instead.

Many companies are focusing on development of tools that expand on instant messaging and e-meetings to provide comprehensive collaborative environments. Among the leading collaborative tools are Notes/Sametime from Lotus, Conference Center 2000 from PlaceWare, TeamFlow from CFM, Centra eMeeting/Centra Conference from Centra, and Caucus Virtual Teams from Caucus Systems. They are building tools in six key areas.

1. Chat and instant messaging applications. These are the basic communication element and where collaboration usually starts. Groups of colleagues or business partners can see who is online and send text messages to each other.
2. Real-time conferencing tools with application sharing. These can be used in conjunction with a conference call and let participants view presentations through a web browser or sketch a diagram or annotate a slide in a "whiteboard". There are many applications in customer service where a remote technician can push a webpage to you with instructions on how to change that printer ribbon or unclog your garbage disposal.
3. Asynchronous web-based conferencing. This includes discussion groups or message boards that are not dependent on real-time interaction.
4. Document and knowledge management tools. This category includes a variety of web based and other groupware applications that enable colleagues to jointly work on documents and keep track of who made what changes.

5. Group calendars. These tools let users coordinate meetings, schedule chat sessions and track other events using a browser or e-mail notification.

6. Web-based project management. These tools show lists of projects and team members as well as the status of their assigned tasks and related documentation.

Tools such as this will become very important in the NGi. The obvious benefit is reduced travel cost but there are equally important but subtler benefits. E-meetings start on time and end on time. The participants can all be in different locations; some at home, some at the office, some at the airport, and some at a client's office. People tend to be prepared. Everyone, by definition, has access to the latest subject matter. And while the e-meeting is going on, colleagues can be sharing information via the instant messaging "back channel".

The most important benefit of e-meetings is that you can actually have the meeting when it needs to be held. How often have you experienced the following problem? You urgently need to have a meeting with someone but that person is "not available". You talk to their assistant and find they are traveling. They'll be back week after next. Meanwhile, you have an urgent matter and you need the meeting tomorrow at the latest. Chances are that the person who is traveling has some slack time at their hotel or at an airline lounge. With e-meeting technology, as long as the participants have access to a PC and a connection to the Internet, the meeting can happen.

The irony of e-meetings is that now you can travel more! In the past you were sometimes tethered to your office. You couldn't take that needed trip to Europe because of an important meeting to take place during that week. Now you can take the trip and still be able to attend the meeting. For the last seven years or so I have been traveling around the world telling people why they won't have to travel so much anymore because of the Internet. That is about to change!

The teenagers will likely continue to make instant messaging an important new social phenomenon but in parallel with that evolution corporate enterprises are beginning to see the potential for profound impact from real time collaboration. Ian Lamont wrote a story in Network World (11/13/00) called "The Coolest

Kind of Collaboration" which focused on how accounting firm Ernst & Young, a longtime groupware advocate, is taking collaboration to the next level. John Whyte, E&Y's CIO, believes that using telephones and e-mail should be viewed as the old-fashioned way for employees to get things done. E&Y is well along on the NGi curve.

Virtual teaming expert Jessica Lipnack goes even further. She believes we are at the brink of a workplace revolution. Improved Internet-enabled features of collaboration applications, combined with the frustrations of more traditional communication tools, will provide the fuel, says Lipnack, co-author of Virtual Teams: People Working Across Boundaries With Technology and co-founder of virtual-teams.com, a management technology consultancy in Newton, Massachusetts. Lipnack says that people need to be able to make decisions and resolve conflicts online, as well as provide leadership, assign tasks, exact accountability and facilitate meetings. "All the stuff we do naturally face to face, we have to be able to do online," she says.

Learning On-Line

Another area that is benefiting from the evolution of instant messaging and e-meetings is e-learning. In practical terms, e-learning is the ability to learn outside a physical classroom. "Distributed learning" such as correspondence courses have been around for a long time but Internet technology is now providing the means for an advanced and wide-ranging e-learning infrastructure. E-learning allows companies to deliver effective, specifically targeted training in a cost-effective way. It can deliver training on a global basis, while tailoring content to suit the needs of individuals. It also allows an organization to regularly assess skills gaps that may exist and make the appropriate investments to close the gaps. A number of the world's leading companies including GE, Cisco, IBM and Procter & Gamble have embraced e-learning and are reaping significant benefits. John Chambers, CEO of Cisco, has described e-learning as "the third wave of the internet." Laura Sanders, Vice President for IBM Mindspan Solutions says, "Having delivery infrastructure to provide e-learning will be as important in the next few years as an e-mail system is today. It will simply be part of what's needed to run a business. E-learning will move from the classroom to the boardroom as a strategic tool to for competitive advantage."

According to International Data Corporation, e-learning will have a significant impact. They expect corporate business skills training in the U.S. to go from 72% in the classroom in 1999 down to 35% by year-end 2004. The technology can be split into three groups. Self-paced or asynchronous learning allows a learner to choose a course independently and learn online, usually alone, like reading a book. Collaborative or synchronous learning makes use of instant messaging technology, which allows a remote learner to interact with others in the group, asking questions and discussing points. The virtual classroom or real-time learning, using video over the Internet, allows a learner to see the teacher and talk to others in the class through instant messaging or an audio link.

E-learning is particularly effective on a large scale – a multinational corporation, for instance, is able to use e-learning techniques to train its entire workforce around the world simultaneously on the introduction of a new product or innovation, with immediate and consistent results. Smaller companies can also benefit by training employees quickly and efficiently in new skills, creating a flexible and multi-talented workforce. Unipart, a company in the UK, for instance, has introduced a comprehensive e-learning system that allows its employees to handle different parts on its distribution line. Theirs is an e-learning system based on "just-in-time" education – where the workers learn something in the morning and apply it to the distribution line in the after-noon. In Unipart's case the innovation has allowed it to widen its product base using existing staff.

Universities Go Online Too

The Internet was born in the university environment and there are many advanced Internet research projects happening there. Probably all universities in the world have websites and many have impressive intranet sites for class scheduling and interactive studies. Some universities such as The Open University in England and the University of Phoenix do most of their teaching online. At The Open University more than 150 courses use Information Technology to enhance learning in various ways including virtual tutorials and discussion groups, electronic submission and marking of assignments, multimedia teaching materials and computer mediated conferencing. OU students read more than 170,000 email and computer conference messages every day. OU researchers have developed new applications of Information Technology for learning from "virtual field trips" and have even created an Internet stadium capable of hosting mass audience events with up to 100,000 students.

The University of Phoenix Online claims to offer "the unparalleled convenience and flexibility of attending classes from your personal computer. In small groups of eight to thirteen, or working one-on-one with an instructor, students are discussing issues, sharing ideas, testing theories, essentially enjoying all of the advantages of an on-campus degree program, with one important exception." And, they also remind us that there is "No commute!" At some point I envision that degrees will be granted based on the "learning space" in which the learning occurred more so than on the educational institution that was attended. For example, a person might say that he or she got their PhD and if you want to see their degree you can go to http://janeqdoe.com/degree. Upon visiting there one would see an e-diploma that might say something like Jane Q. Doe was granted this degree based on the unanimous vote of the following professors. Then there would be a list of professors and their digital signatures that would authenticate that the professors are legitimate. The relevance of the e-diploma I envision is not that of the university but rather of the status and reputation of the individual professors. Suppose a person has gotten a degree in Customer Relationship Management. Even more impressive than a degree from the world's leading university for CRM education might be an e-diploma which is signed by the top ten CRM professors in the world with whom the person studied.

A lot of education will be done on-line but some will remain physical for a long time. Maybe forever. Professor Stanley Birkin of the University of South Florida reminds me that most advanced college degrees today require total immersion. Students operate in an apprenticeship mode and are available at all times for research seminars and presentations. It is this total immersion that has worked so well in developing the research skills necessary to fill or occupy a future role as a professor or a key researcher. Although this archaic approach goes back to the old days of Oxford and Cambridge, it does work, and has resulted in great researchers and faculty members the world over. Online or physical, students can still get together in person to turn the tassel on their mortar boards!

Sprechen Sie Deutsch

Instant messaging, as a technology, is at the very beginning. Much more is possible. Lotus has introduced language translation so that messages can be translated on the fly. For example I might see that my colleague Frank in Heidelberg, Germany is online and send him an instant message. "Frank how is the weather in Heidelberg?" I ask. The message is translated on the fly to German and up on Frank's screen appears a message, "Frank, wie ist das Wetter in Heidelberg"? Frank answers me in German, "John, ist es kalt und regnerisch" and up on my screen appears, "John it is cold and rainy".

Language translation is performed using some very sophisticated mathematics. It isn't perfect. A real person doing translation of what you say as you say it, watching your facial expressions, understanding the various innuendos and body movements is far superior – for now. Machine translation will be good enough for many web applications in the realm of e-business. It is good for conversation but not yet good enough to interpret contracts or provide instructions during a surgical procedure. You could think of it like riding in a taxi cab in New York. The instructions you are able to provide are not in the driver's native language but it is usually good enough to get you where you want to go.

The potential here is enormous. By adding text-to-speech technology both Frank and I could have heard a simulated voice that would speak the translated words through the speaker of our PC. Taking this even a step further, if you combine instant messaging, voice recognition, language translation and text to speech technologies. You get a real time multi-lingual intercom! Think about customer service applications. Think about a person asking a question in Spanish and then that question is routed to the most knowledgeable person in that subject matter, who answers the question in Chinese and the questioner hears the answer in Spanish.

There used to be 30,000 dialects in the world. Today there are about 5,000. Some people say that soon there will be just one. I don't think so. In fact I think the Internet may actually bring back some of those formerly or nearly extinct dialects. People have grown up on a mountain somewhere with a unique dialect. Then they graduated from school and went their separate ways. The dialect dies. Now, with Internet email, these school friends can remain in contact and in fact can maintain their dialect and bring in former graduates to build a community around their common culture.

An Agent At Your Service

Another emerging technology in the instant messaging arena is software agents. Software agents are not new but using them in conjunction with instant messaging is. The software engineers at IBM's Southbury Internet lab began to experiment in 2000 with what they call Buddy Bots. Bot is an abbreviation for robot. The Buddy Bots are software robots. They do things for you. For example, your buddy list may have an entry in it called Blue Pages. It isn't a person – it is a software agent. Blue Pages is the name of the corporate directory at IBM. It contains more than 300,000 entries. If an employee clicks on Blue Pages (which is always connected) and types, "who is Michael Nelson?", the buddy bot goes to the Blue Pages directory, looks up Michael Nelson and sends back an instant message that includes his name, email address, phone number, and office location.

There are, of course, other ways that an employee could get that same information including various intranet applications. However, there is a certain appeal to using the instant messaging program to do it. The IM program is always there; right on the desktop ready for use. Yes, a browser could do the job but sometimes the browser is not a desirable solution. For example, you may be browsing a news story and then your phone rings. You answer the phone and colleague asks you a question. You don't have the answer but you are sure another colleague does and you offer to look up the office location. You go to your favorites list in your browser and look up the information and, your caller being appreciative, you hang up the phone. Back to that interesting news story you were reading. Oops, how do I get back to that page I was on? Sometimes you can go back with a browser – sometimes you can't for various reasons. You could have started a second browser for the inquiry but sometimes having multiple browsers running on your PC gets confusing. Using a simple "who is" command in your instant messaging program could have done the job very efficiently.

I believe this will be an emerging NGi trend; i.e. using an instant messaging program for simple queries and tasks. It is just simpler and faster. How about a weather forecast? Enter "Weather Boston" and back comes "Boston – cloudy with snow showers". How about a stock quote? Enter "stock quote XOM" and back comes "Exxon-Mobil $88.75". The Southbury engineers have prototype buddy bots that bring you your portfolio of stock quotes, allow you to look up the definition of company terms from a reference database, and alert you to your daily calendar and pending to-do items when you first connect in the morning. Buddy bots will make the next generation of the Internet more Natural.

One of the Southbury engineers, Karl Gonzalez, took the concept of awareness a step further. He built a "digital video water cooler" to allow colleagues who work at multiple locations to come together in a virtual space. A video camera and microphone at each of eight locations provides a live stream over the intranet to a single webpage that displays all eight video windows. Colleagues can go over to the camera, wave to another colleague, have a brief chat or just a friendly wave. The result was to increase team camaraderie and a sense of presence and belonging to the same team even though they were physically separated by large distances.

Music Makes The World Go 'Round

Part of the NGi becoming more Natural will come from better integration of media including audio, video, animation, and virtual reality. As more bandwidth arrives for more people we will find that a lot of video content will be available. We will move toward having full-screen, jitter-free, high quality video on the Internet. Over time we will be able to watch video on mobile phones and PDAs. The most significant and practical introduction of media will be music. The reason that digital music (MP3 in particular) has become so popular is that it is possible to transport it in digital form and then play it with no perceptible loss in fidelity. You can convert your CD collection to MP3 format and store it on your PC. A collection of one hundred CDs would require about 5 billion byes (gigabytes) of storage. This is just a fraction of the storage that comes with any PC you buy today. You can then establish "playlists" to organize your collection by genre or composer. You can then connect the output of your PC to the input of your stereo system and the result is high quality stereo music. The quality is not the same as the original CD but most people cannot tell the difference.

That same music collection will be able to be played on your PDA or on any number of different MP3 music players thus achieving excellent portability. Some handheld devices have the ability to store tens of hours of MP3 music and this capacity will continue to rise and the cost will continue to decline as solid state and micro-miniature disk drives continue on the technology curve. The result is that we will be able to carry our entire music collection with us wherever we go. Specialized MP3 servers are emerging for the home at the same time as the handheld devices gain popularity outside the home. These new products enable you to combine your personal music collection with music services on the Internet. Escient Convergence Corporation, for example, is offering products that offer consumers simple ways to manage and access large music CD and/or movie DVD collections without requiring any knowledge of computers or the Internet. Working hand-in-hand with popular name-brand CD changers and hard-disc music products that store large numbers of discs or music files, Escient's TuneBase products have a set-top box that instantly identifies and finds a particular disc, transforming the user's existing TV set or touch-screen display into a "mega-jukebox." With a colorful interface that displays album covers, artists, songs and styles of music, this kind of product will give users instant access to thousands of songs. For years I have been planning to build a database of my CDs including the composer, orchestra, track titles, etc. and in fact I made several attempts at it but never got too far. Much too tedious. Then along came MP3 and the CDDB.

CDDB (compact disc data base) is a service with a database of CD text information. When you put a music CD in you computer's CD-ROM drive, your CDDB-enabled player will access CDDB servers over the Internet to identify the CD and download information about it to your MP3 player. Disc title, artist, track title, and related information is not actually on the CD itself – it is in the database at CDDB. The best part is that now you don't have to type this information in. I am grateful that I didn't waste the hours it would have taken to do it manually!

CDDB[2] is the next generation of the CDDB database and disc recognition service. The new service offers significantly extended information for each CD title in the database. Examples include searchable credits for production, songwriting, and musicians (including instruments) at both disc and track-by-track level; over 250 genres; related web links and associated content; and segments (portions of music that can be smaller or larger than a single track).

MP3 is changing how people think about digital music whether they are consumers, artists, producers, broadcasters, or web casters. Meanwhile there is still a physical/analog aspect to music I don't see going away. Did you know there is a site on the web where you can commission the creation of your own violin or cello? See http://www.msen.com/~violins/

Watch what is going on with music on the Internet. The issue isn't whether the RIAA wins a lawsuit against Napster or whether mp3.com fulfills its business plans. The issue is that the Internet has enabled every computer in the world to be connected to every other computer in the world. As a result people can exchange information very easily. That includes music. What is needed is not more law suits. What is needed is new models for the distribution of music and other media. The explosion of digital music is just the tip of the iceberg. How about creating music on the Internet? A five-piece band may soon have a live jam session with each instrumentalist on a different continent and thousands of listeners who paid to listen in.

Radio Goes Digital Too

Digital radio will be the sound of the future. It will be the best sound on the airwaves in the near future, because digital-radio has the potential to deliver CD-quality, interference-free sound. Digital radio is the transmission and reception of sound that has been processed using technology comparable to that used in CD players. A digital radio transmitter converts its content into ones and zeroes and then broadcasts them. At the listening end, digital radio receivers, containing microprocessors, convert the stream of ones and zeroes back into music or voice with a sound quality that is significantly better than today's radios, just as CDs sound better than vinyl records.

Today's radio, which is analog, can never achieve consistent high quality because of the technology used and the transmission environment in which it is broadcast. Digital radio reception is virtually immune to interference, unlike AM and FM, which means there is no static nor echoes. The microprocessor sorts out the noise from the music.

Because the digital radio has software capabilities it can offer other features too. For example, you can select the station you want from the call letters; e.g. WQXR. There will be no need to select 96.3. In addition, your digital radio will be capable of monitoring signal strengths and then switching you from a fading signal you are driving away from to a stronger signal you are approaching, much like your mobile phone system switches you from cell to cell. It may be possible to drive from coast to coast and listen to your favorite station with no interference or disruption.

Many other features will be possible such as tuning to specific song titles or artists, listening to very localized traffic and weather information, and utilizing paging services or stock market quotations. Whereas today we have two separate bands for AM and FM, we will see the emergence of a single band for digital radio. There may even be a single band globally and both terrestrial and satellite transmission capabilities so we will literally be able to listen to high quality music anywhere anytime.

Digital radio has the potential to revitalize radio as a cost-effective and powerful medium. It is being embraced in the U.K. and Canada. In the United States digital radio may be viewed as a potential threat to existing radio stations, just as MP3 is viewed by some as a threat to the music industry. In the end better-sounding stations will win out.

On March 18, 2001, "XM Rock" was successfully launched from the Sea Launch's Odyssey platform in the Pacific Ocean. This is a precursor to making satellite radio a reality during summer 2001. A second satellite, "XM Roll," is scheduled to launch in early May. XM-ready radios will hit retail shelves across the country. A state of the art broadcast center using IBM's eServers and high capacity disk storage is near completion. Both "Rock" and "Roll" will operate in geostationary orbit above the United States transmitting up to 100 channels of digital quality programming from coast to coast. You will be able to drive from Maine to San Diego listening to the same station!

Pictures Too!

Everybody's got a shoebox of pictures somewhere. Buried in a closet. A drawer. Or stuffed in an album. Now and then, they get taken down, passed around and enjoyed by family and friends. But by and large, the moments that make up life aren't shared nearly as often as they could be. So says Ceiva Logic, Inc. maker of the first Internet-connected digital picture frame. The Ceiva digital picture frame looks like an ordinary 12-inch frame with a LCD screen that displays up to 10 digital images cycling continuously. Plug the Ceiva into a phone jack and it logs onto the Ceiva Website to download any new images posted to your account. It doesn't even require a computer. And anyone you authorize can send pictures to your Ceiva account. Your friends and family can take pictures with a digital camera and upload them to ceiva.com. The Ceiva frame can automatically update and display your new photos everyday. Just sit back and enjoy the show.

And of Course There Will Be Video

I remember in the 1970's when the first color display was introduced for use with IBM mainframe computers. A lot of people said "who needs it"? CFO's were intrigued that it would be possible to see negative numbers in red but many were not intrigued enough to want to spend the extra money they cost. Adoption of color monitors was slow but then they became standard. Can you imagine having a PC today which had only black and white?

Similar to the introduction of color decades ago the introduction of video on the web is greeted by many with "who needs it"? The video available on the web today is in a very small window, it is often grainy looking, and sometimes jittery. After the novelty wears off many have decided to just stick with the web the way it was. That will change with the introduction of Fast as previously discussed. Video will be expected. In fact in the NGi the time will come when you are on a webpage and you will literally say "help" and you will expect a full screen video session to instantly appear on your screen with a live person who smiles and says "how can I can help you"? Full screen, jitter-free, dazzling clarity video. It will help make the Internet more Natural.

Speech Says It All

Imagine a time when you will be able to issue simple verbal commands to run all of the appliances, machines, and systems you use in your home, office, or on the road. In the current decade of the NGi your voice will be all you'll need to prepare meals, shop and bank by phone, invest in the stock market, handle e-mail and even drive your car--without having to turn a key in the ignition or touch the steering wheel. Even security systems will rely on people's voices for computer passwords, access to office buildings, restricted areas, the home, and bank accounts.

Scientists at IBM Research, have already developed a number of voice recognition systems and are now building prototypes for others-which will give a new meaning to the term, "freedom of expression." For example, a test system has been developed that allows travelers to order airline tickets with simple voice commands. Not only does the system understand your spoken words but it also understands the context of what you say. "I'd like the next flight to Austin from New York" and you get exactly that. "Least expensive return flight next Thursday" and you get exactly that. The system not only understands the words "least expensive", "return", and "next Thursday", but also is able to translate them into specific requests that retrieve the data you are looking for. Your spoken words are the system input and the output back to you can be either spoken by a simulated voice or given to you on your cell phone or PDA display where you can more easily recall it.

The Next Generation of Speech Recognition

Significant progress has been made in speech recognition even for large vocabularies of tens of thousands of words. The speech can be continuous – you don't need to have any pause between words. However, the technology to date is most effective only under controlled conditions such as low noise, speaker dependent recognition and speech that is read or dictated as opposed to conversational speech.

That may change with a new approach called audio-visual-based speech recognition. Psychophysical experiments have demonstrated that the shape of your mouth as you say something adds important intelligence to enabling a computer to recognize certain speech utterances. The information is known as visual phonemes or ``visemes''. Visemes provide information that complements the phonetic stream from the point of view of confusability. For example, ``mi'' and ``ni'' which are confusable acoustically, especially in noisy environments, are easy to distinguish visually: in ``mi'' lips close at onset, where as in ``ni'' they do not. Similarly, ``f'' and ``s'' which are difficult to recognize acoustically belong to two different viseme groups. Experiments are underway and in the not too distant future it may be possible to use face detection combined with voice recognition to take things to the next level.

I can still remember the first time I witnessed speech recognition. It was in 1981 and at the time I was assistant to the CFO of IBM. One day he was invited to visit Yorktown Heights, home of the Thomas J. Watson Research Center where hundreds of researchers have created many of the world's great inventions. The main purpose of that particular day's visit was to get an update on the state of speech recognition. A group of us entered a huge room that was full of computers. I had never seen such a large computing center. It was enormous. We all huddled around the console of this "supercomputer" while several PhD's prepared the demonstration. One of them sat at the console in front of a large microphone – looked not unlike a radio station. We were all asked to please be silent. You could have heard a pin drop on the floor. The researcher got very close to the microphone and with a perfect articulation he said the word "nine". We waited and waited and waited. Seemed like forever. Like waiting for a pan of water to boil. Finally, a response came. We all crowded up to see the video console where it displayed a 9. Our mouths dropped open in awe.

Accessible To All

The NGI offers great hope to those who have speech, language or hearing impairments. New therapeutic technologies are being developed too. A computerized language tool called SpeechViewer transforms spoken words and sounds into imaginative graphics. The result is greatly increased effectiveness of speech therapy and speech modification for people who need it. They can select from over a dozen language exercises. Each exercise responds to your voice input with immediate, clear and meaningful feedback that helps you "see how to speak." In addition, the speaker receives animated rewards that reinforce successful responses. This kind of technology can be of great help to help people of all ages who have a variety of disabilities, such as speech or language impairments, cerebral palsy, developmental delay, traumatic brain injury, and speech disorders resulting from a stroke. The technology provides a real boost in effectiveness for professional speech language pathologists, special education teachers, teachers of the deaf, English as a second language instructors, and professionals working with accent reduction.

A Browser That Talks to You

A lot of people take access to the World Wide Web for granted. For the blind, however, accessing the web is a tough task. Chieko Asakawa, a blind researcher at the IBM Tokyo Research Lab, used screen reader technology -- which speaks aloud each item on the computer screen to surf the Web. Initially, she used the reader only for specific research tasks because it was not as fast as point-and-click, but then a team of researchers at the lab created a talking web browser called the "Home Page Reader". It has been released as a commercial product in Japan and is changing the lives of visually impaired people who want to use the web.

The Home Page Reader reads plain text in a male voice and hyperlinks in a female voice, making it easy for users to find the information they need – different voices for different duties. To speed up the slower text-to-speech process, the system includes a quick reading method of text-to-speech. One is a fast-forward function. When the "0" key is held down, the voice goes much faster, like on a cassette tape recorder. But it slows down again for the first few characters after certain types of stops, such as periods, commas, tabs, and hyperlinks, so that users can hear the beginning of each sentence.

The Home Page Reader system also incorporates a method for converting HTML tags into voice data. This is extremely important because there is a lot of "text" on webpages which isn't really text at all – it is a graphic images that looks like text but which was done graphically instead of normal text input. The program even gives users control over answering questions in online forms, which allows them to interact easily with and provide information to all kinds of Websites, from search engines to online shopping malls. I have witnessed blind people using the Home Page Reader and it brings tears to your eyes to see how swiftly and effectively they can breeze through websites gaining the information they want with virtually no limitations.

Limitations In Today's Computing Interaction

Imagine a world where using your computer is as easy as talking with your best friend. Speak, gesture, walk around, point at something that interests you -- the computer hears you and sees and responds to your every wish. Such capability is called "natural computing" and it will surely make the NGi more Natural.

Today we interact with computers in awkward and unnatural ways. We sift through countless instructions, press buttons, and fumble with gadgets, when what we really want to do is create, communicate, entertain, and understand. What we don't want is all the laborious typing, clicking, and memorizing arcane commands. The concept of natural computing is simple: it provides information where we want it, how we want it, and with practically invisible interfaces that adapt to natural human interaction skills. A multi-modal user interface is considered to be one of the core elements necessary in order to reach the level of truly natural computing. Quite simply, the computer responds to humans using the time-honored traditions of human interaction: voice and gesture.

The technology behind natural computing basically gives the computer eyes and ears. For example, IBM's Via Voice speech recognition software can interpret our vocal commands. An embedded camera can send visual information to a machine-vision system that tracks our movement and gestures. Special algorithms developed by IBM Research are capable of then combining and interpreting natural computing environment around us. Someday -- sooner than you think -- natural computing technology could be integrated into offices, furniture, household appliances, cars, classrooms and operating rooms. In the areas of science, medicine, and business, users may be able to collaborate remotely with one another in virtual labs, operating rooms, and factories with both their words and their gestures being naturally interpreted.

Convergence At Last

Pundits have been predicting digital convergence for many years. It was to be a merging of audio, video, images, radio, television, all forms of media and communications with their digital representations. It didn't happen as much or as soon as predicted. However, the tremendous growth in capability and decline in price of digital technology during the end of the last millennium has vindicated the predictors. It is happening. We are on our way to experiencing the NGi and it will be a more and more Natural experience.

Is our media wearing out?

Ever think about media wearing out? I was cleaning out the basement the other day and I came across a box of 5.25" diskettes. Lots of them. They date back to 1979 when I had a Radio Shack TRS-80 Model III. The diskettes stored 80,000 bytes! Seemed like a lot at the time. Are these diskettes worn out? Well, who knows? Probably not but they are "effectively" worn out because I can't imagine where I would find a diskette *drive* that could read them. I also found a box of cassette tapes that I had used as data storage on my Radio Shack TRS-80 Model 1. Fat chance of retrieving any data from them. How about 3.5" diskettes? Sure they are ubiquitous today but how about ten years from now? How about 35 mm slides? I don't know the life of the slides themselves but like the Radio Shack diskettes, I suspect the limiting factor will be the life of the devices with which to retrieve the "data". There will likely come a day when the slides will be fine but there will be nobody who knows how to repair the carousel or obtain parts for the projector.

There are countless other scenarios of similar ilk. So, what's the answer? Let our children and grandchildren worry about it? No, I think we can do better than that. In fact, I have been thinking a lot lately about an Annual Plan for Information Archiving. The idea is simple. It starts with an inventory of all media types in our possession: photographs, movies, slides, audio tapes, and CD's. It also includes data which is already digital and stored on various media types: big diskettes, little diskettes, zip drives, tapes of various formats, writeable CD's, and of course our system hard disks. Each year convert some of your "old" media to new media. I plan to start this myself with 35 mm slides that my mom and dad took in the 1940's. I'll move them to jpegs and store them on disk and tape. I'll also scan some very old family pictures we have that go back into the prior century. Each year review the inventory of media and make a projection of what is "exposed" from a technical point of view. Look at new formats and media types which are emerging. It may also be a good idea to keep an eye on scanning and conversion technologies. It may pay to re-scan or convert files as compression gets better and scanning densities improve. If the oldest media gets moved to contemporary media in bite-sized chunks on a regular basis the effort should be manageable. Admittedly, committing to the discipline suggested here is not easy. Like tax and estate planning, writing a will and reviewing it periodically, and other thankless tasks. If we pass the idea on to succeeding generations, it will hopefully get easier and easier (maybe automatic) to preserve our media and our very culture.

Technical footnote (thanks to my colleague David Singer)

There is also a distinction to be drawn between lossy and lossless conversions. Making a digital-to-digital copy is lossless (assuming you take precautions to avoid errors in the process), and so there is no reason to preserve the original medium. On the other hand, analog-to-digital conversions are potentially lossy (witness the debates about the virtues of vinyl versus CD, since CDs do lose any information above 22kHz), and so it is best to continue to preserve the original and use it as the source for later copies. And on still another hand, some digital formats are inherently lossy (JPEG) and should never be used as the source for a later copy unless there's no other choice.

There is also the issue of preserving more than the bits -- even if you could recover the data on the Radio Shack cassettes, you wouldn't be able to do anything with it, because you wouldn't know how to interpret it. It has been said that NASA has this problem -- they have huge amounts of data to which they've lost the format, so they can't use it.

CHAPTER 8

Intelligent

This chapter included a description of the Extensible Markup Language (XML); what it is and how it works like the preceding descriptions of the Internet and the World Wide Web. Today XML is pervasive. The description in this chapter will help explain why.

One of the examples I used in 2001 was bioinformatics, a science in its infancy. There was no supercomputer, Watson, in 2001 (other than the namesake headquarters for IBM Research). The Watson supercomputer technology has become the embodiment of the big data and analytics initiatives IBM is pursuing in healthcare. The Watson Healthcare group is beginning to have a positive impact in the treatment of cancer and other important healthcare related areas.

Later in the chapter, I described specialized web portals as places to "hang out" and meet up with other people with common interests. When you read this part, you immediately will think of today's social media. It has roots in net attitude.

I discussed the need for webpages to be intelligent. One of the examples I discussed was the need to have a webpage display on small devices differently than on PCs. This was a futuristic prediction because in 2001 there were no small devices powerful enough to browse the web satisfactorily.

A final area I wrote about was autonomic computing. This is a set of technologies allowing computers to self-heal when something goes wrong, much like humans. There have been many advances in this area but the term autonomic faded away, but the concepts are universally implemented in most enterprise computers today.

The Internet has come a long way since its inception, but the links don't always work and it is sometimes hard to find what you want. The Internet needs to work in a more Intelligent manner. The Internet today is a collection of billions of webpages that are more or less randomly organized. Linkages between pages that should be linked seem to be created with "tape and string" or not linked at all – like the hotel's reservations system that is not linked to their frequent guest system or the airline's flight arrival system that is not linked to their gate scheduling system. Searching for information is challenging to put it mildly. The good news is you can find anything and everything. The bad news is you can find anything and everything. Sometimes you are looking for something that seems like it would be easy to find but your search finds ten million matches and you can spend hours trying to narrow it down. When you search on "William Shakespeare" you find things he wrote, books about him, things written about him in discussion groups, personal pages where people list their favorite playwrights, and numerous companies that have adopted Shakespeare's name for their products. The basic reason for both the poor linkages and the difficulty in finding things is that webpages have great format but no context. The result is that it is often hard to cope with the overwhelming amount of information.

A Bold New Standard

Solutions to broad problems such as this are often benefited by standards. TCP/IP (the transmission control and Internet protocols) enabled global networks to become interoperable. HTML enabled universal sharing of documents. A new standard from the World Wide Web Consortium called XML will enable us to cope with information overload – in effect to add intelligence to the web. XML, the Extensible Markup Language, provides a way to add context to a webpage and structure to the web – it is arguably the most important standard for the web since the web was developed. Virtually all new developments going on for the web are based on XML. Just as TCP/IP provided the base on which the web could be built, XML is providing the base on which the web can evolve to a higher order medium – one which is intelligible and useful.

Webpages are constructed using HTML (described in chapter 5) and XML "tags". The tags do not appear to anyone other than the author who created them but they play an important role. Just like tags on pieces of merchandise describe what that merchandise is and how much it costs, HTML tags on a webpage define the format of the page's text; causing it to be blue or red, Helvetica or Courier font, aligned to the left, right, or center, arranged in a table, separated by a horizontal line, made larger or smaller, etc. XML tags on a webpage define what the page is *about* thereby adding context and enabling systems to tell what certain things mean.

For example a tag may indicate that the word "screwdriver" on a webpage is a "tool". The tag doesn't tell how the word is formatted but rather what it means – its context. It also tells us indirectly that this particular instance of the word screwdriver is not related to a cocktail. By utilizing XML tags a webpage can contain very deep context including relationships to other things. For example, different types of screwdrivers could be defined such as large, small, Phillips head, straight head, etc. By consistently applying XML tags to all web content the web will begin to evolve. Once information is properly tagged you will be able to find exactly what you are looking for with much greater speed and precision. It will also be possible to find that small electric frying pan when you can say category=appliance, item=frying-pan, type=electric, size=small. No more electric guitars and fried chicken.

How Is Your Vocabulary?

XML becomes even more powerful when the various tags for defining context get aggregated into higher levels, forming a vocabulary. The carpenter's union might form a vocabulary that defines all the valid tool categories, tools, tool dimensions, etc. that all members and constituencies of the union could understand. Not only could people searching webpages take advantage of this but so could web applications. This would enable the ordering of tools and the inventory taking of tools to be automated. Servers could communicate with other servers, checking inventory levels or order status of tools with no human interaction. The tool tags would be supplemented with tags that describe things like customer number, last name, organization name, postal code, quantity on order, invoice date, and job location. Now the webpages become enabled for e-business and things start to come together in a way that eliminates faxes, manual procedures, computer applications that convert one set of data to another set of data and other redundant low-value operations that add unnecessary lead times.

Contracts Talking To Each Other

Common vocabularies, based on XML, will enable businesses to start taking advantage of the Internet in an expanded way. A new vocabulary called the trading partner agreement markup language (tpaML) will make this possible. The Trading Partner Agreement (TPA) is an electronic contract that uses XML to define the general contract terms and conditions and the valid business processes to be used. Sophisticated software will be able to ensure that all transactions that are conducted over the Internet between the trading partners' business systems are conducted error free. The potential to speed up the pace of business will be greatly enhanced. For example, consider a small auto parts manufacturer that wants to sell to a major automaker. The automaker would create a contract using tpaML and then send it to the parts manufacturer. It would contain all the necessary information about the automaker. The parts manufacturer would then add the essential information about itself to the template and return the completed TPA over the Internet to the automaker. The contract is then processed by each trading partner's systems so that they will be able to transact business. The automaker could issue purchase orders in the form of documents transferred to the parts manufacturer under control of the tpaML document. The whole e-commerce exchange would take place without further human intervention because the buyer and seller previously defined all the parameters.

Taking The High Road

Rolling it up to an even higher level is Oasis, the world's largest independent, nonprofit organization dedicated to the standardization of XML applications. OASIS has several independent initiatives underway including ebXML, which is a joint effort of the United Nations and OASIS to establish a global framework that will enable XML to be used in a consistent manner for the exchange of all electronic business data. "XML standards developed over the next few years will form an essential part of the IT infrastructure for decades to come," commented Laura

Walker, executive director of OASIS. "OASIS is widely recognized as the open forum where industry leaders put aside competitive differences and come together to solve business problems with XML. We have the critical mass to insure standards developed within OASIS will be adopted by industries around the world."

E-Marketplaces Will Change How Business Is Conducted

e-marketplaces will change the very notion of business itself. Corporate partnerships will give way to virtual enterprises. Vertical markets will become a web of supply-demand relationships. And collaborative commerce will blur the line between competition and cooperation. Business as usual will not be sufficient to survive as the new models evolve. So far, e-marketplaces have been mostly press releases. The technology and business guys from an industry – like chemicals, autos, air travel, retail, pharmaceuticals, etc.-- got together and announced that the top handful of players in their industry are going to get together and create an e-marketplace. Some months later the CEO's got together and said to each other, "What exactly is it we are going to do with this thing?" In spite of the early hype and confusion, the real potential of e-marketplaces is very significant.

An e-marketplace is a many-to-many, web-based trading and collaboration model that enables companies to more efficiently buy, sell and collaborate on a global scale and across a whole industry or at least a major piece of an industry. For example, the Worldwide Retail Exchange (WWRE) consists of more than 50 retailers from around the world with combined annual revenue of over $722 billion. The WWRE utilizes the most sophisticated Internet technology available and their goal is to enable retailers and suppliers to substantially reduce costs across product development, procurement and supply chain processes.

The approach to achieving these benefits is to provide a shared Internet-based infrastructure that enables commerce transactions that automate and streamline the entire requisition-to-payment process online, including procurement, customer management and selling; a collaborative network for product design, supply-chain planning, optimization and fulfillment processes; an industry-wide product information database; an environment where sourcing, negotiations, and other trading processes such as auctions can take place; and an online community for publishing and exchanging industry news, information and events. As a result, buyers and suppliers enjoy greater economies of scale and liquidity -- and can buy or sell anything -- easily, quickly and cost effectively. In addition, e-marketplaces will enable companies to eliminate geographical barriers, and expand globally to reap profits in new markets that were once out of reach.

XML provides the lingua franca to make e-marketplaces possible. What remains to be done is the tough job of integrating the many incompatible systems among companies around the world. Major projects are underway in the major industries. The biggest limitation in getting to the ultimate vision is the limited availability of technical skills to do the work. An interesting new company, CommerceQuest, is providing an outsourcing service that may fill the gap for many companies. CommerceQuest created a b-to-b software gateway called enableNet. It is not specific to any industry but rather is a generic kind of capability that can allow transactions from one company to be able to go through the enableNet gateway over the Internet and then be executed on a different company's system even though the participating companies may have totally incompatible information technology systems.

XML will also enable us to easily attach new forms of data to things we do. For example, the advent of small and inexpensive Global Positioning System devices will bring latitude and longitude into our lives. Today we tend to label events with time. We put the day, month, and year on the back of a photograph. GPS greatly expands the possibilities. When a digital picture is taken with a camera that also contains a GPS capability it will be possible to capture the latitude and longitude of where the photographer was standing when the picture was taken. The photographer can also add voice notes describing the picture and digitally sign the picture to establish its authenticity. All of this can be encrypted to ensure that nothing is altered. Intelligence has been added to the art of picture taking.

We all remember exactly where we were when something memorable and significant took place. For example, if you are more than forty-five years old you undoubtedly remember where you were when John F. Kennedy was assassinated -- exactly where. GPS will cause us to think of location as an important dimension. Not just day, week, and month but also latitude and longitude.

P.S. Here is exactly where I was on that fateful day in 1963...

http://www.attitudellc.org/where-were-you-when-3/

Portals for Our Every Need

A physical portal is an entrance to a home or building and a web portal is an entrance to the web or some subset of the web. Portals like Excite, Lycos, MSN, and Yahoo! provide categorized directories of links to vast amounts of web content. Much of the categorization is done by hand – real people at these companies read webpage content and then decide what the context is and determine which category of the directory it should be placed in. Adding new links to the directories sometimes takes months because of this manual process. As more and more content for the web is produced using XML tags, the categorization process can become automated – computers will read the webpages, determine the content and properly categorize them. The "general purpose" portals mentioned will continue to be important around the world for "newbies" -- for people who just aren't sure what they want to browse through or who want to make some general searches for things. They will use these portals as a hub or communication center for many aspects of their lives. These portals will get better and better because of the intelligence XML is adding to the web.

The average person has become more and more web savvy. If they want to learn about a new Ford automobile they heard about somewhere, they will go to www.ford.com. They don't need to go to a portal, and step through a series of menus to eventually get to Ford. They will just go direct.

Specialized Portals

More and more people will be interested in portals that specialize in particular areas of interest; either on a business or personal basis. VerticalNet is a portal for industry professionals. The site has dozens of specialized portals – beverage online, ElectricNet, nurses.com, meat and poultry online, and dozens of others. Each of them provides a community for professionals where they can learn, discuss, look for jobs, issue purchase orders, buy, sell, and find resources to make their jobs easier. Real money changes hands in these specialized portals. They automate the buying and selling processes, save on ordering time, enable people to shop for the best pricing, allow them to secure delivery schedules, track shipments, and gain wider access to the industry in which they work. Similar portals are popping up in almost every industry facilitating a way for people with common interests to be able to have a very intelligent approach to what they're doing.

Community Portals – Hanging Out

There are also community portals. Places that are very people oriented. Mary Furlong, founder of ThirdAge Media calls them "Lifestyle destinations". These are places where people "hang out" on the Internet. Hanging out has emerged as a key Internet technology term. If you have any teenagers at home you will know exactly what I am talking about. Teenagers tend to leave the house late at night at about the time that you are ready to go to bed. As they are leaving you ask them, "Where are you going?" The answer is "Nowhere". "What are you going to do?". "Nothing." And then later, much later, sometimes the next day, they come back. You say, "Where have you been?" "Nowhere." "What were you doing?" "Nothing." "You have been gone for thirty one hours, you must have been doing something!" "I was just hanging out."

People hang out at physical places and they also hang out in the virtual world. More and more, people hang out at life style destinations; places like Blackberry Creek and Nick.com are of great interest to young children. Tripod.com or class-mates.com may be very interesting to people who are 18 to 30 years old. MyFamily.com may be of interest to those a bit older. People who are 45 or so may hang out at HarleyDavidson.com or other motorcycle sites. ThirdAge.com is of great interest to those who are 45 to 102! ThirdAge is where 70 year olds go to find a date or configure a fragrance to match the way a person wants to project their self.

Some organizations have a grand e-business plan to build a portal for their own organization; not any old portal but one that is so great that everyone will come to visit it. With the billions of webpages and large numbers of general and industry-specific portals to choose from, the "we will build it and they will come" approach is unlikely to succeed. An alternate strategy is to reach out and build relationships with the places and portals where the people you would like to reach are hanging out. Where your constituency hangs out is where you want to be hanging out; and by creating marketing relationships with those places, you can provide links to bring them back to your site for what you have to offer. If you build it, will they come? Not necessarily, but if you are hanging out in the right places you will connect to them.

Knowing What You Know

One of the major challenges of organizations of all sizes today, whether it is made up of ten people or tens of thousands of people, is being able to "know what you know". If the 5% most knowledgeable people in the organization could transfer what they know to the 5% least knowledgeable people in the organization, what a tremendous impact that would have on the effectiveness and the profitability of the company. In fact it has been estimated that there is a knowledge deficit of between five and six thousand dollars per employee because of information in the organization that is not known by others. Even is a very large company this is a significant amount of money. For example, a marketing specialist in a company is working on the introduction of a new product and is having difficulty figuring out the optimum distribution strategy for the product. It turns out that a colleague in a sister division of the company in another country had the exact same problem and developed a brilliant solution for it. The real problem is that the first colleague doesn't know about the second colleague. As a result the company may engage a consultant and pay to get a solution they already have!

Companies such as Lotus are developing very sophisticated tools to facilitate knowledge sharing to enable organizations to more effectively leverage the knowledge they have. By combining collaborative, messaging, database, and data mining technologies they are able to create knowledge portals. The idea is to create a window into all the relevant content that a person working on a project may be interested in, not only in all the databases that the organization has but also from the Internet. That person can then find out who else might have worked on or currently is working on some similar project. The project database can be shared and the person with the need can establish an electronic linkage with the other person and collaborate. Company portals built for the employees won't suffer the failings of the "if you build it will they come" syndrome of the web -- in these cases there is a captive audience.

Content Isn't What It Used to Be

Content is a word that became commonplace with the birth and growth of the World Wide Web. It refers to the text, graphics and multi-media that appear on webpages. In the last decade virtually all web content was created using the HTML standard and was designed and published as pages for the browser on a PC. Content on the Next Generation Internet needs to be highly adaptive; i.e. Intelligent. New interfaces and devices are emerging, the diversity of users is increasing, machines are acting more and more on users' behalf, and web activities are reaching a wide range of business, leisure, education, and research activities.

Webpages that are "one size (for the PC) fits all" will no longer be adequate. We need to be thinking of web content in a much different way.

To achieve maximum flexibility and reuse, webpages need to be decomposed into the components that make up the pages or "fragments". Fragments may include banners at the top of a webpage, navigation menus, "boilerplate" legal notices, graphical buttons, images, and pieces of text that collectively represent the page. The fragments can then be recombined and rendered appropriately for the user, task, or context. For example when I go to weather.com to check today's forecast I see a beautifully formatted page that contains a weather map of the entire country plus colorful icons representing clouds, rain, snow, and thunderbolts. If I happen to be receiving weather forecast on a mobile phone or Palm Pilot I don't have the "real estate" to display all of this content. What I really want to see are fewer content fragments - just the temperature and the odds of rain or snow - laid out appropriately for my small display.

A prototype content management system developed at IBM, Franklin, makes the management of fragments possible. It provides an end-to-end process; from content creation and reuse to quality assurance and publishing to multiple devices. Content is broken down to fragments, and the responsibility for managing the fragments is assigned to different experts. The graphic designer produces the buttons, icons and images. The product manager maintains the product descriptions and pricing. The legal department is responsible for the terms and conditions. When creating a product promotion, the web editor only writes any new text and simply points to the fragments already created by the experts.

An important aspect of content management is the separation of content and style. The XML standard enables this: each fragment of a webpage is an XML document tagged with descriptors. A descriptor might tell whether the fragment is a banner, price table or product description, or state its target audience or expiration time. The content management software then uses "style sheets" that lay out the right content for each device. As a result, the end user sees the appropriate content and layout for the device they are using, be it a huge video wall or a tiny display on a mobile phone or pager. In addition, using XML to describe the fragments results in information that is in a format that can be processed by applications as well as presented to end-users. Instead of having to keep the same information in two different formats suitable for automated processing and human consumption, it can be stored just once.

Another critical aspect of content management is detecting change. For example, if a company adopts a new logo or updates a product specification, the change intelligently and automatically ripples through the thousands of pages that may make up the website. Only final pages that include the changed fragment are republished. The efficiency of this approach is huge compared to the old method that relied on people editing each and every webpage manually. Thinking about content in this new way results in a more intelligent approach. Creating and managing websites is easier, more cost-efficient and more automatic for the owner. The content on the resulting websites is consistent, timely to view and appropriate for the user and the new devices.

Life Sciences – The Next Frontier

An often-asked question at technology conferences and in journalistic publications is, "What is the next big thing?" Surely, the many information technologies talked about in this book will continue to amaze us but an even bigger arena may turn out to be the marriage of information technology with Life Sciences. Most of us studied biology, a branch of knowledge that deals with living organisms and vital processes, in high school. It was a relatively broad subject – seems like an overview -- compared to the broader collection of related subjects that are part of the exploding area called Life Sciences. As more has been learned about life, whole new areas of study have emerged – genomics, the study of the genetic material of an organism; proteomics, the study of the incredibly complex proteins that we are made of; bioinformatics, the joining of biology and computer science; and the emerging field of metabalomics, which is the study of substances essential to metabolism. Not only have the topics become more complex but also the very way in which they are studied has changed. Biology has matured from "in-vivo" (observations of real life), to "in-vitro" (test tube experimentation), to "in silico" (experimentation by computer simulation). This transition from "wet" biology to "in silico" biology is inevitable as more and more information becomes available and large scale computing infrastructure becomes available. It is this migration to "in silico" research that promises to enable the greatest advances of our time - the launch of molecular based medicine and the first true understanding of the molecular basis of life.

Proteins control all processes in the cells of the human body. Comprising strings of amino acids that are joined like links of a chain, a protein folds into a highly complex, three-dimensional shape that determines its function. Any change in shape dramatically alters the function of a protein, and even the slightest change in the folding process can turn a desirable protein into a disease. The study of how proteins fold is extraordinarily complex. The simplest investigation with the most advanced tools takes months. The scientific community considers protein folding one of the most significant "grand challenges" -- a fundamental problem in science or engineering that has broad economic and scientific impact and whose solution can be advanced only by applying high-performance computing technologies.

At the beginning of the new millennium IBM announced a $100 million exploratory research initiative to build a supercomputer 500 times more powerful than the world's fastest computers of today. The new computer -- nicknamed "Blue Gene" by IBM researchers -- will be capable of more than one quadrillion operations per second (one petaflop). This level of performance will make Blue Gene 1,000 times more powerful than the Deep Blue supercomputer that beat world chess champion Garry Kasparov in 1997, and about 2 million times more powerful than today's top desktop PCs. Blue Gene's massive computing power will initially be used to model the folding of human proteins. Learning more about how proteins fold is expected to give medical researchers better understanding of diseases, as well as potential cures. Dr. Paul M. Horn, senior vice president of IBM Research said, "In many ways, Deep Blue got a better job today -- if this computer unlocks the mystery of how proteins fold, it will be an important milestone in the future of medicine and healthcare."

Better understanding of how proteins fold can potentially lead to pharmaceutical companies being able to design high-tech prescription drugs customized to the specific needs of individual people. And doctors may be able to respond more rapidly to changes in bacteria and viruses that cause them to become drug-resistant. "Breakthroughs in computers and information technology are now creating new frontiers in biology," said IBM's Horn. "One day, you're going to be able to walk into a doctor's office and have a computer analyze a tissue sample, identify the pathogen that ails you, and then instantly prescribe a treatment best suited to your specific illness and individual genetic makeup."

What we are seeing is a technology revolution in one industry being enabled by advances in another -- information technology has become the driver of experimental biology. The new Life Sciences disciplines are being built on powerful computer systems, massive storage, the Internet and an infrastructure that enables the distribution and sharing of content. Using new algorithms for searching, matching, and aligning information, the basic steps of identifying, purifying, and cloning a gene followed by purification and characterization of the proteins associated with that gene, have been automated and streamlined to a degree that no one could have predicted ten years ago.

To see why information technology has become so fundamental to Life Sciences we only need to contemplate the amount of data involved. The human genome database consists of approximately three trillion bytes of information - equivalent to approximately 3,000 compact discs. Unraveling the interactions and functions of proteins (the products of the genome) will be one of the most computationally intensive problems ever faced and will require orders of magnitude more data and computing power than being used today.

One of the long-standing goals for information technology has been to maximize productivity through enhanced collaboration. That same goal is now fundamental to continued advances in Life Sciences. Researchers now share data, both public and private, and collaborate in virtual environments to meet the increasing pressure to reduce the cost of drug development while also decreasing the time to market. New drugs often cost upwards of $500 million to develop and test. On average, the process from discovery through approval takes between ten and fifteen years to complete. The application of information technology will allow companies to reduce costs associated with creating new drugs, and shorten the development cycle.

Managing Life Sciences data is not just a corporate mandate, but also will become a significant issue for individuals whose genetic information could become available (anonymously or not) through these sources. Protecting individuals' rights by requiring informed consent for any use of their identifiable genetic information is a challenge that information technology must help overcome -- for example, by helping to implement access controls that ensure that only those that should have access to such data, actually have such access.

Autonomic Computing

In this decade there will be billions of devices used by people and there will be trillions of intelligent chips built into or attached to almost everything we buy. The combination of all these devices will generate enormous amounts of data. The passage of the data through the Internet will place enormous strain on the network infrastructure and on the systems used by all kinds of organizations. Operators of e-businesses will find their time being deflected away from finding better ways to leverage their systems for the benefit of their customers, to instead spending their energy on keeping the systems and networks operating properly. The tremendous amount of complexity will lead to more and more human intervention, both at the user interface, at the servers, and at all points in the network. We need precisely the opposite – to hide the complexity, and require less human intervention.

Solving the problem will require a new kind of intelligence. The stakes are big. In a speech to the National Academy of Engineers in early 2001, Paul Horn, IBM Senior Vice President and Director of Research said, ``The future of our increasingly technology-driven society depends on making computer networks fast, reliable, always available, flexible and self-managing. "IBM is working on a broad solution to the problem which they call "autonomic computing".

The basic approach is to create an intelligent network and system infrastructure which acts more like our own bodies. Think about controlling your heart rate, breathing rate, constriction or relaxation of your blood vessels, dilation of your pupils, movement of food through your alimentary canal, the regulation of your body's core temperature -- actually, the beauty is you don't have to think about any of them. They're all regulated and controlled by your body's autonomic nervous system.

This allows you to use information pouring in from the world around you for higher level functions like thinking, deciding, then acting on those decisions. Simply put, you can concentrate on what you want to do, and leave the running of your incredibly complex biological systems to your autonomic system. An autonomic computing network possesses three essential qualities. First, it is responsive -- able to respond to unpredictable events in "intelligent" ways, not just sudden surges in web traffic, but all types of disasters such as fires, storms, earthquakes, etc. that can wreck havoc with networks and systems. Next, it is self-managing and self-healing – able to be adaptive and look after itself, and when something fails or goes awry, correct the problem or get the help or resources needed to do so. Last, it is always accessible -- customers, employees, partners, and suppliers -- anyone that needs to can always get to it easily.

If the network and systems are to have these qualities, all kinds of detection, decision-making and directing functions will be required throughout the network. The information technology industry will need to turn its attention to embedding more "smarts" and functionality in a new array of microprocessors including monitoring chips that detect errors, failures and things about to fail, and network processor chips that can do something about the detected problems. Computers will be built using a new architecture – one that is more cellular and distributed --- just like the human nervous system. The systems and networks will be built from microprocessor "cells" that integrate the functions of computers -- processors, memory and communication.

These cellular architectures will allow the computer to get the computing power out to where the data is – widely distributed to wherever the data is stored. It is likely that in the current decade it will be possible to take dozens or even hundreds of servers in a data center and fit that computing capability into a closet. Software will enable the computing capability to be self-managing and self-healing when something goes wrong. This will enable intelligent computing "utilities" that will allow organizations to tap in and pay as they use it just like they do for electricity and water.

CHAPTER 9

Easy

In 2001, I discussed experiences with websites which made me say, "Why is this so hard?" Fourteen years later, I still find myself saying, "Why is this so hard?" Many websites have gotten easier to use, but there are still many things which remain too hard. This is especially true with electronic health records (EHRs) and patient portals, as discussed in my book, Health Attitude.[1112]

This chapter provided insight about why some things are more difficult than they need to be. Part of net attitude is making webpages easy to use. I described how programmers who write the instructions for webpages think and the various tools they use.

Some web applications are not natural in a browser. I thought by now, it would no longer be the case, but the phenomenon of desktop apps being easier to use than their counterpart on the web remains. The best example is Quicken. Millions of people use Quicken for Windows or Quicken for Mac to keep track of their spending and assets. Intuit, the company that owns Quicken, acquired a web based financial planning and tracking site called Mint.com in 2009. I suspect Intuit's business case for the acquisition included a significant migration of users from Quicken to Mint.com. The Mint.com site is good but not nearly as easy as Quicken on the desktop. I explained why this is the case.

Another contributor to making things easier was the grass roots support of open source software. There are many important lessons in the history and status of Linux. Linux is a programming language many thought was interesting but without a great future. I was very bullish about Linux and urged IBM to adopt it. This turned out to be very good for the company and its customers. I said in 2001, and still believe, efforts springing from grass roots, like Linux, will always prevail and provide continuous improvements. A present example is bitcoin. I feel the same way about bitcoin now as I did about Linux in 2001. It has the potential to make financial transactions much easier for billions of people.

Sometimes I say to myself, "Why is this so hard?" In many cases things actually do work exactly the way they were designed to work but that isn't the way I want them to work! The truth is that when you consider the underlying complexity of many aspects of information technology, including the Internet, it is nothing short of amazing that things work at all. The Internet has been cobbled together, and so have the efforts of businesses to employ and exploit it, resulting in a crazy quilt. We expect it to work as reliably and predictably as the telephone system in America that took decades of planning and building. When we enter information in our PC or at a website we expect the PC or the server to figure out exactly what we meant by what we entered. The fact is that computers are not humans and the programming to enable computers to figure out what we mean is not easy to create. In spite of today's shortcomings, there are reasons to be optimistic about things getting easier. The Internet and the World Wide Web are continuing to evolve based on new standards. In parallel, new software communities, including Linux, are gaining momentum – devising creative new ways to share ideas about software and approaches to creating software applications. The combination of more standards and better software approaches offer the potential to make things much easier.

The browsing experience itself needs to become easier and in fact progress is being made. In the early days of the web you had to be a computer scientist to be able to install a browser on your PC. Today, every PC sold comes with a browser pre-installed and ready to use. Plug your PC into electrical power and a network connection or phone line and you are ready to surf the web. As more and more Internet usage shifts to consumer devices such as mobile phones and Personal

EASY

Digital Assistants things will get even easier – much more like consumer appliances. Consumer companies know how to make appliances easy to use. Although many people still say that a VCR is impossible to program, most consumer appliances are intuitive and require little or no training. If you want to turn your handheld personal stereo off you simply turn the switch to off. Contrast this with your PC where to turn your computer off you must first go to the "Start" button. Then you select "Shutdown" and then various programs running on your PC ask you "Do you really want to shutdown?" If you want to print something with your PC, you must go to a menu that is labeled "File". Computers were designed by very technical people in computer companies who think such approaches are logical. The good news is that things are getting easier. It used to take years for consumers to get feedback to the design engineers that a product was unusable. With the Internet – "Power to the People" -- feedback on products gets back in hours from the introduction of a new product. Not only will things get easier but it will happen more quickly too.

While we can look forward to great progress in PCs and other devices becoming easier to use, a big part of making the total experience easier has to happen at the server – the e-businesses themselves have to be easier. In the 1990s it was not easy to build an e-business, run an e-business or use an e-business. However, just as the Internet is evolving as a medium, the tools for building e-businesses are getting better and better. While we continue to read about major websites that have multi-hour outages, technology is now becoming available to make websites as reliable as the airline reservation and banking systems we have used for many years.

Who Builds Websites, Anyway?

E-businesses, in response to rising customer expectations, are trying to make their websites more sophisticated. Not only do many sites look impressive but they also have some amazing capabilities. "Click here" to do almost anything -- check the inventory level of an item, calculate shipping costs, or initiate a live chat session with a customer support representative. The bar keeps rising as competition ramps up to win over consumers and business professionals. There are two challenges that this presents. First is a shortage of software developers who know how to do the sophisticated things and second is the challenge of using the browser as the exclusive interface for e-business transactions.

The High Priests Et Al

Software developers fall into roughly three categories. First are the "high priests". These technical giants are not only experts in writing very sophisticated computer programs in the more difficult programming languages such as C and C++ but they can also reach into the "operating system" software provided by Microsoft, IBM or Sun et al and modify and extend the basic capabilities that those companies provided. These hard-core experts design, build, and fix large, complex systems, environments, and applications. The really good ones aren't bound to any specific programming language; they use whatever tools fit the task at hand. Some of the "high priests" don't do much programming at all but are experts at diagnosing complex problems and making systems and computing networks do what they are supposed to do. These "high priests" of programming are relatively few in number and in many cases command extraordinary compensation – if you can even find them.

The second category of programmer is much larger in number and typically specializes in developing applications. They are very competent in building programs for specific application areas like business (e.g., payroll), manufacturing (e.g., inventory control) or science (e.g., molecular analysis), but will turn to the "high priests" for assistance in some of the "hard core" problems. Finally, in the third category there are millions of webpage designers, often called webpage developers, who don't really consider themselves programmers at all. In fact some members of this group refer to themselves as "web monkeys".

Software developers in the first and second categories are sometimes called software engineers but are typically called programmers. Whatever you call them, finding good ones is not easy. It is part of a bigger problem. There is a shortage of hundreds of thousands of skilled information technology people in America alone. Europe also has a shortage. There are good skills available in parts of Asia but immigration limits have kept many from being employed. In the year 2000 some progress was made in the United States via the passing of legislation that allowed higher immigration limits but the shortage still remains. Although the first half of 2001 saw many layoffs in the technology industry, the cutbacks were concentrated in manufacturing, marketing, and various indirect support areas – not the skilled programming area.

The key to generating enough skilled people over the longer term lies in a quality education system that can meet the needs of the information economy.

The web was built by programmers -- people who, typically, spend a lot of time thinking about making their programs faster and more capable, but not necessarily easy to use. The users of the web typically don't know (or want to know) the gory details of how the programmers made things work -- they just want to perform certain tasks, like buying an airline ticket or enrolling in an e-learning course. This is where the webpage developers, the third category, come in; putting a simple face on the riches of the Internet, and making it easy for almost anyone to take advantage of it. Webpage developers not only build great looking webpages but increasingly have found ways to make webpages act in dynamic ways to interact with users. However, there are two limitations inhibiting the webpage developers' efforts. One is a lack of programming skills, and the other is a set of limitations imposed by the browser.

Many of the things that webpage developers want their webpages to do require programming. While the webpage developer often has excellent graphic design skills, they generally do not have programming skills. Programming is not visual. It involves thousands of lines of instructions (referred to as code) that then have to be "debugged" -- programming is intellectually intensive. To meet their needs without having to turn to programmers, webpage developers have turned to a form of programming called scripting. Just like there are many different programming languages there are many different scripting languages including JavaScript, Perl, REXX, Tcl, and others.

Webpage developers are flocking to JavaScript and it has emerged as the most popular scripting language. It was developed by Netscape as a tool to enable the browser to have more capability than just browsing. JavaScript is incorporated into webpages just like the HTML or XML tags are. When the browser downloads a webpage, the JavaScript commands are executed. This is very powerful. With JavaScript, a Webpage can react to what the person who is browsing the page is doing: images can swap when you move a mouse over them, menus can appear and disappear dynamically, calculations can be made, or zip codes can be used to automatically look up a city and state.

JavaScript sample programs are readily and freely available on many websites and webpage developers are able to copy these samples and use them without actually having to know the details of how they were created or how they work. The visual aspect of a webpage and the ability to try something and instantly see how it is going to work has enabled some very sophisticated webpages to be developed. By combining JavaScript with various webpage development tools such as NetObjects Fusion or Macromedia's Dreamweaver webpage developers are able to create webpages that can do almost anything you can imagine. Large numbers of webpage developers are becoming empowered with JavaScript – becoming highly productive and able to gain much of the power of programming without having to become a programmer.

Contrary to popular belief, JavaScript has nothing to do with Java. Java was initially developed by Sun Microsystems and was subsequently contributed to by IBM and others. Java is a programming language. Netscape wanted to introduce a scripting language to help webpage developers be able to add more capabilities and at the time Java was very new and becoming popular rapidly. Netscape decided to name their scripting language JavaScript. Some would say this was done to capitalize on the popularity of Java. At this point JavaScript has become extraordinarily popular on its own merits. The fact that JavaScript works in both the Netscape browser and Microsoft's Internet Explorer has made JavaScript ubiquitous. No matter what its name, it is having a positive impact in the world of e-business.

Browsers Are Great For Browsing

There is a remaining problem – JavaScript in webpages is limited by the capabilities of the browser – and the limitations of the browser are significant. Let us start with the positive aspects. The browser has become ubiquitous, it requires no training, and has become second nature to millions of people. In fact it seems that browsing has emerged as a fundamental human trait; one that, until recently, we didn't even know we had. People just click here or click there to do something. Even though the browser was intended for browsing, it is amazing what else they get used for today. Businesses are rushing to "web enable" their entire inventory of computer applications; enabling the applications to be accessible from a web browser instead of the traditional and proprietary interfaces. Corporate CIOs find the browser especially attractive because it reduces the complexity for users and the cost to the organization for distribution of the software (it can be downloaded; no diskettes or CDs) and the resulting support. There is also the advantage that a person can go to any browser anywhere and get access to the company systems and data.

The flip side of this is that the browser is not really well suited for many applications. Millions of people have software programs loaded on their PCs -- Quicken, TurboTax, Microsoft Money and similar programs -- that help them to manage their financial affairs. These PC programs work with Microsoft Windows and have the familiar Windows menus and functions. Just as the browser has become familiar to millions so have these easy to use applications and the Windows desktop.

There are also web-based applications that can enable you to manage your money or taxes using a browser and a website, but the web applications don't look or feel quite the same as a comparable Windows application on the PC. They don't have edit/copy/paste and other desktop functions or don't have them in the familiar way. They don't have "local" data. That means you can't pay your bills or review your budgets while you are on an airplane or if you are at a location that doesn't have good connectivity (unfortunately there are still quite a few of them). They will be only as responsive as the server and the network bandwidth are at the moment.

Applications on your PC feel different. You can click here to pay a bill with the Windows application and the response time is limited only by the speed of your PC and your disk drive. This is typically so fast that it seems instant. Click on a webpage to pay a bill online in your browser and the response time can be a few seconds or, in some cases, much longer as you wait for the server or the network to allow you to go to the next step. Same thing with email; you can use Eudora, Lotus Notes, or Microsoft Outlook and get instant response when you delete an email from your inbox or you can use web based email and spend time waiting for the network or the server. The bottom line is that the browser interface doesn't feel as natural and responsive as native desktop applications and is not adequate to handle all of our needs and expectations

Freedom from The Browser

Fortunately, there are alternatives to the browser interface – and the alternative is the desktop itself. We will soon start to see an explosion of new applications that have the look, feel and accessibility of the desktop but also have access to the web behind the scenes. For example, imagine tracking all your frequent flyer points in a single application that automatically goes to each of the airlines' websites, logs in with your account number and password and downloads your balances. And, if you are offline, still allows you to access and manipulate the data.

All this with an application sitting on your desktop, looking and feeling like a windows -- or Linux or Mac -- application, not like a browser. They will be integrated with the desktop. For example, you may have a small text window in the "system tray" at the bottom of your Windows desktop. You type a stock symbol into it and an application goes to the Wall Street Journal for latest stories, to Edgar Online for the latest SEC filings, to your Quicken portfolio for your current holdings, etc. and pulls it all together in one nicely formatted report on your desktop – no browser. This new kind of application will also operate offline when needed and then update things the next time you are online. We are already beginning to see Internet applications that don't require the browser interface; instant messaging programs, the RealJukeBox and Windows Media Player are examples. Individuals will no longer be shackled to the traditional browser model of the past.

New tools are emerging that are going to trigger yet another wave of Internet applications based on the new "browser free" model. Next generation scripting tools will keep the simplicity of the first generation -- building applications with an easy to use interface but with the power to access the whole range of native desktop capabilities plus all that the Internet has to offer. Using JavaScript, the web developers will create useful applications while the "high priests" will build a scalable, manageable, available, reliable, and secure infrastructure to support the applications at the server. The browser will not disappear -- features in browsers will get better and better for viewing content and surfing the web -- but we may see it return to what it was originally intended for - browsing.

An innovative approach for building these "browser free" applications, called Sash (http://sash.alphaworks.ibm.com), was developed at an IBM skunk works in Cambridge, Massachusetts. Sash enables web developers to use JavaScript to create windows desktop applications that can do all the things web applications can do but which can also take advantage of the start bar, the file explorer metaphor, and other basic windows capabilities. The Sash "weblications" look and feel just like native windows applications while at the same time having the Internet connectivity capabilities of the browser. Weblications can operate online or offline. They "live" on the desktop just like a traditional application but when connected they get live data and interact with the web. When disconnected the weblications can use the data locally. It is a new paradigm for web applications.

In the summer of 2000 a group of summer interns at IBM in Cambridge, Massachusetts developed a Linux version of Sash called SashXB. It was made available to the Linux open source community in August 2000.

The Next Generation of E-Business

Easy is about to take on a new dimension as the web continues to evolve. In the early stages the web allowed for browsing of documents with hyperlinks to other documents. Then with the advent of XML it gained context so that documents could be more easily found and, more importantly, integrated with information technology systems. A new set of standards gained prominence in early 2001 that will allow the web to move to yet a higher level – from a web of documents to a web of documents and applications. The "application web" is now in its infancy but it will expand dramatically and provide a new way for application software to be developed, published, searched, and utilized. Relatively inexperienced software developers will be able to assemble new e-business applications as easily as they do spreadsheets today. They will be able to locate modules of software that were written by others and placed in a global directory organized according to the specific capability of the software. They will then be able to link multiple software modules together to perform the desired tasks. The user will see a webpage at an e-business that simply meets their needs but behind the scenes the e-business server is not interacting with a single website but rather with multiple servers in a network of applications. To understand this important new development, we need to start with some historical perspective on how computer applications get created.

The Early Days

In the 1950s and 1960s computer programming required that the programmer be an expert with the particular computer that his or her employer had. It was like learning to drive a car. Not any car – one specific make and model of car. Being an expert driver of that car gave you no credentials or even capability to drive any other kind of car. If the organization got a new kind of computer, all the programming had to be redone. Users of the system had to make a request by fax, form, or phone and the request would be entered into the application program by someone else and then, at the end of the day, a "batch" of the day's inputs was processed and the user would get the results the next day by receiving a printed report of some kind.

During the 1970s and 1980s the online world simplified things quite a bit. Inputs could be made "real time" while a customer or user was on the phone. A customer service representative could take the information over the phone, enter it directly into a system, get the results immediately and report back to the person on the phone. Some progress was made in making things more compatible from system to system by the establishment of common languages and protocols for databases and communications. However, the programming to do this was still very specific to the particular kind of computing system. In fact things got even more complicated to program because of the real-time nature of the applications and the need to integrate across numerous processes.

The Web

The web took things a big leap forward. At last there was a common way (the browser) for accessing and displaying information, even though the applications that run on the server -- that do the pricing, inventory lookups, shipping estimates, invoicing, etc. -- are still created with various languages which are specific to the vendor or system. The web server applications have also become very monolithic; i.e. in order to fulfill the expectations of customers on the web the application has to do the whole job. Soup to nuts; present the right price, confirm if the item is in stock, calculate shipping, and confirm the status of the order. Increasingly, customers want to get access directly into the supply chain and see exactly where things stand. In short, applications are getting larger and more complicated -- harder, not easier.

The Application Web

The application web (web services is the technical name) will possibly be the biggest change in information technology in decades. Today companies build all of the functions that their website needs. If they are selling their goods and services via the web they have to develop software that can take the order, do credit checks, check inventory, look through the supply chain, arrange for payment, charge the customer, clear credit card transactions, etc. Adding all of this functionality into a website takes a huge amount of time, effort and skills. If they choose to buy the software instead of making it they typically acquire what they need from a single vendor even though that vendor's software may not be the best at all of the individual functions needed. Wouldn't it be nice if there were companies on the web which offered many of the web application functions (web services) needed and you could just link your website into those services and use them instead of creating them yourself or buying them from one source? Just like in the real world, I don't cut my own hair, I look in the yellow pages to find a barbershop and then go have a barber perform that service for me.

For example, suppose that a company called American Specialties Inc. (ASI) specializes in selling American goods for delivery mostly outside of America. They want to create an application to sell their products on the web. The trickiest part of the application is determining the best way to ship the product to ensure it gets there when the customer wants it and at the lowest cost. ASI doesn't have the skills to write this particular part of the application and they haven't bee able to find a vendor with a software package that can do it and which is compatible with the rest of ASI's software.

There is another company called Rates and Costs Inc. (RCI), which specializes in the calculation of optimum routes and the associated costs for shipment to places anywhere in the world. RCI offers the calculation as a service on the web and it is the exact function ASI needs to incorporate into their web application. In yesterday's world ASI and RCI would not be aware of each other. In the new (NGi) world, ASI could discover RCI in a universal directory (the application web) that is accessible to anyone on the web. It is like a Yahoo! for applications (the barber in the Yellow Pages offering hair cuts). Since RCI "published" their application using the new (web services) standards, ASI was able to not only find RCI's service but can also easily see the specifications for RCI's service – what inputs are required and what output does it produce. RCI could have created the calculation service using whatever programming language they want since the standards assure that things can work together.

The programmer at ASI likes RCI's program because it performs exactly the right function that ASI needs and the software has already been written and tested! ASI follows the web services standards to incorporate RCI's service into their web application. Whenever a user goes to ASI's webpage and needs shipment route and cost information, a link is made behind the scenes to RCI's web server to get the information. ASI's customers don't know, nor will they care, that part of the job is being done by RCI's server; not ASI's server. ASI makes an arrangement to pay RCI each time one of ASI's customers uses the RCI web service.

Creating programs by linking to programs written by others – without regard to what programming language was used to create the others' programs -- represents a whole new paradigm. It is one of the information technology industry's holy grails. Standards organizations have been attempting for years to create a "neutral" programming environment. The UNIX vendors – HP, DEC, Sun, IBM, Data General, and others – formed various organizations, councils and consortia over the years attempting to bring things together. Progress was made but none of these initiatives achieved real openness and true compatibility across the information technology industry for several reasons.

Microsoft was out there with a dominant market share on the desktop and promises that they would bring forward the "ultimate" operating system for the server. As long as that threat was there the industry didn't believe that there would be an industry-wide standard. There was also certain distrust that even the handful of UNIX vendors might not stay unified in their own commitment to open standards.

The other reason is that none of the prior attempts were based on a language-neutral approach. Java was a strong attempt at universal compatibility. In the early years of Java it was positioned as the single programming language for all platforms, desktop or server. The promise of Java for the desktop, however, could not stand up against Microsoft and has essentially died as far as a standard for the desktop. On the server, however, it has gained significant traction and is believed by many vendors to be the best programming language for connecting heterogeneous back-end processes in a secure and productive way. Still, Java is a programming language and it is not the only programming language even if it is a very good one.

Standards for web services have attracted a large and diverse backing. Just as the web has standards that make it easy for people to create web content (HTML), find webpages (DNS – Domain Naming system) and connect to websites (HTTP); the key standards for web services bring this same ease of use to developers for the publishing, finding, and utilizing web applications. The web services standards were driven by Ariba, IBM, and Microsoft and more than two hundred other companies have endorsed them. The basic protocols to publish, find, and utilize application services are WSDL, UDDI, and SOAP.

The next generation of scripting languages, such as Sash, will be able to utilize "connectors" that call upon web services using these standards. This will result in webpage developers being able to invoke sophisticated programming – things which formerly could only be done by the "high priests".

More detail on web services can be found at

http://www.uddi.org/ and http://www.ibm.com/developerworks/webservices/

An Even Faster Evolution of E-Business

The web services model is the first language-neutral and vendor-neutral programming model to be developed. It allows applications to be more modular. The new web services standards give complete independence to the programmers who create applications. Applications can now be broken down into "Legoes" and each "Lego" of an application can be written in a different language and can be running on a different server. Application developers can create applications that combine core competencies the developer may have but allow the e-sourcing (web services version of out-sourcing) of functions that someone else may be better at. The web services standards enable the web to evolve from a web of content to a web of content and applications. Web services can enable server-to-server interaction in addition to browser to server interactions. Servers will negotiate with other servers via web services and even complete transactions by themselves with no direct human intervention. These interactions will replace the paper forms and faxes that flow back and forth from company to company today.

E-business has evolved rapidly but web services will speed e-business development and finally create the interoperability between businesses that has been a decades long dream. History has shown that adoption of standards leads to an explosion of usage and that will surely be the case with web services. With the standards in place for web services, the e-business functions for entire industries will be able to be brought together in central directories. These application webs will facilitate the formation of e-marketplaces and enable them to build useful portals. Users of all kinds, business and consumer, will be able to establish interaction with marketplaces more efficiently. The e-marketplaces will be able to deliver business functions to a broader set of customers and partners and pursue new business models by combining applications in new ways. Small companies will be able to e-source to dozens of other companies for public relations, legal, payroll, and other functions they would rather not perform themselves. Large companies will have a much greater range of choice over what they build and what they e-source. Virtual corporations comprised of a federation of smaller ones will form and enable "hyper competition" on a global scale.

Penguin To The Rescue

One last factor that may play a huge role in making things easier is Linux. It is hard to miss mention of Linux in the media – it has gotten a lot of attention and for good reason. It has the potential to radically impact how information technology gets created and used. A student in Finland named Linus Torvalds started Linux in August 1991. His goal was to create a Unix-like operating system which would work on a PC.

Almost all PC's at the time used an operating system called DOS and only larger more sophisticated computers used Unix. Unix was appealing to many students because of its sophistication – in particular its networking capability. What started as a hobby for Linus Torvalds turned out to become appealing to many more than just the students as major information technology companies including IBM, Hewlett Packard, and Compaq have put their full support behind the software with the Penguin mascot.

Linus Torvalds picked the penguin as the Linux logo. He once took a trip to Australia and was captivated by a ten-inch high penguin. Linus said it was, "love at first sight". A few years later people were discussing what kind of logo people wanted for Linux. Many wanted a boring, commercial one. Linux decided on the penguin. "I'm much happier being associated with a fun and slightly irreverent logo than with something static and boring."

Three Shifts

I've seen three major shifts during my more than three decades in the information technology industry. In the early 1980s it was the introduction of the PC. In the early 1990s it was the emergence of the Internet as a serious communications network. In the late 1990s it was Linux. All three existed before those particular timeframes but those are when, from my perspective, the big shift started. Each had some things in common with the others. In all three cases smart people left their jobs at companies and universities to get involved with these new technologies -- and venture capital followed them. In all three areas there was a lot of grass roots activity and the formation of a genuine community. They were not tops down initiatives of major companies or organizations. (Even the PC effort at IBM was led by an independent business unit that was a sort of skunk works.) All three areas were very standards oriented. They were either built on standards or actually created new standards. And one last thing that all three shifts had in common -- some people in the information technology industry said, "Who needs it"? There is a lesson to be learned in this reaction.

Who Needs It?

In 1980, Digital Equipment Corporation had a number of "personal computer" projects underway (some may remember the Rainbow) but there was not a real commitment. Their first PC-like product was called an "applications terminal and small system". In effect the company said, "PC? Who needs it"? Although IBM introduced the first standards based PC there were those in the company that, when it came to serious computing needs, in effect said, "PC? Who needs it"?

In the mid nineties it was clear that the Internet was going to take over the world as far as a networking standard. I was at an Internet Society meeting in Prague in June 1994 and a gentleman from Chrysler Corporation gave a presentation on how his company was going to standardize on TCP/IP for all networking. I am sure there were some at Chrysler that thought this was radical and even some attendees of the Internet Society meeting thought so. At that time there were many networking standards out there – arguably many of them were superior to the Internet standards. But, it didn't matter. The shift was underway and the Internet standards are used by virtually all companies in the world (often coexisting and interoperating with other prior networking standards). Meanwhile, a number of companies that owned those other standards said in effect, "TCP/IP? Who needs it"? And then came Linux. 1999 was the year that Linux began to look serious in spite of a number of shortcomings in scalability, reliability, security, and manageability. Sun Microsystems in effect said, "Who needs Linux, we have Solaris and it is better than Linux. Microsoft in effect said, "Who needs Linux, we have Windows 2000 and it is better than Linux". Along came IBM, which had questioned the need for both PC's and TCP/IP for serious business computing, and said in effect, "Everybody needs Linux". Perhaps it goes to show that only the greatest sinners know how to repent!

The Community

The real power of Linux is not derived from IBM or any other company or organization; it is the power of the community. Linux, just like the PC and the Internet, is built in an open fashion so that all can see how it was done. The communities that emerged to support them added value to what was developed by the grass roots efforts and then a whole industry grew up around them. That may be what some of the companies that did not embrace those shifts in the early days did not realize. They thought it was all about comparing whether the PC, the Internet and Linux were better than the proprietary approaches. In the early days, PC's were much inferior to minicomputers and mainframes; the Internet was much inferior to IBM's Systems Network Architecture or Digital's DecNet; and today Linux is inferior in many ways to Windows and Solaris. But it doesn't matter for two key reasons. First, when a major e-business or an e-marketplace has a choice between proprietary offerings, or offerings built around communities, communities will almost always win. You could say it is the power of democracy. Irving Wladawsky-Berger, of the Presidential Information Technology Advisory Committee, says, "In proprietary offerings, it is 'every man for himself'. In community based offerings, it is the community collaborating in setting standards and building common technologies which will be available to all, and then it is 'every man for himself' in building on top of that, or leveraging the community base".

The second reason that proprietary offerings ultimately lose out is that there is no way that a single vendor can compete against a well-organized community. In the early stages, when the community is not yet well organized, it cannot make progress, and individual vendors can step in and do very well, even establishing natural monopolies as they bring order to chaos. In fact, people have argued that this is the only model that works in information technology, namely the economy of scale and setting of de facto standards that always results in monopolies. But, once the community gets organized, and can start making progress, the game is over. Darwinian evolution takes over; the best ideas survive and the weak ones fall by the wayside. There is just no way a single vendor, no matter how powerful, can have access to as talented and as many skills as the community can bring to the effort all over the world.

Is It Real?

If you still have doubts about how real Linux may be, there are two tests that are easy to apply. First is to visit a bookstore or the web and see what is available about Linux. The 200 books on Java seemed like a lot but for Linux there are more than 500 books! The second test is to visit the campus of any college or university that teaches computer science and ask the students. You will find that they virtually all know about Linux and are comfortable using it. There is a myth that Linux and other open source software is a cult; that it is 90% about culture, 10% serious. It is just the opposite; it is 90% discipline and high quality, 10% culture. Developers who make high quality contributions to the community rise in the unofficial hierarchy; those that contribute poor quality get sent to "programmer's Hell" never to be heard from again. Very high quality software is produced as a result of this self-managing process. That's why people are interested in Linux – it is a community.

Linux has become a "movement". Although there is no central management structure for Linux it has evolved rapidly because almost anyone can contribute to it. This might include a large software sub-system contributed by IBM or some software to enable a new gadget that a student in Eastern Europe contributed. A system administrator at XYZ Company may be looking for a certain kind of software and makes the need known on the Internet. Meanwhile, someone in another part of the world had just written such software and was happy to give it away to anyone who needs it. In theory such global collaboration shouldn't work so well but it does. Developers like the fact that if they find a bug in the software they can either fix it or report it to others in the community. In the end they know, since the software is open for all to see, that it will be fixed and it can be inspected. There's a community behind it that is committed to it.

The other myth about Linux is that it is popular because it is free. There are free versions of Linux available and this makes it easy for students to learn it, but any organization that is going to use Linux for serious purposes will buy Linux from a company that specializes in distributing and supporting Linux. In addition, companies like IBM and others will enable all of their own software to run on Linux platforms, and these companies will not be giving that software away for free.

The Ultimate Test

The ultimate test of course is not what an information technology company or information technology user says about Linux but rather how they vote with real money and contributions of software into the Linux community. In late 1999 the 24th largest super computer in the world was being installed at the University of New Mexico. It is being built using 256 Intel servers from IBM, linked together in what is called a "cluster", running Linux. In early 2001 The National Center for Supercomputing Applications (NCSA) at University of Illinois at Urbana-Champaign announced that they would be installing the largest and fastest Linux cluster in academia. Their two IBM Linux clusters will be able to perform two trillion operations per second and will be used by researchers to study some of the most fundamental questions of science, such as the nature of gravitational waves first predicted by Albert Einstein in his Theory of Relativity.

Linux is also beginning to move into the commercial environment – for real production applications. At the end of 2000 Shell International Exploration and Production announced that they would be installing the largest Linux super-computer in the world. Linux clusters will become more and more common in e-business applications as the demand from large numbers of users and transactions expands. Telia, the largest telecommunications company in Scandinavia, announced that it would be replacing dozens of Unix computers with a single mainframe computer running Linux! The mainframe has an operating system that in turn can enable tens of thousands of virtual Linux operating systems – thousands of systems all running on one computer. Just these few examples show that Linux is no longer just for students – it is coming into the mainstream.

When we think of information appliances we may think of small things like MP3 players, personal digital assistants, and various wireless devices.

There is another kind of appliance that is more significant in size and scope – server appliances. These specialized boxes do a subset of what normal information technology systems do. They provide printing services, manage large amounts of storage capacity, handle network security functions, etc. These are all things that information technology systems can do generally but, by making server appliances that do only these certain functions, the result is much greater reliability. Server appliances using Linux will have extraordinary stability and reliability and that translates into making things easier to manage.

Embedded Computing

At the other end of the spectrum, Linux is finding its way into very small computing devices. TiVo is a personal TV service that transforms your television-watching experience. It allows you to automatically record your favorite shows every time they air—without setting a timer or using videotape. Then you can control your TV watching by pausing, rewinding or instantly replay any program, anytime. TiVo is an easy to use consumer device. Under the covers is a PowerPC microprocessor running Linux. In Taiwan there is a flurry of activity going on in what is called "embedded Linux". Embedded means that Linux is embedded "under the covers" so that the user doesn't even know it is there. Taiwan has developed prominence based on manufacturing efficiency for industry standard products in the information technology industry. They now plan to duplicate that prominence by putting their own designs into products using Linux. I attended a Linux seminar at National Taiwan University in Taipei in June 2000. The seminar was focused on embedded Linux for all kinds of handheld and Internet attached appliances. The opening keynote speaker was very bullish about Linux. He said that existing industry standard operating systems for PCs are "big, expensive, and unreliable" but that Linux was "small, inexpensive, and reliable". Since no one company controls Linux, it is available to all companies in the world to use, contribute to, and exploit. We can expect to see Asian countries approach this opportunity very aggressively.

At the extreme end of the spectrum, IBM researchers have built a "smart watch", running Linux, that can communicate wirelessly with PCs, cell phones and other wireless-enabled devices, view condensed email messages, provide users with calendar, address book and to-do list functions. Future enhancements will include a high-resolution screen and applications that will allow the watch to be used as an access device for various Internet-based services such as up-to-the-minute information about weather, traffic conditions, the stock market, sports results and so on. Dick Tracy's watch is finally here!

Making Things Easier

The industry commitment to Linux is growing rapidly. IBM is betting its future on Linux and has said publicly it will invest nearly $1 billion in Linux in 2001. Fifteen hundred engineers at IBM are working on adding Linux capability to the company's products and services. HP, IBM, and NEC are setting up an Open Source Development Lab in Portland, Oregon. This independent, non-profit center will provide the open source community a place to test enterprise-class Linux software. This will help ensure that Linux will be "hardened" and ready for serious e-business. Over time Linux will do for operating systems what the Internet did for networking and communications – make them truly open and interoperable.

A lot of effort is expended in organizations today on an activity called "porting". Porting means moving an application from one software "platform" to another: from a mainframe to Windows, from Windows to Linux, from Unix to the Mac, from the Mac to the mainframe, etc. This activity does nothing for the user and yet it requires scarce skills to get it done. As Linux becomes more and more prevalent the porting can decline and those scarce resources can add more value for users.

In addition, many information technology services companies, including IBM, see a big opportunity in making things easier for companies wanting to exploit Linux and they are opening new services practices to capitalize on it. The combination of mainstream acceptance, continued contributions of software from many organizations around the world, the widening availability of skills and services, and the high quality of Linux software will all contribute toward making the next generation of the Internet easier.

So is Linux going to replace all the other operating systems anytime soon? No, but is Linux a disruptive (in the positive sense) technology? There's no question about it. In the market for server operating systems, Linux is growing the fastest and steadily gaining share. Windows still dominates the desktop operating system market but Linux is even making some inroads there with several open source initiatives including Gnome, KDE, and Eazel that are creating personal productivity applications and making the Linux desktop easier to install and use.

CHAPTER 10
Trusted

On December 16, 1994, six IBM, DEC, and a few other companies staff met at MIT with Tim Berners-Lee, the inventor of the World Wide Web. Our small group co-founded the World Wide Web Consortium (W3C), the organization that created and maintains standards for how the web works. We made a list on a whiteboard of what was missing from the web. At the time, most of what we have today was missing. The list included the need for tables, different fonts and colors, and various technical capabilities needed to create and publish shared web documents. When I suggested we add privacy to the list, I got strange looks. Sir Berners-Lee got it immediately and endorsed an effort to develop privacy standards. Facebook is still grappling in developing publically accepted privacy controls. Part of a net attitude is respecting the privacy of others. This chapter explained why.

This last chapter of Part 2 described the elements of privacy and security. As with the Internet, web, and XML, I explained authentication, authorization, non-repudiation, and the critical element of encryption, what they were and how they worked in layperson terms.

Many of the issues about Internet security have to do with policy and procedures. These have to do with net attitude. I described the importance of a user being able to establish on the web they are who they say they are. I was confident the principles of digital signatures I described would be widely adopted by now. This is the biggest gap of any topic in Net Attitude between then and now. In July 2015, I went to Intuit.com to change my email address *from john@patrickweb.com to john@attitudellc.org. After filling out a web form with the new information and my contact information for verification purposes, I was asked to upload an image of my driver license. The purpose was to establish I am who I said I am. This chapter offered many insights about ways to make our interactions on the web secure.*

O f all the issues which will affect the future of the Internet, the safeguarding of our personal information when it travels on or over the Net is likely the most important because it is at the heart of Trust -- and without Trust the Net will not be able to realize its full potential. This means that information about an individual needs to be handled in a way that is consistent with the privacy and security expectations of the individual -- if not, there will be no trust.

Privacy

MyFamily.com is a very useful site for families to share information, calendars, photos, and to learn about genealogy. As part of the registration people are providing the site with their registration information and also the name, email address, and (optionally) the birthdays of their children. This represents some very serious information that a person is entrusting to this website. The management of MyFamily.com is committed to their privacy policy but what happens if MyFamily.com gets acquired? What assurance do we have that the policy will survive? How do we know that the site is safe from hackers? How do we know we can trust the I/T staff not to look at our personal family information? There are numerous questions of this nature that are not Privacy Policy per se --they are actually more about security in many cases -- but questions about which people will eventually get worried when they begin to think about the fact that they have placed potentially their entire family history and photo gallery on a website.

One element of privacy on the Net is Opt in versus Opt out. When you register at a website you will often see a small box to be checked giving you the "option" to be included or not included in subsequent emails making offers to you. Opt in means you proactively choose to be included. Opt out means you are included by default and you have to take action to be removed from the list of those who will automatically receive the emails. In some cases, you have to read the words very carefully to determine which case is the default. This is part of Trust. Is the site really opening up to you and making it very clear what your options are, or are they making the words a bit fuzzy and hoping you won't figure out what the default actually is?

Citibank recently introduced a new service called c2it that enables the sending and receiving of cash via e-mail. You simply visit the c2it site, specify which of your checking, savings, or credit card accounts you want the money to come from, and enter an email address for someone you want to send the money to. That person then receives an email, is asked to enroll in c2it, and then can accept the money from you directly into their checking, savings, or credit card account. This seemed like a potentially useful service to me when I learned about and so I enrolled. Only after I enrolled did I find out that there were fees involved. Then I discovered that incoming amounts are not credited to your account for five to six days, which is longer than if I had received a check and deposited it myself. Then I discovered that there is no fee to receive into a Citibank credit card but there is a fee if it is another bank's credit card. I am not saying the fees are unreasonable – the competition from PayPal and other services will determine that.

The issue is trust. It would be easy to get the feeling that Citibank was not being forthcoming about their offering. Now comes the good part – Affiliate Sharing. The enrollment page on the website said "Citibank FSB is allowed by law to share with its affiliates any information about its transactions or experiences with you. Please check this box if you do not want Citibank to share among its affiliates any other information you provide to us or that we get from third parties". We are talking about a sweeping allowance to provide a broad and undefined amount of information about you with a broad and undefined audience. Should the default be "check this box if you do not want" this? Seemed to me that this was an obvious case where it should have been opt in not opt out. Trust might wane a bit further.

Then comes the Marketing Offers. "Citigroup may still send you marketing offers by telephone, mail and e-mail. If you do not want to receive such marketing offers, please write to the address below and include you name, address, social security number and tell us you don't want offers by mail and/or phone and/or e-mail". Write to us? This highly automated website that can transfer money in and out of any account can't have one more check box; preferably with "check here if you would like us to make offers to you"? I sent the letter and am not sure how long it will take to get "processed". In the meantime, I am already receiving unsolicited marketing offers. Citigroup is a superb marketing oriented company but the approach with this new Internet offering may not build trust with new enrollees even though the company is a highly trustworthy organization.

A World Where Everything Is Connected

When every computer is connected to every computer a lot of things are possible. Some of them are not pretty. Trust will become critical. Brands will become more important than ever because they will signal to us what level of trust we can expect. How will we know whether we can really trust a website? Trust goes hand in hand with good security and privacy. Offering good security and a solid privacy policy will be the bare minimum but we will also follow how an e-business acts over time. What is their commitment? Do they listen to their constituencies? Do they respond to concerns about privacy and make things better? These actions will separate the good guys and the bad guys.

> Brand used to be a feeling conjured up by how a company's product was physically packaged or how you imagined yourself using it. Increasingly brand is a feeling conjured up by your experience on that company's website. It ties directly to Trust. Companies that have a website that provides an end-to-end positive experience and which enhances people's quality of life by saving them time will gain enhanced brand equity. The converse will become obvious.

Privacy, Confidence, And Trust All Go Together

In a December 2000 speech in New York, Lou Gerstner, chairman of IBM Corporation said, "We know that trust is a fundamental element of every positive brand experience. It is fundamental to all consumer behavior, to the willingness to buy and to brand loyalty. All of it is based on trust." Websites already have a repository of huge amounts of personal data that represent the byproduct of not just our registrations but also our surfing habits and our purchases. In the near future our medical records will be on a website somewhere and beyond that will come real time data streamed from pacemakers and other medical instruments that are attached to our bodies. All of this data can bring significant benefits to us but only if we are able to trust the holders of the data and have confidence that they will protect it and respect our preferences about how and when it can be used. Lou Gerstner summarized it well when he said, "The answer here must begin with a responsible marketplace. Through our policies and our practices, industry has to send an unambiguous message that tells people: 'You can trust us. You have choices. They will be respected. And you'll know in advance how any information that you give us will be used.'"

The Cookie Monster

When you click on a link to a webpage, a request is made to retrieve a document from a server and the server sends the document to your browser. If you then come right back to that server for another document, it is an independent request – the server has no knowledge that it was you that had just requested the document. This is fine for surfing but for e-business there are numerous reasons why the server does need to know that you were the one that had just made the request. Some of the early web pioneers had realized the need to be able to retain information about who had made requests of the server and they also saw the need to maintain the "state" of things going on at the server so that if there were multiple steps to an e-business process or if a user became disconnected from the Internet, they would be able to return to the site and pick up where they left off. The technical invention to make this possible was called the "cookie".

When you visit a site the server sends a cookie to your PC. The cookie is a small data file that can contain information about you and the transaction you are participating in. When you come back that second time the server reads the cookie, looks up some data about you in a database if needed and then allows you to continue. The cookie was a great idea and most websites use them. In fact, cookies have facilitated e-business. However, in some cases the use of cookies has become an invasion of our privacy – a tool to be able to track our every mouse click. Cookies have been used by some companies to analyze your web visits and then target advertising at you based on what sites you have recently visited. Some people like this and others find it a large invasion of their privacy.

From time to time I see an editorial or story suggesting that anonymity should not be allowed on the Internet. The motivation is usually associated with concerns over pedophilia. This is certainly an important concern but so are the concerns of those who feel they need to be anonymous. A battered wife or an alcoholic that are seeking help and finding it in discussion groups on the Internet have a very valid reason to be anonymous. We have to be careful that we don't react to "bad things" that happen on the Internet with a cry for regulation. There are laws that address many "bad things" and law enforcement agencies need to use the Internet more effectively as a tool to enforce the laws that already exist. This is happening but more needs to be done.

Platform for Privacy Preferences

A new standard has been developed called P3P, the platform for privacy preferences, which provides a simple, automated way for users to gain more control over the use of personal information on Websites they visit. At its most basic level, P3P is a standardized set of multiple-choice questions, covering all the major aspects of a website's privacy policies. Taken together, they present a clear snapshot of how a site handles personal information about its users. P3P-enabled websites make this information available in a standard, machine-readable format. P3P enabled browsers can then "read" this snapshot automatically so that the user can compare it to their privacy preferences. P3P enhances user control by putting privacy policies where users can find them, in a form users can understand, and, most importantly, enables users to act on what they see. P3P will allow you to establish the degree of privacy you want to have. Some of us may want to be anonymous. That's okay. Some may conclude that they really like the idea of getting e-mails and personalized webpages. Some may even like the idea of an e-business which sorts through past web purchases and then makes buying recommendations based on the history. They may be very busy and don't have time to shop so if somebody can make suggestions for them it may be a valuable service. That's okay too. P3P will enable us all to express our preferences in the browser and then help us to find those services that meet our individual privacy requirements. If a website doesn't meet our privacy requirements, we will be advised and have the choice to move on to a different site.

Part of Trust comes from seeing people up close and personal. Looking into their eyes. Observing whether they look back into yours. Body language. I often get asked whether the Internet as a new medium will reduce people's desire to get together in person or whether people will just sit in front of their PC and never go anywhere. I don't think so. Perhaps the ultimate proof point is websites for seniors like SeniorNet (http://www.seniornet.org) and ThirdAge (http://www.thirdage.com) that have been responsible, at least in part, for numerous marriages. People will have a lot of e-meetings but I don't think people will give up on meeting in person as a result. There is too much that would be missed.

Internet Security – The Glass Is Half Full Not Half Empty

Mention the word Trust and many people immediately think of security. We hear so many negative questions about Internet security. Is it strong enough? What will happen to my credit card number? What about hackers? We would like to implement this or that application but we can't because of "security". The list goes on. This is one area where some "old fashioned" attitudes are actually healthy. Security is critical and needs to be taken very seriously -- but not in a restrictive sense. In fact, the question that business and government leaders should be asking is about how security on the Internet can become the *enabler* of global commerce, the enabler for meeting peoples' expectations, and the enabler for Trust.

In one sense, the Internet is actually completely insecure. It is similar to a "party" telephone line (for those old enough to remember them) where multiple parties are actually sharing the same network. You might pick up a "party" phone line and find out your neighbor is already using it. The Internet is a shared network also. Our emails, webpages, and IP telephony calls are broken up into "packets", containing 5,000-10,000 zeroes and ones each, and the packets travel over phone lines hopping between specialized computers called routers to get from their origin to their destination. A clever "snoop" could use various "sniffers" to "listen" to the packets and if they are very clever assemble them back into the email, webpage, or IP telephony call.

Enter encryption technology; one of the most powerful technologies on earth. Using very sophisticated mathematics, the contents of packets can be scrambled (encrypted) in such a way that only the intended recipient is able to unscramble (decrypt) the packets. Millions of people have discovered that this technique has enabled them to put their credit card number into a secure web transaction in a way that only the server at the other end is able to read it. In fact more and more people are realizing that their credit card number may be safer on the Internet than it is when they give it to a total stranger over a toll free number or to a waiter in a restaurant. The "strength" of encryption is incredible. There is no known case of anyone "breaking" full strength encryption or even a practical theory for how to do so. At some point in the future there may be some combination of people, networked computers, and schemes that will enable information encrypted with today's technology to be decoded but by then the strength of the encryption technology will have advanced even further. The bottom line is that using encryption enables us to do things very securely using an insecure network.

It's Not The Technology

The real issue with regard to Internet security has to do more with policy and procedures and these in turn have to do with attitude. I spoke with a group of CEO's recently and one of them asked me what a firewall is? I said, well that's a specialized computer that stands between your company and the Internet, and it allows your employees to be able to go out to the Internet and see what's out there. It also allows the other 200 million people out there to come into parts of your business you don't want them to come into if it isn't set up and managed properly. By the way I asked, "Do you know the state of the morale of the person who administers your firewall"? When did they get their last salary increase? Are they a disgruntled employee? A security study once showed that the most common password for operating firewalls is the word 'password' which comes shipped as the default password when getting new firewall hardware or software!

We all know how we feel about en employee who cheats the company by claiming reimbursement for a meal or travel expense they didn't actually have. We don't tolerate it. End of discussion. How do we feel when an employee puts a stick-on memo on their PC screen or under their mouse pad with their password on it? We should feel the same way as with the expense fraud because that employee has compromised the security of the company. Is it condoned for employees to share passwords? How about the physical security of your server room? Is it ok to leave the door open if it gets warm in the room? Can visitors get into the server room? Does the audit department make periodic attempts to "break in" to the server room and see if they can turn something off or walk out with some backup tapes?

One of the fastest growing businesses at IBM is the "ethical hacking" group. For a fee they will try to break into your servers from the Internet. If successful they tell you how they did it and offer advice for how to prevent it in the future. Unfortunately, they are usually successful. At PC Forum, an exclusive I/T industry conference of top executives from around the world several companies volunteered to be guinea pigs while a team of IBM "ethical hackers" attempted to break into their servers. This was done on the condition that the company name would not be revealed. An IBM expert stood at the podium while talking over a speakerphone with the "ethical hacker" team that was at a technology center far away. The discussion was broadcasted over the sound system to the audience. The first break-in took eleven minutes after which the IBM engineers were looking at the driver's license of the daughter of the CEO of the company. The second company attempt took seventeen minutes after which the engineer had access to the company payroll file. These were not failures of technology. They were failures of process, procedure and, audit. The source of the problem is attitude about security. It should not be feared – it should be embraced. The right attitude will not restrict the opportunities but in fact will enable more opportunities and enable them to be handled in a more secure manner.

Who Are You – Really?

There was a cartoon by Peter Steiner in the July 5, 1993 issue of The New Yorker showing a dog at a PC speaking to another dog watching from the floor. The caption was, "On the Internet nobody knows you're a dog." Very true and in fact nobody really knows for sure just who you are. Nor do you know who is at the other end of a chat session or e-commerce transaction either. In the NGi we will have Digital IDs that will change this. There has been a prevailing attitude that digital IDs would mean that the "government" would issue an ID that would then enable them to spy on us; read our email, track what we do on the web, or invade our privacy in some way. A bit of knowledge plus a healthy net attitude would actually instead lead us to a very positive view -- that digital ID's are not to be feared but in fact should be embraced. They represent the empowerment that can unleash the full potential of e-business. They will allow us establish that we are who we say we are and to validate that the web server we are doing business with is really who they say they are. Security is not the issue. Authentication is.

It is true that large numbers of people have learned that security technology can encrypt their credit card number in such a way that only the web server at the destination is able to decrypt it. When people see the solid lock or key at the bottom of their browser they implicitly know that their credit card number or other private information is being encrypted using the public key of the server at the other end. And, since only that server has the corresponding private key then only that server is able to decrypt the private information. An important question however is who is that web server on the other end? How do you know it really is the merchant or university or government agency that the server's home page said it was? Answer? You don't. It could in fact be a hacker who has "spoofed" the website; i.e. the site could be an imposter. Likewise, the website at the other end doesn't really know for sure that you are who you say you are. What we are talking about here is authentication. For the most part we do not have it on the Internet today. Yet, it is one of the core capabilities needed to achieve the ultimate potential of the Internet and enable us all to fee we can Trust the Internet.

Today we use the login ID and password as a substitute for authentication. We all use them every day but the problems with them are nontrivial. First is the password sharing problem that enables someone else to be you. If you leave your password on a stick-on on your PC or under your mouse pad then one of your children or a colleague can become you. They can get into your bank account, buy a book at Amazon, or engage in a chat session as you. Assuming you keep your password to yourself, there is another set of problems. Websites have different rules for login Ids and passwords. Some require that you use your email ID as your login, some require you to use your social security number, others allow you to pick anything you want as long as it is at least so many characters or in other cases as long as it is no more than so many characters. For good reasons they all require that your ID be unique. Sorry, but jjones is already taken. The same thing is the case for the password. Some require at least so many characters, some require that a password must contain at least one numeric character, some require that it be all numeric, and others require that contain no numeric characters. The variations are vast and the result is that you end up with a lot of different IDs and passwords.

Digital Ids to The Rescue

There are basically two ways to deal with managing this problem and neither of them is a good solution. First is to devise an ID (and password) that conforms to nearly all website rules but which is also unique. Maybe you design an ID or password something like k7jyt14s that seems to work just about everywhere and surely nobody else will already have it. On the surface your multipurpose universal ID or password seems to be a good idea until you realize that if one of your web merchants turns out to be a scofflaw or if someone somehow steals your ID and password he or she now has access to your bank account, brokerage account, and every other website where you have registered! By making things simple for yourself you have compromised yourself with every web relationship you have.

The other potential solution, which many people use, is to create a small database of all your IDs and passwords. Where to put it? On a piece of paper? Where to put that? On the desk. Then it falls off of the desk and dog eats it. You now have No ids or passwords! Then you decide to get serious and buy some database software and create a PC database of your IDs and passwords. Hmmm, this is a really important database --. maybe you need an ID and password for your ID/password database? Hmmm. Maybe you need a backup and recovery scheme? You have now become a database manager!

In case you aren't discouraged about IDs and passwords yet there is one more peril. Whatever your ID and password are, when you send them they are almost always sent "in the clear"; i.e. not encrypted. Even sites that use encryption for all transactions normally do not use encryption to receive your ID and password. This means that an unscrupulous person might be able to "sniff" your ID and password from the Internet. They wouldn't need to even know who you are. They just know they have a way to gain access to many websites as an impersonator of you. There has to be a better way. Fortunately, there is.

In the near future most people will have a digital ID along with an accompanying biometric link such as a fingerprint, face print, voiceprint, iris or retina scan. The combination of digital ID and biometric match will enable you to establish yourself as a completely unique person. At last you have the ability in the digital world to establish that you are who you say you are just as you can in the physical world! Step one is to get a digital ID from someone that knows for sure who you are and who is trusted by others as a reliable source for authenticating you. And who would this someone be? The Certificate Authority, or CA, is the place. The CA will ask you for information to validate that you are who you say you are. The degree of certainly they require will depend on your intended use. For routine things like email perhaps asking your mailing address and mother's maiden name will be adequate. If you are going to use your digital ID to make millions of dollars' worth of purchases for your employer, then a personal appearance may be required where you show multiple forms of identification and then the CA gives you a diskette or other form of digital ID.

Over time there will be many CAs. Governments will operate them as will banks, companies, and institutions of all kinds. In theory there could be one CA that authenticates everyone and you would have just one digital ID. In theory you could have a "national" drivers' license in your wallet (actually, most countries outside of America do) or a "universal" credit card and that one card could be used for all purposes. In theory, but not in practice. Can you imagine that VISA or MasterCard or American Express will give up their logo on the card and be part of a generic ID? I don't think so either. Not only do they not want to give up their marketing presence on the card they also don't want to take on the liability for providing a general purpose digital ID that you could potentially use to go to the hospital for a leg amputation. If the hospital happens to take the wrong leg off of the wrong person, the credit card company will surely not want to be liable for having validated that you are who you say you are. Just like we have multiple physical IDs in our wallet we will have multiple digital id's.

The important thing is for a CA to be able to be quite certain that you are who you say you are before they issue you a digital ID. This can happen in various ways. For example, Equifax is a consumer credit reporting company that has information about 200+ million people. They know your name, your last few addresses, your phone number, and in many cases your mortgage balance! So when they ask you for certain information they can compare it to what is in their database and if there is a match the odds are very high that they can indeed be sure that you are who you say you are. With this assurance they can issue you a digital ID or provide the information to another third party who can THEN issue you the digital ID.

Digital IDs are actually being issued already in some parts of the world. Singapore and Taiwan have established guidelines that provide for CA's. Europe has established a directive that will enable CA's across the continent. In fact, the Ministry of Finance in Spain issues digital ID's that allow citizens to make their tax payments over the Internet. A Spanish citizen can log on to the site by entering their password into their browser. The digital ID is stored in the browser and does not have to be passed over the Internet in the clear. Once authenticated, the Spanish citizen can pay taxes or check the status of tax payments. The U.S. government in July 2000 passed legislation that will allow CA's to be established that can enable digital signatures to be used anywhere in the country.

Once you get a digital ID, where do you keep it and how does it work? There are two parts to your digital ID; a public part and a private part. The public part is something you want to make easily available to anyone. This will be described in more detail a little bit further on. The private part of your ID is something you will keep very private and never share it with anyone. Where will your digital ID be stored? There will be a lot of choices including on our PC hard drive, in our mobile phone, in smart cards in our wallet, in a PCMCIA card, in an electronic ring on our finger, or in a token we wear around our neck. A company called KeyNetica is developing products that will enable a broad spectrum of Internet users - everyday people who do everyday things like banking and shopping - to move among many different Internet access devices during the course of a day using a portable personal identification tool that they can use on almost any computer via a "USB flash memory key". Since all PC's shipped today have a USB "port" used to plug in printers, digital cameras, and other devices, the USB flash memory key could enable you to plug your digital ID into any PC anywhere. Wherever you keep it, the digital ID is a very empowering capability.

> Does a digital ID mean we lose our privacy? No, quite to the contrary. By having a Digital ID you can establish not only who you are but what privacy preferences you want to stand by. If you choose to be anonymous you will be able to.

Authentication (You Are Who You Say You Are)

There are five important attributes in a world of digital IDs. The first is authentication. Once you have a digital ID you will no longer have to send your login ID and password over the Internet. Your password goes no further than your smart card, token, or your PC. Instead you will use your password to enable an encrypted exchange of digital data between your PC (or phone or other information appliance) and the other party. The result of the exchange is that both parties will be able to confirm that the other party is indeed who they say they are. If you have also provided biometric data the person will know not only that it was your ID but that it was actually you who initiated the transaction and not someone who may have "borrowed" your login/password. Digital IDs are stored in a digital certificate (hence the origin of the certificate authority) and during the initial exchange of information you will see some of the data that is stored in the other party's certificate. For example, you will see who issued the ID to them and you can use this information as an additional input to determine whether you want to trust the other party. Authentication is the beginning. If you want to be really sure you can examine the other party's "fingerprint". This is analogous to the small key number embossed on your house or car key. Your credit card statement, for example, may have the "fingerprint" printed on the statement so if you wanted to you could check it against what appeared on the webpage to be 100% certain that the credit card company's website was indeed them.

Authorization (Who Can Do What)

Now that you have established that who you are who you say you are (been authenticated), various service providers such as banks, merchants, and others can authorize you to do various things. This might include reading a subscription to a publication, banking, investing at an on-line brokerage firm, establishing an account with a merchant so you can buy things without having to register each time you purchase something, or voting in local or national elections. Authorization goes deeper however. Since you are authenticated, you can be authorized to authorize others! Let's suppose your company has an intranet application that allows you to enroll annually for various medical and dental benefits. Suppose you wanted to allow your spouse to do this for you. How would that work? In today's world, unfortunately, many people don't think twice about giving their password to a friend, colleague, or relative. In tomorrow's world that is not a good idea. A digital ID gives each of us great power and enables us to establish our privacy at the same time. Sharing our password with others dilutes that power. An alternative approach is simply to have a web application that allows a person to authorize someone else to do something on their behalf without giving up their own identity. You authenticate yourself and then you authorize your spouse to be able to enroll or change your medical and dental plan benefits. Then the health care provider or insurance company knows not just that a valid ID and password were used to enroll, but that in fact, the person using the application was authorized by an authenticated person.

If you read the fine print at on-line banking sites you will find that you agree that as long as your ID and password was used to execute a transaction that they are not liable for it not being you. If one of your children finds your ID and password and sells your portfolio (or doubles the size of it on margin) the on-line brokerage is not liable. It was *you!*

Confidentiality (Only The Intended Recipient Can Read Your Messages)

The killer application on the Internet is arguably still email. Unfortunately, of the trillions of emails sent each year most are sent "in the clear". In other words, they are not encrypted. Think about writing your most sensitive personal thoughts about someone on a plain postal card and dropping it in a postal box or the slot at the post office. You would have no idea who might be able to read it as it travels from postal box to post office to post office to mail room to intended recipient. That is how it is with all the emails you send! You really have no idea who can read them. When we all have Digital IDs there will be a better way. If you want to send Josef a very private message that nobody but Josef can read you will go to a Certificate Authority and get a copy of Josef's public key. You will then use your email program or other encryption software such as PGP (Pretty Good Privacy) to encrypt your message to Josef. When Josef receives the scrambled message he decrypts it using his private key. Nobody has Josef's private key but Josef so you and Josef both know that nobody but Josef was able to read the message.

Integrity (You Both Know Nothing Got Changed)

How does Josef know that the email really came from you and that it wasn't altered in some manner on its way to him? A by-product of using the encryption keys is a function called "hashing". A calculation is made based on all the characters in the message you create. This calculation is encrypted along with the message. After the decryption takes place, the calculation is compared to the one that was made at the time of the encryption. If they agree then your software will in effect tell both you and Josef that the message was not altered. Also, the message was "signed" by you using your private key. Josef gets your public key from the CA and decrypts your digital signature to confirm that it was actually you who "signed" it.

Non-Repudiation (No One Can Deny A Conversation Or Transaction)

Have you ever been told, "We did not receive any request from you to make that stock sale" or have you had to say, "I did not receive that confirmation notice"? If you receive an encrypted message from someone that is "signed" with their Digital ID (with their private key) and you are able to decrypt it with their public key then you know that the message must have been signed with their private key. Only they have their private key, so they must have signed it. They cannot deny it. This works in both directions, of course. Many major countries of the world have now passed legislation that makes digital signatures as good as signatures with ink. They will stand up in court. Soon we will realize that they are actually much better than ink.

Digital signatures are not perfect. Bruce Schneier, founder and CTO of Counterpane Internet Security Inc., has pointed this out in great detail in various writings. This is because computers and computer software are not yet perfect. In order to trust the digital signature, we implicitly trust the hardware and software that enabled us to use our digital ID to create the digital signature. In spite of the imperfections there are many instances where digital signatures are adequate and in fact a clear advantage in efficiency and effectiveness versus current methods. Where the dollar value that depends on the signature is very high, strict security measures need to be taken in proportion.

Back to The GE Wire Transfer

Remember my saga with GE Capital in trying to wire money to my attorney? Let's contrast that process with how it might have worked using a public key infrastructure approach with the five security functions described above.

Authentication. Yes, I was authenticated by the bank. They looked at my driver's license and put a rubber stamp on the fax request form. The only difference was that instead of a mouse click or two it was a harrowing forty-five minutes running around the streets of New York on a hot summer day.

Authorization. Yes, I was authorized by GE Capital because once they received the authentication they could look up my account, see that I had adequate funds, and therefore authorize the funds transfer.

Confidentiality. Sort of. If I call GE Capital and the person I am talking to is standing at a fax machine and I am standing at a fax machine and I say "Ok, here it comes" and they say "Ok, I see it coming" then arguably we could say it is a confidential transfer of information. In reality faxes tend to go from an outbox to an assistant who takes it to a fax machine where someone could be looking over their shoulder. And then the document is faxed to a number and received in a "fax room" to be read by anyone who happens to pick it up. And of course there was the hassle of finding a fax machine and the time delay. Hardly a mouse click.

Integrity. Definitely not. This is the real flaw in the manual paper based process. When the fax was taken by me or someone else to the fax room I may have placed in on a table and made a quick run to the men's room or gotten distracted by a phone call. Meanwhile someone sees the wire transfer form and changes $500 to $50,000. Then the form gets faxed. What amount gets wired? $50,000. No integrity.

Non-repudiation. You bet. The transaction will stand up in court. As far as GE Capital is concerned I requested the wire transfer of $50,000. I was authenticated, the transaction was authorized and the fax form was transmitted "confidentially". If I contested the transfer I would probably lose in court.

So what is missing? Why couldn't I have done this transfer on the web with a few mouse clicks or mobile phone clicks? Technology problem? No. Security problem? No. It is time for the leadership of institutions of all kinds to move forward to make digital IDs available to their constituencies so that Trust can be achieved.

Open Standards Need To Continue To Rule

Another dimension of Trust has to do with standards. The Internet is the only thing I know of that works the same everywhere. Most things work differently in different parts of the world. The side of the road we drive on, the side of the car we drive from, the width of the railroad tracks, the plugs that we put in the wall; all work differently around the world. But not the Internet; it works exactly the same in every corner of the world. It is based on standards. There are a lot of debates during the process while Internet standards are being developed but once published as a standard every vendor implements the standard. The vendors compete on how well or how fast they are able to implement standards but they do not compete by changing an Internet standard. As an application developer, when an application is built with open standards you can have a high degree of Trust that the application will interoperate with other applications, that technical support will be available in the event of problems, and that there will be flexibility to change vendors if appropriate.

An open standard means a standard that is supported on all information technology platforms. XML and HTTP, for example, work with Windows, Unix, Linux, Apple, IBM, HP, and all PC's. There are other important technologies like IBM's mainframes or Microsoft's Windows that are dominant in various ways. They support open standards, like XML and HTTP, but they are not themselves open standards.

So Many Issues; So Little Time

The final element of trust comes from public policy. There are many policy issues that will affect the Internet -- taxation, trade rules, jurisdiction over transactions, protection of intellectual property, privacy, and others. Although the Internet is transferring "Power to the People" there is still an important role for governments and global organizations. Generally speaking, regulations are not needed but thoughtful standards and cooperative policy work are. The private sector needs to provide aggressive leadership. We can't delay. We have to anticipate the impending issues such as privacy and run hard and fast to address them. The alternative is to wait until the political pressures result in regulation that, in many cases, may be difficult and costly to implement.

Part Three

Attitudes for success

Part 3 of the original book was all about attitude. Technology and apps have changed dramatically since 2001, but the need for a net attitude has not changed. If you want to be ahead of the competition, the need for a net attitude is greater than ever. The principles behind a net attitude, so far, are timeless.

In the first chapter of Part 3 I described in detail the culture behind a net attitude. What is it? How do you get it? The second chapter was about organizing to get things done. The things I described about a "skunk works" approach to innovation continue to serve me well. The idea of small teams working together in which it is okay to fail is fundamental to success. My mantra was and still is, "Think big, act bold, start small, and iterate often". This simple mantra is often re-tweeted by those who are believers. Healthcare.gov has shown what happens when you do not follow this mantra It was reported the management behind healthcare.gov purposely did not want to get the site out there early for fear of political criticism of bugs.

The second chapter of Part 3 is about kids and seniors getting a taste of the culture. They both provided many lessons. The final chapter was about what to do once you get a net attitude. It contained a checklist of actions and philosophies managers can adopt to leverage a net attitude. I modified the list in Health Attitude somewhat to include newer technologies, but the principles remain valid and are more important than ever. I would say how you modified it.

My first keynote speech about the future of the Internet was at Internet World in December 1994. Compared to today the web at that time was very crude. It didn't make the dramatic change in one big step though. It evolved. Seems like every month there has been a new technology, a new version of a browser, the introduction of Java, JavaScript, streaming audio; a lot of things that cumulatively added up to what we think of as the Internet today. That same path is continuing to happen to the next generation of the Internet. As breakthroughs are made in the laboratories of companies, governments and universities that progress gets incorporated into the Internet and it thereby morphs itself into a commercial version of the prototypes that are in the labs. And then the process repeats. Constant evolution is the hallmark of the Internet.

Meanwhile, the Internet has transferred "Power to the People" and their expectations are rising by the day. More and more people are coming to the Net but an increasing number are not satisfied. The NGi is under development and the fast, always on, everywhere, natural, intelligent, easy and trusted new medium will provide many of the capabilities that can satisfy people in new and exciting ways. But there is a big IF. The technology will only do the job if it is applied in the right context – call it attitude – that lines up with the cultural aspects of the Net. Mastering the technology and the new business models is difficult but achievable. The hard part is mastering the attitude that is necessary to both attract the talent needed and to satisfy the expectations of customers and all the other constituencies. Getting the people on board to help build successful e-businesses and e-marketplaces will require that same attitude. Once you recruit them the attitude becomes even more important so that you can motivate and retain the best talent.

CHAPTER 11

Getting an Attitude

This chapter described how to get a net attitude. Some of the characteristics of a non-existent net attitude, unfortunately, still abound on the websites of major organizations of all kinds. Some websites and emails still use ALL CAPS because they want to place EMPHASIS on something. FUNDS RECEIVED. ACCOUNT PAST DUE. Most people don't like getting ALL CAPS in their face. It is unpleasant to read and hard on the eyes.

In my book Health Attitude, I wrote about the difficulty of truncated abbreviations used in explanatory sections of healthcare benefit statements. These statements showing only truncated abbreviations make the benefit explanation statements almost impossible to understand.[13] The reasons for the unreadable documents are partly technical, but I attribute it mostly to a lack of net attitude in the people who are responsible for designing the statements. It appears they don't think it is important to make them easier for customers to understand.

The classic example of a poor net attitude, the call center, which I used 14 years ago, still hasn't improved. The pre-recorded voice begins with, "Please pay attention because our menus have recently changed." If you press "0", you get a response saying, "You have pressed an invalid key". "Please enter your 16-digit account number" is often followed by, "What is your account number?" These annoying, often repetitive responses are not due to a technical problem. They are due to a lack of net attitude.

This chapter explored the dimensions of Netiquette. Netiquette is a combination of "Net" and "etiquette". Netiquette has evolved over the years but its role to make electronic communications more pleasant, as well as more effective, continues to be a key element of net attitude. Many other examples of Netiquette also were discussed. The vocabulary of net attitude is more important than ever as users find it easier than ever to change to a competitor's website.

Net attitude means thinking about things in a way much different than the way many of us grew up. We need to think along the lines of the development of the Internet; to think like those who were part of the grassroots development of the Internet. We need to think more "outside" than "inside". Thinking big is important but starting simple and growing fast are even more important. Good security starts with attitude – not with technology. We need to utilize the rigid six sigma quality thinking for some projects but leave it at the doorstep others and adopt a just enough is good enough approach -- trial by fire – for others. We need to learn how to get requirements directly from the market – not from complicated processes and studies. We need to believe in small teams and give them maximum freedom of action. We also need to think differently about information technology systems; in particular, to adopt an attitude for rapid deployment and integration of applications. The Net makes it possible to communicate in new ways and an attitude of over-communications is usually the right one. Last but not least a healthy net attitude can best be adopted if you get a real taste of the culture. The best way to do that is to talk to your kids.

A New Vocabulary Is Needed

Business vocabulary needs to change in a hurry. "Please call during our normal business hours of nine to five Monday to Friday" doesn't even come close to the realities of a connected world. The source of the problem is usually based on an attitude that is centered in the past – and many years of habit. It is ingrained into business vocabulary. Even some new Internet startups have somehow adopted the old language. You find the old vocabulary in newspapers, you find it on the doors of stores, and you find it on the web. You won't find it on many homepages but if you drill down far enough on most websites you will eventually get to something that essentially says "Oh, if you need to know that, then call us nine to five Monday to Friday".

Companies should ban the old hours of operation from their websites. Make 24 x 7 service the mantra – faxes by special request only. Send the signal that your e-business is progressive and ready to serve customers around the clock and using modern communications methods. Some may say, "But nine to five is really when we are open. This is when we have always been open." They are thinking about when they are in the office instead of when people are out there on the web looking for help. Some corporate managers even say that they can't afford the extra labor cost to handle all the inquiries that may come from an around the clock website. People with net attitude salivate about the possibility of such a problem! As more and more customers come online it may call for a restructuring of work hours. Careful monitoring of web traffic can be used to map the availability of on-line chat support to the pattern of web visits. Support resources can telecommute to provide the support.

Then there is the fax. Here a fax; there a fax; everywhere a fax. The vocabulary of the fax is equally ingrained as the hours of operation – the words just roll of the tongue. Even businesses that have email systems routinely ask for your fax number when you request information. It is a habit that is hard to break. Email messages surpassed "snail mail" messages in the last millennium. Getting an email account is a free service offered by many sources and email is still the most popular use of the Internet and yet, when it comes to the "forms" of the world, the fax continues as a mainstream communications tool. The information that gets delivered via fax often gets entered into a computer; sometimes the same computer that the information came from! It's habit and attitude. Make email information delivery the norm and offer fax by special request only. Change the vocabulary. Highlight the availability of price quotes, product information, and support requests by email. Think of email as an advertising medium. Most email programs now support HTML mail, which means that an email can look like a webpage, complete with color, graphics, and multimedia. Every email can have an epilogue with company specials or additional product information. Get rid of the old medium and pizzazz to your communications.

The concept of a "maintenance window" for a website is also an old habit. The vocabulary is ingrained – "down for maintenance". If the site is not yet up to 24 x 7 standards technically, then at least express a net attitude when explaining to customers; "We apologize to any of our valued customers in parts of the world that are seeing this system outage while we make some necessary improvements".

Just Say NO to ALL CAPS

Part of vocabulary consists of the words we use and part is how we present those words. As information gets relayed between buys and sellers in the supply chain it often gets converted to all uppercase letters. Some people create ALL CAPS because they want to EMPHASIZE something. Most people don't like getting ALL CAPS in their face; it is unpleasant to read. FUNDS RECEIVED. ACCOUNT PAST DUE -- and other unfriendly snippets. Some companies even send you email in the same manner. GREETINGS. GET RICH QUICK. Typing in all CAPITALS is like shouting or yelling in someone's ear. It is time to make user-friendly text the rule and use upper-case words only to make a point and, even then, to use them in a very restrained manner. If you'd like to emphasize certain words, consider highlighting them with **asterisks**.

Some of us can remember when messaging was still a matter of sending a FEW ALPHANUMERIC CIPHERS from one dumb terminal to another. And, of course, we wrote in ALL CAPS -- a charming holdover from the industry's roots in the old keypunch days, before lower case letters existed. Proper use of letters, abbreviations, and symbols is part of Netiquette. As the term implies, Netiquette is a combination of "Net" and "etiquette". Netiquette has evolved over the past few years and its role is to make electronic communications more pleasant, as well as more effective.

David Singer, senior technical staff member and guardian of Net culture at IBM Corporation, offers some additional basics:

The basic rule of netiquette is to show consideration for the other party. Stop and think how the other person is likely to receive your communication.

Use white space to make things easier to read. Don't run your entire message into one long paragraph.

If you're replying to a message, only quote as much of it as you need to make your point. Don't quote the entire message and then add a one or two-word comment like "I agree". You can also preface paragraphs with the sender's initials.

Be brief. Your recipients are probably as busy as you are!

"Emoticons" can be useful but, if you say something not so nice and try to take the sting out of the remark by using a <g> to represent a grin or :-) to represent a smile, it usually doesn't work. If you think your phrasing might offend the reader, fix the language -- don't rely on a "smiley" to convey your feelings.

Abbreviations, like btw for "by the way" or imho for "in my humble opinion" or iac for "in any case" can be helpful and save typing, but should not be overused.

There are times to use e-mail and times to use the phone. E-mail is generally NOT good for solving conflict or for emotionally charged subjects. Messages should be concise and to the point. Think of your memo as a telephone conversation that you are typing instead of speaking.

Communicate, Communicate, And Communicate

In 1993 a number of us were talking about the Internet at IBM and someone said "How do we make money on the Internet? We all agreed we had no idea but one thing we all knew for sure was that Internet was surely the greatest tool ever for communicating both to our employees and to our external constituencies. Gone forever were the words in an internal announcement "For more information see your manager" or for external announcements "For more information, please contact your IBM Marketing Representative".

Effective communications is a challenge in any organization, large or small. Key messages from the top often get "filtered" on their way down the chain of command. An email, on the other hand, can go directly from the CEO to all employees to personally make a point, introduce a new idea, explain a shift in company strategy, or congratulate and recognize a significant accomplishment. The email can be replete with hyperlinks to webpages on the company intranet. The email becomes the "push" mechanism to drive people to the intranet where they can find much more information.

In July 1995 IBM made a hostile takeover of Lotus Development Corporation. The announcement was made to the press at ten o'clock in the morning and at that very same moment an Internet website came alive to enable Lotus employees to see a picture of Lou Gerstner, IBM's chairman, and hear his words through a recorded "webcast" as he described IBM's vision for acquiring Lotus. The employees didn't have to read the Wall Street Journal or the Boston Globe to get a reporter's version of what Lou Gerstner said at the press conference – they could get it timely and "straight from the horse's mouth"! All major companies have issues that arise from time to time; mergers, product liability or employee suits, government investigations, or financial surprises. There is no substitute for getting the information to employees first hand.

The webcast has emerged as a powerful way to communicate. The concept is to capture the audio and video of a speech, convert it to digital form (encoding), and then "stream" it (web version of broadcast) over the intranet or Internet. Many organizations don't take advantage of webcasting because of fears of inadequate bandwidth to deliver the content with good quality. This is often a valid concern but there are clever ways to get around the problem. A webcast does not have to be live. Chances are all the employees are not available to watch it live anyway. At IBM, speeches are captured and then stored in a "video jukebox". When a major speech by the CEO or other executive is to take place an announcement goes out via email and encourages employees to participate in it if they are able but if not to visit the video jukebox and watch it at their leisure. During the live webcast, the number of employees allowed to "get in" to the webcast is limited just like seats in an auditorium are. This allows for controlled bandwidth usage and good quality for those who are able to get in. Others watch it later in the day or the next day or whenever they get a chance. The video jukebox becomes an invaluable library of content over time.

A personal website can make your life very interesting. In 1995 I was getting a lot of calls from people asking for a copy of the presentation I was giving at Internet World and various places. I decided to build a website of my own and launched www.ibm.com/patrick as a place to put copies of my presentations. It evolved to become an efficient way for me to share and become part of the community at large. There is a lot to be learned by being "out there" – actively creating content for your own site and especially from the feedback people give you. It is also a good feeling to be able to lend a hand to people who come to the site looking for something. My "Gadgets" section has a lot of things in it but the one that has gotten the most attention for some reason is the Pepper Ball (an ingenious gadget that grinds pepper as you squeeze its two handles). Numerous people have sent me email asking where I bought it and more than one have sent me mail asking how to refill it with pepper! One woman wrote "Mr. Patrick - thank you for responding about the pepper ball. I have been searching the world over for how to refill it and no idea I would finally get the answer from a vice president at IBM."

Staying Connected to The Real World

Numerous newspaper stories have commented about employees at companies who are spending too much time on the web. Charts and graphs have shown the hours per day or week that these employees are surfing, the implication being that they are wasting time. I have heard multiple middle managers and CEO's say things like "I don't want our people surfing the web. We have real work to get done around here!" The presumption is that the people on the web are shopping or trading stocks or chatting with friends or a family member. If that is true (and surely it is to some degree) is it bad? Do people bring a newspaper to work in their briefcase? Do people ever do any shopping on their lunch hour on the phone? Or do they take even more time away from work by driving somewhere for an errand they could do on the web instead?

In a big organization it is so easy to spend all of your time talking or emailing with colleagues. That is how big companies can lose touch with customers and markets. The Internet has transferred power to people. They can now communicate across management layers, have discussion groups about technologies or products, learn what is going on at competitors, find out who is hiring what skills, learn of new research initiatives, explore new product ideas, provide real-time focus groups to get a lead on requirements, and link directly to any company of their choosing to facilitate sales or purchases. More important than the use of the Net as a new medium for efficient communications is that by spending time on the web they stay connected externally and generally become much better informed about what is happening in the real world. Most of the people in the world are outside the organization. Let people in your organization stay connected to them. The alternative is to cut off Internet access for employees (which some companies actually do) and in effect put all heads in the sand. Worry if your people are not spending *enough* time on the web.

"Outside-In"

The concern over employees spending too much time on the Internet is a classic "Inside-out" attitude. It is a focus on what is going on inside the company or organization. There are still many executives and managers who don't realize that the key to being effective in markets is understanding the competition, knowing what is going on at key universities in technology areas that are important to their business, and experiencing new trends and new business models first hand. Is it possible that if executives from the music industry, or financial services industry, or publishing industry had spent more time "outside" than "inside" that they may have developed new models for their businesses instead of later getting on the defense about the web and in some cases losing focus and spending large amounts of money trying to stop the new models?

Inside-out is a pharmaceutical company website that contains information about a new drug only from the perspective of what the company wants you to know. All the links on the site are to company publications and company perspective. An Outside-in approach would acknowledge that there are sources outside of the company that may be of value. An outside-in site would provide links to key universities where joint work is being done, independent healthcare sites, and even discussion groups that are focused on the company's products. There is in fact a lot of information out there that may be useful to customers and if the product is truly a good product, its merits will emerge in discussion by others and add creditability to statements made by the company. Providing an external link should not imply that the company "suggested" that you go there and should not make the company liable if a person goes to a discussion group and takes an action that results in negative consequences for the person. Providing external links should be viewed as a service and an acknowledgement that there is a lot of information outside of the company.

There is a lot being said on websites and Internet discussion groups about virtually every subject and organization. Do you know what people are saying about your organization and your products? A key decision is what approach do you take to dealing with the information that exists. One approach is to just monitor it, but a more proactive approach is often better. By participating directly an organization can gain great creditability – assuming you are always completely forthcoming. Any attempt to put one over on a discussion group will be detected almost immediately and recovery from it would take a very long time. Interacting, listening hard, empathizing, explaining, describing actions that will be taken to resolve problems discussed, etc. can lead to a level of trust that can endure.

Name That Product

There are many dimensions to Outside-in versus Inside-out. Product naming is a good example. I have always wondered about the model names of various consumer electronic devices. Anybody ever ask you what model Discman or Boom Box you have? You take a look and find it is the Model QLP-5810 CSi. Now there is a memorable user-friendly model number! It was named inside-out instead of Outside-in. There are probably some good internal reasons, perhaps based on engineering or distribution channel factors, for the model being called the QLP-5810 CSi. It is what someone Inside wants to call it instead of what someone Outside can remember. It makes perfect sense to people Inside and no sense at all to people Outside the company. Apple is a great example of Outside-in thinking in their product naming. I suspect there were at least some product development engineers at Apple that thought naming their neat new computer after a fruit was a really stupid idea.

There are currently billions of webpages out there. Which is easier to remember? http://23.124.65.129 or netattitude.org? The Domain Name System (DNS) was invented so that people would not have to remember the Internet Protocol address (like 23.124.65.129) but rather could just use a name. The name is Outside. The IP address is Inside. Part of communications is giving names to people that they can remember. The shopping site at IBM is

http://commerce.www.ibm.com/content/home/shop_ShopIBM/en_US/home_840.html

Hardly something anyone can remember. The printed ads of the company refer people to ibm.com/shop. There are good Inside technical reasons why the URL may need to be long and ugly. Coming up with simple aliases allow visitors to think in their own terms, not the terms of the server administrator or systems people.

The Call Centers We Love

The ultimate in inside out mentality is the automated call center. What is going on with call centers? They are Inside-out. The call center is in charge. The menus from inside are controlling you. Don't dare to second-guess the menus or you will waste even more time. The company is saving time. You are getting frustrated. There is hope on the horizon and in fact many companies are moving fast to integrate their call centers with the web. The integration is a big step toward the outside-in model. At IBM there is an automated call center for annual enrollment in the employee medical and dental plans. It has countless choices, options, and menus. I used to dread that time of year when I would have to go through the enrollment. In the year 2000 an intranet application was installed that shows all the options on a webpage. You look them over, check the options you want, click for help as needed, and click submit when you are satisfied with your choices. You know what you want and the webpage lets you have control over the process. Outside-in.

Groovin' With Peer-To-Peer

Perhaps the most profound Outside-in model will be peer-to-peer computing. The advent of powerful PC's plus an Always on Internet makes this new model practical for many purposes. There is no central authority. While the peer-to-peer model lacks connections and integration with the vast amount of enterprise data and is only a small piece of the full collaboration needs of the enterprise, it will clearly have value for many people. Much like the PC and Local Area Networks allowed users in the eighties to by-pass the CIO and meet their own needs, peer-to-peer computing may enable users to share files and documents without "permission" from any central authority. The hype in the media may be overdone on peer-to-peer but it clearly represents a new computing model that will add value. Many CIO's had the attitude that PCs and LANs were not "real computing" and they ignored what was happening. By the time they were forced to embrace it, a lot of control had been lost and it took more than a decade to get things back under control. The Internet has shown us that new models can emerge quickly and so a good net attitude would be to take any new computing model seriously, get an early pilot going, and evaluate the potential.

Peer-to-peer is a case of "It's all in the name". While peer-to-peer is very real as a potentially emerging shift in information technology, it isn't quite what meets the eye. While various kinds of computer files can be transferred directly from one PC to another, most of the peer-to-peer technologies actually have some reliance on a server. Napster uses a server to provide a directory of who has music to share and Groove has a central server for registration and to provide users the latest version of their software. Dan Powers, a former I/T manager and now director of early stage Internet technology at IBM says, "There is no such thing as pure peer-to-peer. I haven't found a case yet where there wasn't a server involved".

Think Globally and Act Locally

The Internet is the ultimate decentralized system. It is often said that the reason the Internet works so well is that nobody is in charge! Many organizations still run their websites in the same way. Organizations with numerous divisions, groups, departments, etc. often want to allow for autonomy in the creation of web content. There are obvious merits to enabling autonomy but the results can backfire in a major way. While the Internet provides the best ever method of communications, the autonomous sites may create multiple images, multiple messages, or worse yet conflicting messages about what the organization in total is about. Some organizations don't see this as a problem and in fact do not want any overall identity but increasingly organizations are finding that consolidating and centralizing offers economies of scale they can't afford to pass up. It can also enable them to be more competitive.

Fortunately, the Internet can let you have it both ways. Decentralize the creation of content but centralize the way that content gets placed on the web. Creating templates so that all departments, divisions, etc. will have an identical look and feel to their webpages can do this. This results in a strengthened and consistent image of the organization overall. There is a caution, however. Avoid thinking Inside-out. Regardless of your internal wrangles and inconsistencies within an organization, someone has to have the presence of mind to have empathy with the people visiting the site and say "what do we want people to think of our company?" -- how should it look to the outsider? Templates give the uniformity that gives the impression of "one voice", but it requires some editorial control to ensure that conflicting messages aren't being presented inside of a great page structure and color scheme.

Actually, the operation of the Internet is more organized than you may think. Although no one "owns" the Internet there are in fact a number of organizations that propose and develop standards that make it all work.

One of the original design principles of the Internet was to make it work even if parts of the network were to fail. As long as both ends of a communications session remain connected, the session will survive internal faults in the core of the network. Brian Carpenter, former chairman of the Internet Architecture Board and now chairman of the Internet Society, says "That was an engineering choice, but by the Law of Unintended Consequences, it turns out that as a result the Internet doesn't need central management in the same way that (say) the telephone network does. So operationally, nobody is in charge". Thousands of Internet Service Providers compete and but also collaborate. Hundreds of hardware and software vendors supply technology to the ISPs and users, millions of systems get plugged together -- and somehow, it all works.

This doesn't happen entirely by chance. There are technical standards such that when two, or two million, boxes get plugged together, the packets can flow and applications can interoperate. The technical standards come from many organizations, including the International Organization for Standards (ISO) and the International Telecommunication Union (ITU), both in Geneva, Switzerland.

The basic standards that define how the Internet actually works come from a group called the Internet Engineering Task Force (IETF). The IETF is unusual because it is not a legal entity with defined membership - it is simply a world-wide group consisting of a couple of thousand very committed engineers from many companies and universities from all over the world, who meet three times a year in person, and 365 days a year by email. They argue, debate and ultimately agree on the basic technical standards of the Internet. The motto of the IETF is "rough consensus and running code", meaning that rather than taking a formal vote, the IETF's working groups make decisions on the basis of argument and practical experience. Brian Carpenter says, "This isn't always the fastest or simplest way to make a decision, but it does lead to good engineering choices".

A unique feature of the IETF is that it is self-governing: its management committees (the Internet Architecture Board and the Internet Engineering Steering Group) are nominated by the active membership of the IETF, not by stakeholders such as governments or companies as in most other standards organizations. The IETF's standards are published in what are called "Requests for Comments" known in the industry as RFCs. The name reflects the open-mindedness of the IETF. RFC 1 was issued in April 1969 and RFC 3001 in November 2000.

Another important source of Internet standards is the World-Wide Web Consortium (W3C). This is a more traditional organization with corporate memberships. Tim Berners-Lee and a handful of companies, including Digital Equipment and IBM, founded it in 1994. The W3C concentrates on specific technology standards for the web and these standards have a lot to do with how webpages actually look and what they can do. Other major contributions of the W3C have included standards for privacy and for the rating of content.

So the IETF and the W3C are in charge? "Hardly", says Carpenter. There are dozens of technical organizations around the world that help to keep the Internet alive and well.

CHAPTER 12

Organizing to Get Things Done

This chapter outlines net attitudes which can help managers accomplish work more effectively. A net attitude is more than a way of thinking. It is a way to get results. I discussed the importance of having a skunk works for innovation and how to use small teams with maximum freedom of action. I describe some additional net attitude principles which continue to be invaluable: "Fail and fail often", "Just enough is good enough", "Avoiding the one-size-fits-all approach", and "Trial by fire". Each was described with examples.

The most important ingredients to accomplishing great things as an e-business are to find, attract, recruit, hire, motivate, and retain really great people. Every year the crop of students gets better so you have to continually raise the bar -- look at every movement of staff and ask yourself if you are improving your hand. Everyone has to not only bring something to the table but bring unique value to the overall equation. When things are working right the whole organization breeds and feeds on itself. If the caliber of your team is high, there's a much greater likelihood of being able to attract additional high caliber people. Once you have them it is critical to nurture and support net attitude and to have creative programs to take advantage of their skills.

The Skunk Works

Every CEO I have met has asked how to make e-business web projects go faster. Every CIO I have met worries about e-business web projects going too fast. The CIO has spent decades getting information technology under control and making it reliable. Fast moving projects are sometimes in conflict with that goal. The solution to the dilemma is multifaceted but one key element is to have a "Skunk Works" where rapid prototyping is the modus operandi.

As far as I can tell, the origin of the term Skunk Works was at the Lockheed Corporation. For over a half century, the Skunk Works built a reputation that is unique in the world. Almost routinely, this elite group has created break-through technologies and landmark aircraft that redefined the possibilities of flight.

The Skunk Works was created to design and develop the P-80 Shooting Star, America's first production jet aircraft. Since then they have created a string of firsts. In the 1950's was the U-2, which to this day defines the possibilities of high-altitude jet aircraft. Then there was the SR-71 Blackbird which, with its titanium airframe is still the fastest jet aircraft in the world. The F-117A Stealth Fighter, which incorporated low-observable technology into an operational attack air-craft, created a revolution in military warfare. Its capabilities were demonstrated dramatically in combat during the Gulf War.

The company, now Lockheed Martin, says the key has been to "identify the best individual talents in aviation, blend and equip them with every tool needed, then provide complete creative freedom so they may arrive at an optimum solu-tion in short order." This simple formula is highly effective not only for creating state of the art aviation but also for any kind of corporate endeavor.

Lockheed Martin Skunk Works continues to serve as a wellspring of inno-vation for the entire organization and as they build advanced aerospace pro-totypes, and contribute to technology research and systems development. Lockheed Martin says this happens because they are "not big on titles or proto-col - just getting the job done, regularly meeting schedules on time and under budget."

The Skunk Works got its name from the "Skonk Works" of Al Capp's L'il Abner comic strip, where they had a hidden still in a secluded hollow. The name still fits, because exciting things continue to "brew" there.

Small Teams With Maximum Freedom Of Action

Product development is typically managed in a very structured organization with multiple levels of management and a lot of controls. This can be effective in many cases and is probably necessary for extraordinarily complex projects like putting a man on the moon but this approach will likely not bring any breakthroughs. The Skunk Works uses a different model. Small teams with maximum freedom of action, very flat management structure, and minimal controls can lead to breakthrough ideas – if the people are allowed to work below the radar tracking level of the larger bureaucracy. (Small teams of really top people are also more productive, and have more fun, than a significantly larger team.)

Skunk Works are also good at figuring out what key problems there are in existing systems -- because the Skunk Works members have no vested interest in the success or failure of those systems. They can often solve problems that the larger organization can't solve because the larger organization is too close to the origins of the problem. It is usually best to let the Skunk Works figure out what things they should work on as opposed to "assigning" problems or projects to them. Problems the organization thinks are most important may not be optimal ones for the Skunk Works to invest in. The formal requirements processes typically used to determine what should be developed don't always anticipate some of the most profound issues and problems. The Skunk Works often just stumbles into profound things if you trust them and give them freedom of action. The instant messaging system being used by over 200,000 people at IBM did not come about because anybody asked for it or because a strategic planning or requirements process called it out. A few Internet software engineers stumbled into it, tried it out, built a prototype, and then nurtured it. In a couple of years, it became an indispensable application for the company.

A subtle but critically important element in a successful Skunk Works is executive support, or "air cover". There needs to be a well respected and highly placed executive who trusts the "lunatics" who are out on the edge. At times the executive will be scared to death that a project the Skunk Works is pursuing will fail, but has to have the nerve to place a bet on it and trust the team to come through. Visiting the team late at night or on a weekend, bringing pizza and soda, showing that he or she cares and has a clue about what the team is working on, even if they don't really understand the details, are critical ingredients. The little touches motivate the team beyond belief.

Impedance Matching

One of the biggest challenges with a Skunk Works is figuring out how to take the prototypes developed by a small team with a "just enough is good enough" mentality and integrate it with a more disciplined development process of the larger organization. In effect you have a tiny gear spinning at high speed trying to synchronize with a much larger and slower turning gear. One approach to solving this dilemma is to use an "impedance" matcher. Think of it as placing a third in-between-sized gear between the small one and the large one. Rather than a gear, of course, it is a small group of people whose mission is to adapt the prototype to the standards of the larger organization. Their focus is not developing it but rather adapting it, smoothing over the rough edges, and getting it into good enough condition that the larger organization will look at it and say it is good enough to be adopted and taken to market or put into production. The result is a speed to market that is a little slower than pure prototype but much faster than the full-blown process. Without the impedance matcher the larger organization is more likely to view the prototype as a virus and seek to eradicate it.

Fail and Fail Often

A successful organization has to be willing to have projects that are going to fail. A process designed to keep failures from happening is antithetical to a net attitude for innovation. But you need to be able to declare a failure, move on, and not punish the participants for being assigned to (or even creating) the failure. A good process encourages people to submit ideas into the mill as quickly and as often as possible and allow others downstream to figure out which ideas are worth pursuing further. There should be no penalty for putting in an idea that gets rated "close - no action required".

Skunk Works are a vehicle for developing new things, or for bringing alternative ideas forward – they are not a universal answer to all problems of innovation. For Skunk Works to succeed, the company at some point may have to be cannibalistic. Children that come to life through the Skunk Works have to be able to eat their parents. In many companies there are countless examples of brilliant ideas and technologies that came to life in Skunk Works fashion but were then squashed by the mainstream part of the company. These same innovations are often successful when they are brought to market outside of the company.

alphaWorks

There are a number of Skunk Works scattered around IBM Research laboratories and other parts of the company. One thing they have in common is the challenge of finding a path to market for some of their ideas which have no clear destiny. During an early 1996 visit to one IBM's Research laboratories, Irving Wladawsky-Berger, then general manager of IBM's Internet Division, noticed a particularly interesting streaming audio technology that had potential use for Internet applications. In fact he saw numerous technologies that seemed to have potential. While the technologies were quite impressive, there was no clear "business case" to take them to the market. Irving asked me to figure out how to reinvent the process of getting these research-phase (often referred to as "alpha") technologies out of the lab and into the market. I thought about it all that weekend and then it hit me like a ton of bricks -- all the bells and whistles went off in my head. Put these technologies on a website and offer them as free downloads and let the market tell us what they think the technologies are good for. We could put basic legal protections in place, create an easy mechanism for feedback, and perhaps even build a community around these early stage technologies. Without much planning, reviews, or analysis, we decided to implement alphaWorks quickly.

There were a lot of questions. Aren't we giving up control of the technology? How about if someone takes our idea and turns it into a big business? By putting great technologies on the Internet for anyone to download, are we giving up intellectual property and will we later regret it? Yes, it is surely giving up some control but we believed there was more upside than downside. The technology candidates for alphaWorks were in some sense "orphans". If the business case was clear for them they would be adopted by a product line of business and would be developed into products. These orphans seemed to be brilliant ideas but the application for them was not clear. If a lot of people download them and find them useful we will get feedback on what they found them useful for. This could help us go the next step toward product development. If nobody downloads them or the feedback is negative we could kill the project and redeploy the resources to other more fruitful areas.

There was no formal organization; it would just evolve. That is how most important ideas flourish. If there is conviction in the idea, just do it, don't' study it. Don't focus on who reports to whom. Just focus on getting something into the market and then let the market tell you what is good and what isn't. If the idea takes hold you can build a more formal organization later -- organization can kill an entrepreneurial idea if it is formalized too early.

A full-blown website for alphaWorks was built in weeks. A couple of college interns who didn't know things like this were supposed to be hard created a very impressive site. The legal team created a very simple agreement that said that if someone downloaded our technology they could do whatever they wanted to with it – except sell it. A process was put in place to enable IBM researchers to introduce one of their technologies onto alphaWorks. Executive "air cover" was in place and alphaWorks came to life – downloads started happening and feedback started to pour in. Outside-in.

alphaWorks morphed from a site for "cool orphan technologies" to an effective way to surface emerging technologies and create paths to market for them. A community of hundreds of thousands of early adopters, entrepreneurs and innovators emerged that provided "headlights" to enable the company to see how people are thinking about the technologies, what challenges they face, and what features and support they would like to have. As a byproduct of reaching out and forming a community the company received positive press coverage and was able to build mind share about its technology.

We Are All in This Together

One important piece of a net attitude is a very people-oriented thought: "We are all in this together." A system or a web application isn't a success if only one participant in the transaction wins -- there have to be benefits for all sides. Customers and companies aren't at war here -- customers benefit from faster access to data, and companies benefit because it costs them less to deliver the information. Because customers see speed as a direct benefit to them, they're likelier to come back -- and the company gets to save money. Similarly, a doctor with a net attitude won't feel threatened if patients use the Internet to find out more about their conditions -- in fact, the doctor can work better with an informed patient, and again, both parties win.

Unfortunately, many companies don't have a net attitude -- they view their customers as resources at best, adversaries at worst. You see this when you encounter a website or application which asks many questions just to get in the door, and then burdens you with more "required" fields when you order or request something -- fields which are only required so that the company can best exploit your information.

One way to focus on "we are all in this together" is to spend time and money listening to your customers -- your partners. That doesn't mean a "contact us!" link is enough, either -- you need to listen to subtle input, such as unanswered or bogus fields on your forms (you don't really believe that half of your customers are named "Bugs Bunny", do you?). .

Planning Ad Nausea

There are four phases of e-business to consider. Planning for an e-business, building an e-business, running (operating) an e-business, and using an e-business. We have talked about the importance of planning. It starts with sorting out your business strategy, figuring out what your value proposition and business model are, committing yourself to meeting the expectations of people who visit your e-business and finally establishing a framework that provides for an e-business which is scalable, manageable, available, reliable, and secure.

In a world where so much is possible, it is really important to think big. The challenge is to both think big but to start with a simple implementation and grow it fast toward the big idea. Many organizations have planners. Planners like to plan -- that is their job. New ideas require a plan before they can be implemented. The problem is the plan expands and expands to encompass the big thought – the entire vision. The result in many cases is that the plan gets so big that it can't be implemented or by the time it does the whole world changed and then the plans have to be scrapped and things go back to square one.

Prior to the Internet becoming commercialized, the model for creating new I/T applications was Plan, Build, Deliver -- eighteen-month cycle. With technologies and markets now changing at Internet speed, the new model has to be based on a net attitude, Sense and Respond – 18 hours cycle. Sense what is happening with the project or your website and respond to it. Seek feedback, listen to it hard, and act on it. Iterate with baby steps but on a fast cycle. Evolve as fast as possible toward the big thought. The traditional model yields a second release of the product a year or two after the initial release. Net attitude takes you down a different path. Deliver a release .1 product. A month or less later, deliver a release .2 product. After a year you are at "Release 1.0". Chances are good that your Release 1.0 after one year is way ahead of where a traditional Release 2.0 would be after two years

Just Enough Is Good Enough

This shouldn't be taken to mean to do sloppy work or throw something against the wall and hope it sticks. It is a fine line. You've got to know or even sense when to "Just Ship It", and when to be sure things need to be really well engineered. Many new technologies that have been introduced on the Internet including streaming audio, Java, and even the protocols of the Internet itself were arguably inferior to alternate approaches that could have been developed or even that already existed. However, they all "did the job". Just enough turned out to be good enough to get the idea out there and enable people to start to benefit from it. Early adopters are happy to get a hold on new things and are very willing to spend hours providing their feedback on bugs and suggested improvements. This same net attitude can be applied to projects of all kinds in any size organization. You can actually use the model and culture of how the Internet was developed to develop any idea – using the Internet itself as the platform for feedback, review, collaboration, and communication. There have been many examples of this approach on the Internet over the past five years. When the National Center for Supercomputing Applications released the first alpha version of Marc Andreessen's new web browser (called "Mosaic") in February 1993, it was a bit crude. Likewise on May 23, 1995, when John Gage, director of the Science Office for Sun Microsystems, and Marc Andreessen, then cofounder and executive vice president at Netscape announced that Java technology was real, it was hardly ready for prime time. Ditto for many other technologies. In all cases the early adopters greeted the technologies with open arms, provided feedback and reviews to the developers, and actually collaborated with the developers to iteratively improve things until they were usable by larger numbers of people.

Avoid The One-Size-Fits-All Approach

While explosive developments in all aspects of the Internet were happening out in the public domain there were an equally important set of things happening inside of organizations of all kinds around the world. Internal networks using TCP/IP, the protocols of the Internet, were constructed and firewalls were erected to protect against unwanted intrusion from the Internet. The internal networks became known as intranets. Web technology is relatively low cost and relatively easy to implement and this enabled the intranets to mushroom. They were initially used to publish information such as reference manuals and employee directories.

As the web application tools have become more sophisticated the intranet applications have too. CIOs of organizations have embraced the use of web applications and many have also begun to apply the disciplines of more traditional information technology application development including requirements planning, system architecture, design specifications, development, testing, systems integration, etc. This is good on the one hand but potentially can impede rapid progress if taken too far.

For some applications the "quick and dirty" approach of the early web days is still adequate. A good net attitude is to avoid a "one size fits all" approach. A payroll application that allows an employee to set up deductions on the web needs all possible rigors. An application to enable an employee to signup for next weeks blood drive doesn't. The risk of harm to the organization or to the customer needs to be weighed against the time and effort to apply all the processes to creating the application.

In addition to sensing and responding it is also a good idea to be proactive. Many organizations have put everything but the kitchen sink on their websites. This is not all bad but it is time to clean it up. I recommend hiring a college student for a few afternoons per week whose job is to scour your entire website and find all the things you can't do. While they are at it, have them find all the instances of "fax me the form" or "call us nine to five Monday to Friday".

Trial by Fire

A few things are certain about a new website -- you don't know how many people are going to visit, you don't know when they are going to visit, and you don't know what they are going to do when they do visit. In the "old days" of the sixties, seventies, eighties, and early nineties, it was relatively easy for the CIO to test things before putting them on line. Most of the users were "hard wired" to the mainframe or central mini-computer. Since the CIO actually controlled the applications, he or she knew exactly how many users there were and knew which applications would be used and when they would be used. With the web it is much more difficult to plan. In many cases the best approach is to put something out there and see what happens, gain some feedback from users on their experience on the site, monitor constantly, measure the performance under load, and then use all the input to build a truly scalable and reliable system.

Trial by fire is dangerous because you really don't know what is going to happen. Therefore, it is really important to set expectations – and set them low. In 1999 Victoria's Secret, a retailer of women's undergarments, proudly announced it was going to have a live webcast of models showing off their latest products during the Super Bowl football game. Talk about setting high expectations! The number of people who watched the webcast was a record but the numbers who were disappointed was probably larger. The site just could not handle the load. Another approach would have been to announce that an experimental prototype of a modeling webcast was going to be introduced "in the near future". Plenty of people would have "discovered" the webcast. No "announcement" was necessary. Instant messages would have been flying around the Internet. "Yo, Bill, check out http://victoriassecret.com".

Good communications to set the expectations are critical. "This will be the first time such an event has taken place on the web and we are proud to introduce it. Because of the experimental nature of this we are not sure how many visitors there may be and what the resulting performance may be. We look forward to your feedback and apologize in advance if you are anything but delighted with the experience". Based on the feedback and measurements of system load and performance a more aggressive marketing approach could be taken on the next webcast after the appropriate systems design was incorporated.

Kasparov 1, Deep Blue 0, Website In The Ditch

In 1995 IBM began to experiment with sporting events on the web. Everything they did was a first of a kind; never done before for large audiences. It was perpetual learning. One of the first events was the U.S. Open in 1995 when a small team of Internet engineers worked in a construction trailer at Flushing, New York and put the tennis scores on the web. They also used live video cameras on multiple tennis courts and gathered real-time data from radar guns that measured the speed of the tennis balls as they flew across the net (not Net). There was no basis, no textbooks, no data from which to plan for such events on the web. It was pure trial by fire. After each event the team was smarter -- they learned the effect on the server when something exciting was going on and a large number of people started interacting with the website. This enabled them to optimize the structure of the databases and fine tune the server.

That same year was the first match between the world famous Gary Kasparov and a supercomputer from IBM named Deep Blue. An advertising agency in New York City hosted the website because the Internet team was busy getting ready for the following summer's Olympic Games. After the first chess match the headlines proclaimed "Kasparov 1, Deep Blue 0, website in the ditch". No one had any idea that a chess match on the web would be so popular. The website at the ad agency was not well designed and the system that was running it was not prepared for scalability. The IBM team raced to New York, gathered up all the information for the site, and took it back to IBM. They then went to the head of the supercomputer division of the company and made a request to borrow a supercomputer. After thirty non-stop hours of frenzied programming and systems work, the team built a replacement website and the chess match continued offline on the chess board and online on the web. Deep Blue won match #2. After the third game, the headline was "Game 3 chess match a draw; IBM site up".

The chess matches enabled IBM to learn a lot about how to build scalable websites. They devised a method for handling large and unpredictable numbers of incoming web requests by deploying software that could intelligently distribute the requests across multiple servers in order to balance the load. This in turn enabled the site to provide stable and reliable performance. The technology developed that weekend later became crucial to the Atlanta and Nagano Olympic Games sites (both of which held world records traffic) and then went on to become part of IBM's flagship WebSphere web application software product. It may have been possible to invent it in a laboratory environment but using a trial by fire approach certainly got it to market faster.

Another attitudinal aspect of websites has to do with registration. More and more sites require that you register in order to explore the site or to receive an email newsletter. The motivation is to get demographic information for analysis and marketing. There is nothing wrong with that as long as you have a really solid privacy policy that you adhere to. The flip side is to make it really easy to unsubscribe. Some sites make it nearly impossible. The right net attitude is to not just make it easy to unsubscribe but to make it really easy -- at least as easy as registering in the first place. People will remember. (Besides, the people who want to be subscribed are more likely to be the ones who will accept offers, promotions, etc.)

Make Easy Things Easy!

Making things easy is a key net attitude. It doesn't come naturally, you have to plan for it, test it, and refine it. Some of the hardest things are subtle. Most of the people visiting websites are going to be doing simple things – click here to buy, make a payment, check the status on something, and other basic transactions. It is important to make those things easy to do. One simple idea is to make URLs easy to remember and type. For example, it would be nice if ups.com/track worked, but it doesn't -- ups.com/tracking doesn't work either. The URL that does work is ups.com/tracking/tracking.html. Fortunately, you do not have to type the http://www Not to pick on UPS – there are many examples around the web – but hitting the Enter button on the ups.com/tracking/tracking.html screen gets you a screen where you can enter more tracking numbers instead of giving you tracking information for the numbers you've already entered -- especially if you've only entered one number.

Making things easier applies to your employees, too. Part of net attitude is treating your own people's time as valuable -- time they spend fighting your internal web is time they can't spend working on customer problems.

One way to find out what users really want is to use focus groups. Focus groups have served the world well. Get a specially selected group of people behind a glass wall and videotape them while they are interviewed or shown a presentation. Today the Internet allows a focus group to be self selected in real time. People on the web who participate in discussion groups are brutally honest. Get out there proactively and talk to them. It is much more real world than the old focus groups. You may not like what you hear but it will likely be the truth. People who take the time to give feedback are usually the most discerning users and have the most valuable input.

Think Integration

Application integration is the Holy Grail of e-business. Designed separately at different points in time on different platforms the preponderance of systems can't talk to each other. Most of the transactions on the web today are between people and servers. By thinking Integration an e-business can be built where servers talk to servers. Today's typical approach to solving the integration problem has been to utilize business process reengineering (BPR). BPR is certainly critical long term but the problem is that it takes a long time to get the resulting new systems implemented. Most organizations, for competitive reasons, don't have time to wait for a BPR solution. Fortunately, there is an alternative.

BPR will eventually result in an updated hotel and airline reservations systems that incorporate the frequent guest or flier systems so that things are totally integrated. In the meantime there is an approach called Message Queuing (MQ) that enables incompatible systems to communicate with each other. Going back to the hotel reservation scenario, recall that I had made a reservation for a hotel room and wanted to pay for it with frequent guest points. Imagine the reservations system sending a "message" – think of it as an email – to the frequent guest system. "I have this guy here who just reserved a room for one night in New York City. He wants to use his points to pay for it. His guest number is 1234". A message goes back from the frequent guest system to the reservations system. "Yes, guest 1234 is a valid account and he has a balance of 125,000 points. The New York City room would cost 30,000 points". The reservations system now sends another message. "Ok, please deduct 30,000 points from guest 1234 and confirm". A final message goes from the guest system. "Points deducted". This all happens in less than a second and then your webpage gets updated and it says, "Your reservation has been confirmed. 30,000 points have been deducted from your guest account. Happy travels"!

Neither system was reengineered. They were just enabled to communicate with each other. Each system could have been operating in a totally different software environment. The integration took place in the web server that provides the interface to the customer. Implementing the messaging is not trivial but it is much simpler than reengineering the two systems. Japan Airlines has used this approach to enable their gate scheduling system and their flight arrival system to communicate. They solved a problem that greatly annoys large numbers of people. Sometimes you order something that isn't coming directly from the manufacturer or the distributor and the delay can be extensive. Typically you will get quoted four to six weeks for delivery. The long lead-time isn't because the item is not available but because the supply chain involved in getting it to you does not have integrated systems. One participant may fax a form; a second may enter into their automated system that then generates something which gets mailed to a second participant. That participant then faxes it to another participant, etc. Incompatible systems are at the root of the problem. Utilizing message queuing interim to, or in some cases instead of BPR, is a form of "just enough is good enough". It can mean transactions that make our life easier and result in us waiting less or standing in fewer lines.

Build On a Framework

To sense and respond at Internet speed is critical but to do so by throwing things against the wall and hoping they stick is not a good idea. E-businesses must be built to "scale". Remember we are 3% or so of the way into the Internet. The biggest potential problem facing many e-businesses is success! The infrastructure technology that exists today isn't ready for what is coming. We are going to see ten times more people using the Net, one hundred times more network speed, 1,000 times more devices and a million times more data! Expectations of the users are going to be very high and so the information technology planners in all kinds of organizations are going to have very large challenges.

Things are compounded by the fact websites are overwhelmed with "maintenance" of their software. Many of the e-businesses, even the startups, have built a huge base of programming and content over the last six years of the web's evolution. Many of them decided not to standardize on commercial products and architectures and the web services model did not exist. They adopted an approach, somewhat out of necessity, of "we can build it better from scratch ourselves". This is not a good attitude for the long term. What many of them have now as a result are incredibly complex systems based on their homegrown system. One of the results of this approach is that now many of these companies take a very long time to fix things and add new features to their sites – they are too busy performing maintenance of what they already have. The cost of development and time to make changes has gone exponential on them.

Like the sports sites discussed earlier, e-businesses are going to find that they too don't know how many people are going to come to their site, when they will come, nor what they are going to do when they get there. Peak performance needs will be very hard to predict. Having the many devices the next generation of the Internet is facilitating is going to exacerbate this. People with devices of all kinds that they can use wherever they are will greatly increase the number of transactions. Scalability will become paramount in importance. The typical e-business today puts in some database software and some web servers and when demands increase they add more servers. This will work to a point but eventually the management of the large numbers of servers becomes a problem.

Building an e-business is a big job. The website needs to be comprehensive – built to handle the end-to-end needs of the constituencies. In addition, it needs to be connected to and integrated with the existing information technology systems --

bringing the "front end" (the web) together with the "back end" (the existing systems). Stability must be maintained while this is done – and while transaction rates and numbers of visitors are growing rapidly. It is like changing the tires on a car while it is speeding around a curve on two wheels. The solution to the challenge is to build the e-business on an architecture that provides a SMART infrastructure. A SMART infrastructure includes Scalable servers that you can not outgrow, Management tools to allow you to identify and fix problems, Availability options that provide self-healing failsafe operations, Reliability for all the components so the weakest link doesn't bring you down, and Total Security so you can protect all the data for you and for your constituencies.

Various information technology vendors have blueprints or architectures that meet these needs to various degrees. Whatever architecture you select it is essential to pick one that embraces open standards including the Internet standards and the web standards of the World Wide Web Consortium. As new ideas evolve on top of the Internet there are more and more proprietary implementations. Wherever open standards exist, however, it is a good idea to demand that your information technology vendor support them. Standards are evolving rapidly and it is important to have someone in the organization responsible to closely follow the standards processes and to test the commitment of vendors to contribute to them and follow them.

Where Is The Leadership?

Leadership is a core net attitude. It is all about making it happen versus watching it happen. I am looking forward to the day when I can have all of my medical records on the Internet where I will know that at last they will be safe. I went to Yale University Medical School for my annual physical and while checking in (filling out forms with information that I had filled out during each of the prior years) I observed the large number of manila folders containing medical records. I wondered who the people were who had access to them and on what basis. I wondered if the son or daughter of my next-door neighbor might work there and whether they have been reading my medical records. I was thinking about how referrals work. Your doctor suggests you see a specialist about some condition. A copy of your medical records may be forwarded to the specialist in a manila envelope. Who opens the envelope? Who will be able to read the contents? No idea.

I wondered if I borrowed my daughter's stethoscope and put on a white jacket, if I could walk behind the counter and pick out a dozen or two manila folders and walk out with them.

Suppose my medical records were encrypted with my own public key. That would mean that they could only be decrypted with my private key. Only I have my private key so only I could enable access to my medical records. I spoke to my doctor (now retired) about it and he said he thought it would be hard to capture the "real" conditions and observations because each doctor likes to record the information in their own unique way. If my choice was to have encrypted information coming from a marginal doctor versus unencrypted handwritten information coming from a great doctor I would of course take the latter. But isn't there some way we could have both? Isn't it possible to record medical conditions with voice recognition and to capture blood pressure data, test results, and even a doctors hand written notes and make them part of a digital record that is encrypted and securely stored on an Internet server?

Why don't we have digital ID's that can allow us to keep our medical records on the Internet, to wire money with a mouse click, to open new accounts without having to fax forms, make online funds transfers, online vehicle registrations or driver's license renewals? Is it a lack of technology? No. Lack of leadership with a net attitude? Yes, and at multiple levels.

The governor of a mid-west state once told me that he believes that the votes he may lose from constituents displaced by on-line services would be more than offset by the votes he would gain from constituents who were delighted with new Internet based services. That is leadership and net attitude. Unfortunately, this may still be a minority opinion in many jurisdictions of the world.

You Are Not Normal

How about financial services? I had lunch with the CEO of a major insurance company and described to him how the only thing standing between me and being really satisfied with his insurance company was his agent! When I want to do business the insurance agent is not working. When he is working I don't have time to focus on insurance. I described how I would like to see a webpage where I could check off all of my needs for coverage; cars, house, liability, etc. and then I would like to iterate on various coverage options until I got what I wanted. He said, "You aren't normal". I then described how I had a home in one state and a vacation cottage in another state but I had to have two different agents and I couldn't understand why I couldn't just deal with one. He said, "Well, there are some 'regulatory' issues".

If I were to speak to the firms involved in my wire transfer about why wire transfers can't be done on the web I am sure I would hear about more "regulatory issues". When I asked First Chicago why I couldn't transfer a share of stock without a "gold medallion" signature from a bank, they told me about "regulatory issues".

There are "regulatory issues" for sure, but I think the real problem is lack of net attitude. There is fear and misunderstanding and a lack of leadership to make it happen. Major institutions have been dealing with regulatory issues for decades. They have found ways to educate and influence regulators to enable them to do business in developing countries, break into new markets, get approval for new products, and get investment tax credits. But they can't convince regulators that it is a good idea to automate wire transfers or securities transfers using digital signatures?

Entrepreneurs Don't Know It Can't Be Done

Clever entrepreneurs are attacking the "regulatory issues" with a vengeance. One of the most highly regulated areas of commerce is the ordering and shipment of wines and liquors to consumers. Every state has different regulations and most of them are highly restrictive. Some states have regulations that specify that liquor or wine can only be sold to a consumer by a retailer, who in turn can only obtain the liquor from a wholesaler. It is a form of protectionism. Nevertheless, entrepreneurial companies are finding clever (and legal) ways to get around the regulatory restrictions by using various distribution intermediaries.

When California passed a digital signature law in 1999 E-Trade proclaimed that this would enable them to open new securities accounts for anyone anywhere since E-Trade is a California company. The Wall Street Journal quoted New York attorneys saying that they were not so sure. Could they have been part of the established firms? Charles Schwab has a MoneyLink feature that allows their customers to move money to or from a Schwab account and any bank account – 24 x 7, no faxes, no phones. I don't know of any banks that do the same.

In the U.K., all the banks are members of The Banking Automated Clearing System (BACS) that does funds transfers between any bank and any bank every night. It has been running for years. You can deposit a check at any bank and it goes to your own bank account at your own bank. The U.S. banking system has a long way to go. It is not a technology or security problem.

Escrow.com has a simple webpage approach for setting up an escrow account for selling your car to a stranger or any other purpose. You fill out an on-line form with the conditions and it is emailed to the other party. When they agree the escrow is established. When the conditions are met the money is released. All on-line. All secure. The fee is $100. Seems like it should be profitable for them. I am sure there were "regulatory issues" but some entrepreneurs took the leadership to make it happen.

Established institutions have the choice to stand by and watch things happen or to use their considerable influence to accelerate the process of regulatory reform and make it happen. Everyone would benefit. If they don't the entrepreneurs will gain market share from the established institutions.

Organizing to get things done in the fast paced world of the NGi cannot be done by the textbook. It takes a new way of thinking – net attitude. Moving out a bit closer to the edge – where things are somewhat uncertain; where you don't have the control you would like to have, but where innovation is happening continuously. On the edge is not the place to live but a place to visit often to get a sample of the culture – or at least have someone assigned to visit there for you and keep you a breast of what is happening.

CHAPTER 13

Get A Taste of The Culture

There is a lot of culture underpinning a net attitude. It is partly a way of thinking. You learn the attitude by hanging out with those who have it. This next to last chapter discussed where you can find those who have it. One of the best sources is young people. You don't have to be young to have a net attitude but you are more likely to find it in them. This chapter also described some ideas on how to recruit the right people into your organization. It finished with a source of net attitude you may not have thought of – seniors. Seniors represent a fast growing segment of the economies of the world. Many seniors have the time and motivation and have learned the skills needed to be proficient on the web. They have high expectations based on decades of experience.

In May 1994 a colleague, Dave Grossman, and I gave a presentation to a group of senior managers at IBM. It may sound hard to believe but back then most people had not yet seen the web. We showed an artificial hip simulation from a medical site at Cornell University, some pictures from the Vatican Library, some dinosaur pictures from Honolulu Community College, and the very first release of ibm.com. These were all impressive but the most impressive part of the demonstration was Andrew's webpage. Andrew is Dave's son and at the time he was seven years old. After Dave showed him the dinosaur pictures at home one night Andrew wanted to make his *own* webpage. He drew a picture of a dinosaur and gave it the name "thorcolervo" (after the name of a robot in a book he had just read). Dave helped Andrew scan the picture and turn it into a webpage. Andrew then recorded a sound byte; "Hi, this is Andrew and you are looking at my drawing of a thorcolervo". This totally blew people away. Seeing a picture of dinosaur come across the Internet and get displayed on the screen and then to hear a voice come across the Internet describing it and then to find out it was done by a seven year old! In 1994 Andrew thought that making web makes was *normal*.

> When Lou Gerstner saw the new IBM homepage, his first question was, "Where is the BUY button?" The term e-business had not yet been invented -- there was nobody buying anything on the web back then -- and here was the CEO of IBM asking how people were going to be able to buy things! He had the insight and intuition to see what was possible long before most major companies of the world. Later he was the first CEO to publicly say that the Internet is for business; not email or surfing, but for business transactions. Another first was the audio recording on the homepage that said, "Hi, I'm Lou Gerstner. Welcome to our homepage. I hope you will come back often."

A few years later I was talking to Dave one day and asked how the kids were doing. He said the family had a nice weekend skiing and that during the trip to the mountains Andrew had a great time chatting with his buddies back home. I asked what he meant. He described how Andrew was in the back seat of their van with a ThinkPad connected to the Internet using a wireless adaptor and he was using IBM's "instant messaging" program and his "buddy list" to have an on-line chat session with his friends. So as Dave was driving seventy miles per hour to the mountains, Andrew was having an on-line chat session with his friends and Andrew thought that was *normal*. This was in 1996. At the time a lot of people were still amazed that the Internet worked at all and here was a ten year old using instant messaging in a car and he was completely unimpressed.

Dad, You Should Know More

One day at home I was trying to get a new SoundBlaster audio card working in my PC. For a variety of technical reasons that I won't go into here it was proving to be quite difficult. It had to do with deep technical parameters that most people don't know exist (and shouldn't have to). I got myself totally confused and frustrated trying to get the parameters set properly. To my great relief my son Aaron arrived home from school. He was 15 at the time. I told him the problem. He walked over to my PC and in about 15 seconds had everything working. After I thanked him, Aaron said, "You know Dad, for someone at your level in IBM, you should really know more about PCs". The kids wonder why we think technology is so hard. I want to know less. He thought I should know more. He thought it would be *normal* to know more.

Visiting colleges and universities is a great way to learn what is going on today and more importantly where things are headed. Occasionally I get an invitation to visit a campus and speak about the Future of the Internet. One summer I visited Lehigh University (my alma mater) and spoke at a combined session of the ACM and IEEE membership – a very technical audience. I asked how many were writing Java programs and all the hands went up. This became an important proof point for me as skeptics about Java emerged. Professor Ron LaPorte of the University of Pittsburgh in Pittsburgh, Pennsylvania invited me to visit the College of Epidemiology. Ron is leading a terrific project called the Global Health Network. I got the chance to meet some wonderful and creative graduate students who are collaborating to improve the health of the world. During this visit I learned how non-technical people were getting as much out of the Internet as the technical people I was used to spending time with. A visit to The J L Kellogg Graduate School of Management at Northwestern University was nostalgic since I had attended their executive program some years ago. More importantly I got to meet with a group of students and hear their questions during an extended Q&A session. They stimulated my thinking about where things are going. Similar sessions at MIT, the University of Pennsylvania, and Stanford have inspired me greatly. There is no formal training program or company experience that can compare with an hour of Q&A with bright students – they ask questions that really make you think. When I leave one of these sessions I always feel that I have gained at least as much as they have. I tell them they are the most fortunate graduating class in many years because they are about to enter a networked world of e-business and they can be the technical and business entrepreneurs who can help create it.

What Is Normal?

What we consider esoteric or even bizarre our kids consider normal. When we think of an insurance agent we think of a person. They think of a Java applet that runs on the Internet finding the optimum deal for insurance coverage. When we think of opening a bank account we might think of sitting in front of a desk while someone is filling out a form. They think of "click here to open an account". When we hear someone say they had a chat with a friend we are thinking of them doing so in person and the kids are thinking of instant messaging on the Internet. The kids talk about Napster and Gnutella and we don't even know what they are talking about.

There is so much we can learn from the kids. They represent the way e-business is going to be. I recommend to CEO's and CIO's that they hire a student for a few afternoons a week and make it their job to review the company website and look for things *that you can't do*. There are plenty of them. Listen to the students; ask for their suggestions. They think about things differently – like most of your customers are beginning to think.

Extreme Blue

In early 1999, an Internet engineer at IBM named Ron Woan had an idea to bring in a group of a couple of dozen computer science students to be part of a really unique summer program. Ron's idea was to go out to the top ten Computer Science schools in America and recruit the best of the best students. His idea was to create leading edge projects for the students to work on and to set up a mentoring program whereby the students would work closely with IBM's best technical leaders; Senior Technical Staff Members, Distinguished Engineers, and IBM Fellows. A further part of Ron's idea was to give the students the latest IBM technology to use, provide housing for them, and generally make their life as fantastic as possible. We all thought this was a great idea but questioned whether we could actually pull off the administration, find the budget, and manage all the details. There were doubting Thomases but in the main many of us thought it was a great idea. The management team; Dave Grossman, from a technical point of view, and Jane Harper, from an operational point of view, believed in Ron's idea and made the commitment to make it happen.

The project became known as Extreme Blue. Wired Magazine wrote a story about it called "Big Blue Reinvents Internships". The vision was to enable some of the world's brightest computer science students a chance to spend a fast paced summer working on real, cutting-edge IBM projects. Not running the copying machine or "make work" projects but real projects; things IBM was actually quite interested in making happen. The students were split into teams of three and each team had a mentor who was a senior technical leader from a product group somewhere in IBM. The mentor had a very specific technical project that may have been on their dream list but for which he or she had not been able to get funding or skills.

Getting some top computer science students to tackle the challenge would have all upside and no downside. The students exceeded everyone's expectations. The thing about students is that they have no "baggage". They don't know all the things that didn't work in the past or all the reasons why something can't get done in a short period of time. No blinders. Totally uninhibited. They have the summer – all of twelve weeks or so. Whatever it takes, they will get the job done. Students are fearless and tireless. Yes, I am sure they learned a lot about IBM and from their mentors but I think IBM learned even more from the students. How they think and work together. Their attitudes about technology. The trends they see. Their view of the future. It is so uplifting and enriching to talk to the students and learn from them.

Talk To The Kids

So, talk to your kids. Look over their shoulder. Ask them what they do on the Internet. Talk to them about their values. What do they think of intellectual property rights? What do they like most about the Internet? What do they like least? What sites are really with it? Which are brain-dead? What do they think the Internet will be like in five years? How do they expect they will use it after they get a job? If what they tell you makes sense, think about how you can incorporate some of their kind of thinking in your business or institutional planning. If what they say doesn't make sense or you don't agree with what they say, talk to your kids some more. If you don't have any kids, borrow one! If you can't find any kids to talk to then talk to some ThirdAgers.

ThirdAgers

If you can't find any teenagers to validate your business plans for the web, look for some 60 year olds. When I visited the Heritage Village retirement community and went into their "web room" I saw a huge banner across one wall. It said "Keeping Pace in Cyberspace". That is their motto. They are not intimidated in the slightest by technology. A petite elderly lady looked up from her keyboard to say hello. She was helping a friend learn how to send email to her grandchild. At their monthly meeting a seventy-year-old gentleman made an announcement that the "Hardware" special interest group (SIG) was going to start a new project whereby each participant would be building their own PC from scratch and he asked if anyone would be interested. Dozens of hands were in the air to join the group.

ThirdAgers are generally between the age of forty-five and sixty-four. The heart of the group is made up of those who Mary Furlong, founder of ThirdAge Media, describes as being in their "transitional fifties". Some are going through job changes or a divorce. Others have aging parents, health issues, or are experiencing the birth of grandchildren. These are all issues which change the lives of the ThirdAgers and create a desire to join a support group, go to a class or pick up a hobby. In many cases, explains Mary Furlong, the changes "lead to a quest for a more spiritual life and more focus on one's interior life. The result is that people become more intrinsically motivated". For all these reasons ThirdAgers are flocking to the web. They are not intimidated by the technology. They have goals and the web can help them cope. ThirdAgers are going to MyFamily.com to share family pictures and learn about genealogy. They are going to ThirdAge.com to get career or health advice or check the romantic tip of the day. There is no substitute for the loss of a loved one but these websites are helping people find others with similar interests and enabling them to create new friendships. In some cases, these have lead to marriages.

ThirdAgers represent a fast growing segment of the economies of the world. They have a lot of personal challenges but they also have time, motivation, and decades of experience. As the next generation of the Internet evolves as the new medium it will enable members of this highly skilled workforce to come back to work part time from their retirement communities via telecommuting. They may prove to be crucial in filling the huge skills shortage that is facing the information technology industry today. For those who don't choose to come back to work the Internet will enable them to fulfill their lives in various ways and to find help in meeting the challenges they face.

CHAPTER 14

What to Do Next

The last and most important chapter of this book explored what to do once you adopt a net attitude. I compiled a checklist of action items. They can help you stimulate your organization to the highest possible level of performance. The concepts apply whether you are running a small business, a large business, a government organization, a non-profit, or a hospital. I edited the list and included it as the last chapter in Health Attitude because the healthcare industry desperately needs a change in attitude. The technology available to help you deploy a net attitude throughout your organization has changed. Social media offers techniques not practical in 2001. However, the principles, the philosophy, and the spirit behind net attitude have not changed. The need for a net attitude is greater than ever.

Once you have a Next Generation Attitude and a grasp of the coming technologies of the Next Generation of the Internet, what do you do next? Here are some very simple ideas, organized in five categories, that I hope will help you survive and thrive on the Internet in the days, weeks, and months ahead.

First and Foremost, Communicate, Communicate, Communicate

✓ Leverage the power of email for communication with customers, suppliers, stockholders and business partners. Add staff to handle external e-mail on a 24 x 7 basis, and find ways to justify the cost based on increased business, improved customer satisfaction, and offsets to paper-based processes. Use flexible, pre-drafted responses and use software to categorize the email by department or product and by whether it is feedback, a question, or a complaint. Automatically route the email to the right part of the organization. Ensure that every email is answered within 24 hours. Use a follow-up system to ensure closure on issues.

✓ If you use an email form on your website instead of providing an email address, give the sender the option to receive a copy of their email message. People often don't use the email form because they have no confidence it will get delivered and they have no record of having sent it. Allow them to attach a document that may contain more information about a situation at hand.

✓ Set up an email directory search capability that enables people outside of the organization to find email addresses of employees and departments. When some question whether this is giving away proprietary information, remind them the company switchboard already gives out phone numbers and email is usually more efficient. Accept the principle of opening up your organization and allowing outsiders to easily send you e-mail. Become the easiest organization in the world to communicate with.

✓ Set up an enterprise-wide Instant Messaging system that provides encryption of messages. Make it available to all employees. Provide the infrastructure to enable them to have e-meetings in addition to messaging.

✓ Make your website a comprehensive information resource for customers, prospects, industry analysts, consultants, editors, and your employees. Include not just press releases, but owner manuals, white papers, and technical and customer support information about your products and services. Put someone in charge of keeping things current and managing the archives. Establish a company standard, such as the Adobe portable data format (PDF), for publishing all information. (If you choose Adobe, provide a link to get the free Adobe Acrobat software to enable any visitor without one to quickly be able to read your content.)

✓ Provide external links related to your products and services. Include links to your customers and business partners, to universities doing research in areas affecting your business, to third parties who write about your products or services, and to relevant discussion groups. Don't make your constituencies find these places on their own. If you provide plenty of links away from your site, people will remember it and they will return often.

✓ Establish an "Experts and Executives Online" program to enable your constituencies to engage in open electronic dialogue with your executives and subject matter experts. Use electronic forums, discussion groups, chat rooms, and e-meetings. Have offline approaches where answers can be staffed out and posted after the appropriate executives or experts have approved them, but also have periodically scheduled online dialogues. Realize that you don't control these groups and that your conversations with them are not private.

✓ Use the threads of the electronic dialogues as a sort of electronic town hall meeting from which you can learn first hand what your constituencies like and dislike. Use the dialogues to deliver key messages about your organizational philosophies, the principles you are dedicated to and the plans you have for the future.

Outside-In

Always think Outside-in. Outside is where all the people are; they have the power, walk in their shoes.

✓ Make sure key people are well connected outside of the organization. Encourage product development executives to spend a lot of time with customers but also attending conferences where they can learn what competitors and influencers of your industry have on their mind. Encourage them to network outside of the organization. Make trip reports widely available on the intranet.

✓ Use the Internet as the world's largest focus group. Analyze incoming email in detail and take it seriously. Realize that extreme or even insulting views may be directed at your organization from the Internet but that these messages often represent the leading edge of opinion. (People on the Internet are passionate about their areas of interest.) Listen really hard to what people are saying -- you may save a lot of time and money and be able to anticipate problems that the masses will later experience.

✓ Create a privacy program that enables you to know where your data goes and who's responsible for it. Have a solid privacy policy and appoint an accountable person who ensures that the policy gets implemented (Chief Policy Officers are the rage -- and they should be empowered to talk to people inside and outside the company)

✓ Audit your privacy policy. Make sure it is a comprehensive one, that you are following it, and that it has teeth in it from a compliance point of view. Ensure that safeguards are in place over data that belongs to others.

✓ Examine how you have linked your brand to your web presence. Make sure the policies and actions on your website are consistent with the values and principles of your organization.

✓ Employ open standards and require that your vendors do. Assign someone in your organization to follow Internet and web standards. Conduct periodic standards reviews to ensure you are compliant.

✓ Follow key Internet policy issues in those areas where you have expertise or a vested interest. Visit the Global Internet Project at http://www.gip.org for an overview of some of the current Internet policy issues.

Think Big but Start Simple and Grow Fast

Use trial-by-fire, just-enough-is-good-enough, and sense and respond approaches where it makes sense.

✓ Inspect all of your core business processes in marketing, distribution, order processing, application development, human resources, etc. Make sure that you are using the plan-build-deliver model only where you have to and are using the sense-and-respond model wherever you can.

✓ Set up a Skunk Works somewhere where it can't get snuffed out or attacked by the white corpuscles of the organization. Give it top-level support.

✓ Use the Internet to introduce new product and services ideas. Iterate to improve the ones that get good feedback. Stop development or quickly change development on the ones where feedback is negative. Move from idea to proof of concept to prototype with a subset of customers as fast as you can.

✓ Evaluate the role digital IDs (a big idea) will play for your organization. Start a pilot project with a subset of your constituency to experiment and get feedback. Establish long-term goals, iterate from the pilot toward them, and fine-tune them as you learn more.

✓ Use incentives, recognition and communications to encourage knowledge sharing. Consider appointing a "chief knowledge officer" with responsibility to evolve a system that facilitates broad and deep sharing of knowledge across the organization.

Information Technology Infrastructure

Build an information technology infrastructure that enables you to have a scalable, manageable, highly available, reliable, and secure e-business on the Internet and the intranet.

✓ Assume your constituencies will be using an Internet that is Fast, Always on, and Everywhere and that those constituencies are going to be interacting with your e-business 24 x 7. Build or buy or e-source an infrastructure that you cannot outgrow – one that can handle the spikes of demand and is intelligent enough to handle the unexpected, perform diagnostics, and heal itself.

✓ Make your e-business Natural, Intelligent, Easy, and Trusted. Constantly seek feedback from visitors and constantly improve the site based on what visitors tell you. Do it often and in small increments. Make your web interface at least as easy for the customer as talking to a real live, experienced and well-informed sale representative.

✓ Select a content management system to create and manage content for your e-business and intranet websites. Standardize on XML to give context to your content and give you the flexibility to publish to the many devices that will be part of the NGi.

✓ Include multimedia capabilities in your infrastructure, including audio, video, and animation, to provide constituencies with product photos and videos, demonstrations, infomercials, and tutorials on how to assemble or install a product. Set and manage expectations for what you can deliver with the multimedia. Do not assume that all of your customers have the capacity to handle multimedia.

✓ Put as much energy into creating a powerful intranet for your employees as you do for your external customer website. Identify all processes from signing up for the blood drive or health care benefits, to ordering business cards, to using e-meetings for more effective collaboration. Encourage the formation of communities within your organization. Make sure all employees have access to the web and email -- provide training for all new employees.

✓ Consider issuing a notebook computer to all new employees so they can be connected when they are at home or traveling. Provide a docking station so that the notebook can be connected to a display and keyboard when they are in the office.

✓ Consider a wireless infrastructure to enable employees and visitors to connect their notebook computers to the Internet wherever they are in the organization. Offset the cost by eliminating separate phone lines that people use to connect today.

✓ Look at all the functions in the cycle of everything a constituent can do with your organization – end-to-end. Evaluate how many of these functions are available on your e-business, prioritize the ones that aren't, and develop plans to get them in place.

✓ Identify key applications that are not integrated (like the hotel reservation system and the frequent guest system, or the gate scheduling system and the flight arrival system) and evaluate the use of message queuing to enable your incompatible systems to communicate with each other in a seamless way that adds value to your customers.

✓ Establish a plan to consolidate all employee information into a single directory. Do the same for your customers, suppliers, and other constituencies. Use these directories as the single "hub" of information and then build applications that all use the same directory. Create a "single sign-on" for all applications.

Internet Culture

Last, but certainly not least, get a taste of Internet culture – and then change the culture. Ensure it has a healthy component of net attitude. Let people know you care about net attitude. This can be done tops down or bottoms up.

✓ Setup an advisory council composed of some of your new, young employees in the organization (and maybe a couple of sixteen-year-old high school interns). Meet with them quarterly. Give them assignments to look at key business or organizational problems and have them come back with ideas on what solutions they would apply. Take their suggestions seriously.

✓ Hire a college student to review your site on a regular basis and look for signs of "Fax this form" or "Call us nine to five Monday to Friday". Use your expanded email support structure to replace the old methods.

✓ If you are in a position of leadership, establish strong executive commitment to the new communications program. Electronic communications has the effect of flattening the organizational structure, thereby potentially threatening some middle management groups. The commitment from the top is critical to keep the grassroots teams energized and to avoid bureaucratic resistance to the implementation of new ideas.

✓ Eliminate fax machines from the organization. Numerous fax-email gateway software solutions are available to replace the paper-based system. The announcement of this change will send a strong signal that net attitude is alive and well in the organization. If you don't have the authority to do this tops down do it bottoms up. Get an account at eFax (http://www.efax.com) and then spread the word through the grass roots.

✓ Pick a time of the week, Saturday morning, Tuesday night, sometime that can be reasonably consistent and spend an hour on the web on a regular basis. Do this whether you are a programmer or the chairman of the board. Try something you haven't tried before. Use Yahoo! or Excite or Google or other search engines and look for something about a product or a service or any subject of interest. Follow the links and see where they lead you. Look at surveys like Media Metrix (http://www.mediametrix.com) that regularly rank the most popular Websites to help you identify the new sites people are visiting. Explore and learn.

✓ Get an email account (from one of the free Internet email services such as Hotmail or Yahoo! mail) that disguises your identity and then do a transaction at your e-business every week. Buy something, look for something, or ask a question. If you find any disappointing results, convene a meeting to have the responsible people in your organization explain why things are the way they are and what can be done to improve.

- ✓ When you have a meeting with important people in your organization, ask an unsuspecting person what the best thing was they saw on the web this week. Chances are they will begin to avoid getting in that awkward spot each week. The culture will begin to change.
- ✓ Grassroots support. Many different kinds of skills are necessary to implement the concepts of *Net Attitude*. Some are technical, some are communications-oriented and some are marketing-oriented. This program most likely cannot be implemented with only a top-down approach. Grassroots teamwork must be encouraged, nurtured, and supported. Every organization has a grass roots contingent somewhere. See if you can find yours. Have lunch with the grass roots leaders. Listen to them and give them tops-down support. The most profound long-term positive change may occur when key initiatives come from people on the front lines.

Getting a net attitude can help you energize your organization and allow you to transform it to meet your vision for doing business into the next century. The challenges are real, but the benefits are spectacular – if you get a net attitude. If you want to find some early indicators of what e-business will be like in the months and years ahead, talk to the kids – as often as you can. They may not know anything about e-business per se but the way they think, the way they interact with their friends, and the expectations they have represent the future.

Epilogue

The epilogue was not about net attitude. It was about giving back to the community in which you had built or were building your career. Since 2001, the gap between rich and poor has widened. Millions of people are in need of housing, education, health, and assistance. For those fortunate enough to have benefited from the advances of technology over the past decade, we have an opportunity to give back to those who are less fortunate. Like the increased need for the adoption of a net attitude, the need to help one another is great. A giving attitude can make a real difference.

Assuming you have been wildly successful in building an e-business you might want to think about how to give something back. I think we are all aware of how well the economy has been doing in recent years. The unprecedented growth has resulted in prosperity for many people beyond what they may have imagined was possible. For many people the amassing of a million dollars of net worth was a dream they didn't really expect to happen. Now many of those same people likely dream of $10 million. Those with $10 million dream of $100 million and those with $100 million dream of being billionaires! Much is being written about the wealth of so many – even after the huge drop in the early part of 2001. At the same time there are much larger numbers of people who have not been so fortunate. There are many people who go to bed hungry. Even in "affluent" communities there are long lists of people waiting to gain access to barely habitable Federal housing. For reasons of health, location, skills, misfortune, or disadvantage there are large numbers of people in need.

Who is responsible -- the government or those who are more fortunate? Many would agree it is at least in part the latter? What can be done? A lot. For those of us who have been fortunate there is a range of ways to help out. Basically, there are so many ways to help that there are no excuses for not doing so. The means to help follow a hierarchy as do so many things. At the base of the pyramid of helping is giving money anonymously. This can be done through the United Way, churches or synagogues, private foundations, various national appeals, or directly to pinpointed charities. Websites abound.

A second level up the pyramid is to not be anonymous; to directly support causes that are meaningful or important to you or your. friends and family. A couple of years ago I attended a reception of the Society of Alexis de Tocqueville, a group of contributors to the United Way who exceed a threshold of $10,000 in giving per year. At the reception I was astounded both at how many people were there and how many people were not there. It was initially impressive to see a group of 150 or so in the room. Some quick arithmetic suggested that the giving represented was probably greater than $2 million. On the other hand seeing that there were just a very few people (literally) from any one of the major companies represented (GE, IBM, Merrill Lynch, Chase Manhattan, Texaco, etc.) made it pain-fully clear how small the participation really was.

Given that the stocks of all these companies (and many more) have appreci-ated so much and the additional fact that these companies all provide a corporate match of the employee gift shows how much potential there really is. Suppose, for example, an employee had options to buy company stock at $25 per share and the current price of the stock was $50 per share. A gift of just 100 shares of stock would be worth $5,000. The company match would make the gift worth $10,000. The cost of the donation to the employee would be $2,500 to exercise the options plus a capital gains tax (assuming the donated shares had been held sufficiently) of roughly $750 minus a tax savings of $2,000 (assuming a 40% tax bracket) or a net cost of $1,250. The leverage of the gift: 8 to 1!

A further extrapolation of the leveraged giving idea is the formation of a pri-vate foundation. On October 21, 1998 the Senate passed a bill that made perma-nent the section 170(e)(5) charitable deduction for gifts of appreciated stock to private foundations. This means that any person can establish a private founda-tion and use appreciated stock to do so. This can be a very useful way to reduce tax obligations in the event of a bonus payment, retirement payout of restricted stock, or any "spike" in income. At the same time the foundation can be used to provide charitable donations for subsequent gifting or even to receive and distribute charitable donations from others. There are a few catches but they are reasonable. One is that your foundation must give away at least 5% of its average net assets per year. Another is that you have to file a tax return for the foundation. If all this is too daunting, you can donate to an existing foundation that someone else has established. Some links to resources can be found at http://www.jcdowning.org/

The Alexis de Tocqueville reception was hosted by Jane Pauley (NBC) and Bob Wright (GE), I was quite impressed with the short speech made by Jane. She talked about the positive impact people can have by publicly revealing the amount of their contributions. Put modesty aside, she said, and let others know. It will challenge them and spur larger gifts. I think she is right. As the United Way and others publish their gold/silver/platinum giver lists the top categories seem to be growing.

And then there is the most important gift of all; our personal involvement. Our time is our most scarce resource and giving even a small amount of it is very difficult. In the end however this is the greatest gift and the greatest leverage. An hour of time donated to a board or committee makes the 8 to 1 leverage seem small.

How can we get more people thinking about all this? One idea is e-philanthropy. It is not just "click here to donate". It is a larger idea. Creating a local community of interest, a charity portal that can enable charities to make their needs known and where those with resources can make their abilities known whether it is an anonymous gift, targeted visible funding, or volunteer time. If the idea were to spread it might mean enabling people to contribute to charities where they grew up, went to school, or have a vacation home. It might also be a resource to help people set up their own private foundations or contribute to existing ones. It might also be a way for the smallest of charities with no executive director, corporate sponsors, nor advertising budgets to make themselves visible.

The bottom line is simple. Incomes and assets are up. So is need of those less fortunate. Let's give e-philanthropy a chance. Take a look at http://www.greenstar.org/e-philanthropy/

Acknowledgements

In the acknowledgements I thanked the agent, editor, and numerous friends and colleagues who helped me bring Net Attitude to readers. My appreciation continues. I would now like to thank those who have helped me maintain a net attitude over the past 14 years. Irving Wladawsky-Berger, my former manager at IBM, and I have lunch every few months and compare notes on developments in technology. I continue to appreciate his inspiration. Mike Nelson, a former member of my team, lives and breathes net attitude every day. I appreciate his active communications in the social media and his occasional tweet or post to keep me on my toes. Jane Harper and Mary Keough were key members of my team who were the operational gurus who enabled the WebAhead group to innovate. I am grateful to remain in contact with them. I would like to thank Skip Prichard for his suggestions and encouragement for re-publishing this new version of Net Attitude. Finally, I am grateful for Kathleen Imhoff's invaluable review and editing.

There are so many people to thank for making the book possible. First and foremost is Nick Philipson, my tireless editor, for his countless contributions, corrections, and helping to me to make my writing more readable. His questions were painful at times but helped me to clarify and organize my thoughts. Thanks to John Dvorak for introducing me to John Brockman, my agent. John Brockman appropriately questioned whether I had anything relevant to write about but I thank him for taking time to visit our Internet Technology Laboratory, see the work we were doing on advanced technologies, and take the time to listen to the story I wanted to tell. I also thank him for leading me to Nick.

I want to thank the executives at IBM who were in a position to restrain me but instead encouraged me to live out on the edge of the Internet even though we had no idea where it would lead or how or even if we would ever make any profit from it. These included Jim Cananvino, Fernand Sarrat, and Dennie Welsh in the early days and Irving Wladawsky-Berger over the past five years. Irving, more than anyone, constantly encouraged me to spend as much time as possible out in the marketplace, learning from others and sharing the IBM vision.

And thanks to my friends and colleagues for reading my drafts and giving me their candid feedback about where I had gone astray or missed key points. I express my gratitude to Jeff Auger, Tim Blair, Brian Carpenter, Andy Stanford-Clark, Joe Eckert, Sara Elo, Dave Grossman, Mark Harris, Mike Maney, Dikran Meliksetian, Mike Nelson, Harriet Pearson, Dan Powers, David Singer, and Irving Wladawsky-Berger. Thanks also to Matt Graham for his assistance in researching various trends and statistics and to Sarah James, a package engineering intern at Nestle, for contributing references about advances in the packaging industry.

I would also like to acknowledge the numerous fine companies I have referenced in the book. Many of the scenarios I describe in the book, not all of which are positive, are drawn from real experiences I have had with various companies as a consumer. Most of these companies are highly valued customers of IBM. I have chosen the examples to illustrate how even the most progressive and dynamic companies may still have trouble seeing the true power of the Internet and how it is affecting their relationships with customers or, in some cases, see it clearly and are in the process of building out their capabilities. At this stage I would say most companies, including my own, are wrestling with the many extremely difficult challenges that the Internet presents. Hopefully, In Internet time, most of the examples will be ancient history by the time you read this book.

Speaking of Internet time, there may be other things that changed between the time I finished writing this book and when you started reading it. That is where http://netattitude.org comes in. Once the book was out of my hands and into the publisher's, I began to make notes about things that happened sooner or later or differently than I thought they would. There were also new developments that I had not anticipated. I have tried to capture all of these changes and post them at http://netattitude.org. It will help the book stay dynamic. There are various sidebars – I call them "Reflections" -- throughout the book. I am sure you have many reflections of your own. If you would like to share them or any comments with other readers of the book and me please visit http://netattitude.org and post them.

References (2001)

Alpert, Bill. Optical switches will be the next big thing in data transmission. Barron's. 4 December 2000.

American Bankruptcy Institute. U.S. Bankruptcy Filings 1980-1998 (Business, Non-Business, Total). http://www.abiworld.org/stats/newstatsfront.html

Barta, Patrick. With Some Exceptions, Dot-Coms Score Poorly on Customer Service. The Wall Street Journal. 27 November 2000.

Berst, Jesse. Why You're Craving an Internet Appliance. Ziff-Davis Network. 11 November 1999

Burbeck, Steve. The Tao of e-business services. IBM Corporation. October 2000. http://www.ibm.com/patrick/webservices

Digital Radio -- The Sound of the Future! The Canadian Vision. Task Force on the Introduction of Digital Radio. Ottawa, Canada. Minister of Supply and Services Canada 1993-1995, Cat. No Co22-132/1993E, ISBN 0-662-20678-

Hedtke, John. MP3 and the Digital Music Revolution.

"Internet Growth Statistics," Internet World Stats (2015), http://www.internet-worldstats.com/emarketing.htm.

Kunii, Irene M. with Baker, Stephen. BusinessWeek Online. 17 January 2000.

Lamont, Ian. The Coolest Kind of Collaboration. Network World. 13 November 2000.

"List of Social Networking Websites," Wikipedia (2015), https://en.wikipedia.org/wiki/List_of_social_networking_websites.

"Monthly & Annual Retail Trade," United States Census Bureau (2015), https://www.census.gov/retail/ecommerce/historic_releases.html.

Reddy, Raj. Infinite Memory and Bandwidth: Implications for Artificial Intelligence. 19 October 2000.

Parmar, P. J. "Who Still Uses Faxes? The Medical Industry Does," *KevinMD.com* (2014), http://www.kevinmd.com/blog/2014/10/still-uses-faxes-medical-in-dustry.html.

Patrick, John R. Health *Attitude: Unraveling and Solving the Complexities of Healthcare.* Palm Coast, FL: Attitude LLC, 2015.

Patrick, John R. *Net Attitude: What It Is, How to Get It, and Why Your Company Can't Survive without It.* Cambridge, MA: Perseus Publishing, 2001.

Scourias, John. Overview of the Global System for Mobile Communications. http://ccnga.uwaterloo.ca/~jscouria/GSM/gsmreport.html erloo.ca

Shim, Richard. Is the BlackBerry your next pager? Ziff-Davis New Network. 28 April 2000.

Strom, David. Making Beautiful Music on your PC. http://strom.com/awards/166.html

Whitlock, Natalie Walker. Accelerating e-business. Casaflora Communications. September 2000. http://www-106.ibm.com/developerworks/library/w-uddi.html?dwzone=ws

Webmergers.com. Year 2000 Dot Com Shutdowns: A Webmergers.com Special Report http://www.webmergers.com/editorial/010201_shutdownreport.php

Notes (2016)

1   John R. Patrick, *Net Attitude : What It Is, How to Get It, and Why Your Company Can't Survive without It* (Cambridge, MA: Perseus Publishing, 2001).

2   "List of Social Networking Websites," *Wikipedia* (2015), https://en.wikipedia.org/wiki/List_of_social_networking_websites.

3   "Monthly & Annual Retail Trade," *United States Census Bureau* (2015), https://www.census.gov/retail/ecommerce/historic_releases.html.

4   "Internet Growth Statistics," *Internet World Stats* (2015), http://www.internetworldstats.com/emarketing.htm.

5   Ibid.

6   John R. Patrick, *Health Attitude: Unraveling and Solving the Complexities of Healthcare* (Palm Coast, FL: Attitude LLC, 2015).

7   P. J. Parmar, "Who Still Uses Faxes? The Medical Industry Does," *KevinMD.com* (2014), http://www.kevinmd.com/blog/2014/10/still-uses-faxes-medical-industry.html.

8   Patrick, *Health Attitude: Unraveling and Solving the Complexities of Healthcare*.

9   "Company Story," *Stew Leonard's* (2015), http://www.stewleonards.com/about-us/company-story.

10   Justin Reich, "Mooc Completion and Retention in the Context of Student Intent," *EducauseReview* (2014), http://er.educause.edu/articles/2014/12/mooc-completion-and-retention-in-the-context-of-student-intent.

11   Patrick, *Health Attitude: Unraveling and Solving the Complexities of Healthcare.*

12   Ibid.

13   Ibid.

Index

A

account number, 44, 45, 135
adopters, early, 190, 192
alphaWorks, 189, 190
Amazon, 8, 33, 35, 160
American Express, 42, 162
answer, 12, 34, 51, 59, 91, 92, 99, 100,
    110, 120, 154, 160, 177, 211
applications, 36, 67, 71, 93, 94, 135, 136,
    137, 138, 139, 141, 148, 167, 193, 214
architectures, 198, 199
artists, 29, 30, 102, 103, 104
attitude, 34, 37, 51, 158, 159, 169, 170–
    73, 180, 203, 207, 209
attitude problem, 6, 37, 41, 42, 43, 45,
    46, 48
attorney, 4, 166
authentication, 13, 46, 159, 160, 163, 166

B

backbones, 61, 62
bandwidth, 11, 21, 56, 57, 58, 60, 65,
    101, 226
banks, 4, 5, 10, 13, 34, 40, 45, 50, 51, 105,
    161, 164, 166, 201–2
banner, 56, 122, 208
bits, 21, 29, 55, 56, 58, 59, 60, 61, 62, 63,
    65, 72, 73, 111
Bluetooth, 21, 73–74
Bluetooth wireless technology, 74
Bots, Buddy, 100, 101
BPR (business process reengineering),
    8, 196–97
browser, 35, 36, 69, 70, 71, 78–79, 93,
    100, 129, 130, 131, 133, 134–36,
    155, 162
browser interface, 135, 136

browsing, 42, 78, 91, 100, 133, 134, 136, 137
buddies, 90, 91, 93, 204
business failures, 9
business process reengineering. *See* BPR
button, 75, 81, 83, 85, 93, 122, 196
buyers, 7, 8, 26, 40, 50, 51, 116, 117

C

CA, 161, 162, 165, 175
cable companies, 28, 55, 57, 58, 59
cable modems, 19, 59, 60, 62, 63, 69
cables, 11, 20–21, 57, 58, 59, 62, 68
calculations, 23, 133, 139, 165
calendars, 30, 31, 80, 148, 152
Call Center, 43, 45, 180
Cambridge, 98, 136, 137, 226, 227
CAPS, 171, 174
CD, 28, 29, 30, 39, 102, 110, 111
cell phones, 19, 47, 73, 78, 80, 81, 82, 83, 84, 85, 86, 106, 147
CEO, 10, 20, 96, 117, 158, 159, 175, 176, 177, 186, 200, 204, 206
cereal, 48, 49, 74
charge, 29, 50, 73, 77, 138, 180, 181, 182, 183, 210
CIO, 89, 92, 180, 186, 193, 206
click, 19, 22, 27, 30, 36, 37, 38, 67, 69, 70, 71, 93, 134, 135, 180
click here, 33, 43, 45, 131
coffee, 36–37, 73, 74
community, 50, 57, 58, 100, 119, 143, 144–45, 177, 189, 190, 208, 214, 217
community portals, 120

companies
consumer, 85, 131
insurance, 164, 200
satellite, 59
compression, 29, 110
computer companies, 131
computers, 12, 20, 21, 22, 27, 70, 78, 103, 108, 124, 127, 130, 131, 154, 173
connect, 19, 26, 27, 50, 61, 68, 69, 71, 72, 73, 84, 86, 101, 120, 214
constituencies, 4, 7, 14, 15, 115, 154, 167, 170, 198, 199, 211, 213, 214
consumers, 6, 8, 34, 35, 47, 48, 49, 51, 57, 60, 61, 102, 103, 131, 201
content, 58, 60, 63, 79, 83, 119, 121, 122, 123, 176, 177, 181, 198, 199, 213
content management, 122, 123
countries, 23, 24, 25, 80, 104, 121, 122, 162, 166
culture, 13, 110, 145, 169, 172, 192, 202–3, 214, 216
customer number, 37, 115
customer service, 10, 12, 36, 39, 40, 44, 45, 94, 138

D

database, 102, 121, 138, 155, 161, 162, 194
decrypt, 74, 157, 159–60, 165, 166
Deep Blue, 124, 194, 195
departments, 93, 181, 210
desktop, 54, 71, 100, 129, 135, 136, 140, 149
developers, 134, 140, 141, 145, 192

devices, 19, 20, 21, 72, 73–74, 77, 78, 79, 80, 83, 84–87, 113, 122, 125–26, 198

digital ID, 13, 25, 46, 81, 159, 160, 161–67, 200, 213

digital subscriber line. *See* DSL

diskettes, 109–10, 134, 161

DNS (Domain Name System), 140, 179

DoCoMo, 81, 82

doctor, 3, 20, 63–64, 72, 124, 190, 199, 200

documents, 27, 38, 39, 70, 93, 94, 114, 116, 137, 155, 167, 180, 210

Domain Name System (DNS), 140, 179

download, 27–28, 30, 39, 55, 59, 63, 84, 92, 105, 135, 189, 190

DSL (digital subscriber line), 57–60, 62, 63, 69

E

eBay, 8, 27, 40, 50, 51

e-business, 6, 7, 8, 15, 41, 42, 51, 131, 155, 156, 191, 196, 198, 213, 216

successful, 13, 48, 170

e-businesses, 8, 137, 141

e-commerce, 7, 22, 34, 48, 51, 67

e-learning, 96–97, 133

electric frying pans, 42, 43, 115

email, 39–41, 50, 51, 56, 57, 60, 68, 91, 135, 152–53, 157, 165, 173, 175–77, 209–10

e-marketplaces, 8–9, 117–18, 142, 144, 170

e-meetings, 93, 94, 95, 96, 157, 210, 211, 214

employees, 83, 96, 97, 100, 121, 158, 175, 176, 177, 178, 180, 193, 210, 214, 218

Europe, 22, 39, 40, 70, 80, 81, 83, 87, 95, 132, 162

expectations, rising, 4, 14, 15, 34

experts, 11, 28, 63, 64, 92, 122, 132, 137, 211

F

failures, 9, 35, 127, 159, 187, 188

fax machine, 3, 4, 5, 6, 7, 9, 37, 38–39, 68, 137, 141, 166–67, 173, 197, 201

feedback, 107, 131, 189, 190, 191, 192, 193, 194, 196, 210, 212–13

formats, 110, 111, 115, 122

Friday, 7, 35, 36, 40, 42, 44, 172, 173, 193, 215

G

GE, 4, 5, 6, 96, 218, 219

GE Capital, 4, 5, 6, 166, 167

Gerstner, Lou, 154, 176, 204

governments, 14, 22, 24, 31, 34, 159, 161, 162, 168, 170, 183, 218

Groupe Spécial Mobile. *See* GSM

GSM (Groupe Spécial Mobile), 80, 81, 226

H

headlines, 9, 50, 195

healthcare, 3, 18, 113, 124, 226, 227–28

home automation, 67
homepage, 41, 63, 70, 204
hospitals, 11, 14, 34, 71–72, 162, 209
hotels, 21, 34, 39, 72, 73, 77, 81, 91, 95
hours, normal business, 7, 36, 39, 40, 44, 172

I

IBM, 61, 89, 92, 140, 143, 144, 146, 148, 158–59, 176, 195, 204, 206, 207, 222
IBM's Internet Technology Laboratory in Southbury, 90
ICANN (International Corporation for the Assignment of Names and Numbers), 25
IDs, 159, 160–61, 163, 164
IETF (Internet Engineering Task Force), 182–83
industry, 9, 117, 118, 119, 140, 141, 144, 147, 154, 183, 211
information
personal, 152, 156
private, 159–60
information technology, 93, 97–98, 123, 124, 125, 130, 138, 142, 145, 181, 186
information technology companies, 142, 146
information technology industry, 38, 126, 140, 143, 147, 208
information technology infrastructure, 213
information technology systems, 118, 137, 147, 172

innovation, 57, 78, 97, 169, 185, 186, 188, 202
instant messaging, 56, 57, 68, 83, 90, 91–97, 99, 100, 194, 204, 206
instant messaging programs, 89, 90, 100–101, 136, 204
International Corporation for the Assignment of Names and Numbers (ICANN), 25
International Organization for Standards, 182
International Telecommunication Union (ITU), 182
Internet access, fast, 56, 58
Internet appliances, 84
Internet applications, 69, 83, 136, 189
Internet Architecture Board, 182, 183
Internet communications, 83
Internet companies, 9, 10
Internet Culture, 214
Internet Engineering Task Force. See IETF
Internet engineers, 194, 206
Internet Growth Statistics, 225, 227
Internet kiosks, 77–78, 86
Internet Protocol. See IP
Internet Security, 151, 157, 158
Internet Service Providers, 63, 67, 73, 182
Internet standards, 14, 83, 143, 167, 183, 199
Internet startup companies, 9, 10
Internet startups, 9, 14
Internet Technology, 96
Internet time, 222
Internet users, 163

Internet World, 170, 176
Internet World Stats, 225, 227
intranet, 101, 176, 192, 211, 213, 214
IP (Internet Protocol), 56, 86, 114, 143, 144, 192
IPv6, 86, 87
ISP, 67, 69, 182
ITU (International Telecommunication Union), 182

J

Java, 134, 140, 145, 170, 192, 205
JavaScript, 133–34, 136, 170

K

key
private, 159, 165, 166, 200
public, 159, 165, 166, 200
kids, 51, 90, 169, 172, 204, 205, 206, 207, 216
kiosks, 12, 25, 85–86

L

Life Sciences, 123, 125
limitations, 108, 118, 133, 134
Linux, 146, 147
embedded, 147

M

mainframe, 144, 146, 148, 193
manufacturer, 26, 47, 116, 197

Massive Open Online Courses. *See* MOOCS
matter, 19, 21, 27, 39, 45, 60, 61, 68, 85, 91, 93, 95, 143, 144, 145
media, 11, 12, 57, 101, 103, 109, 110, 142, 180
medical records, 154, 199–200
Message Queuing (MQ), 197, 214
microprocessors, 103, 127
Microsoft, 74, 132, 140, 141, 144
miles, 11, 12, 36, 58, 60, 61, 62, 64, 69, 82, 84, 92
mobile phones, 12, 71, 74, 78, 80, 81, 82, 83, 85, 101, 122, 130, 163
model, 14, 26, 27, 28, 29, 30, 124, 137, 145, 180, 187, 191, 192, 194
money, 4, 5, 6, 23, 26, 39, 40, 45, 46, 50, 51, 153, 175, 201, 202
MOOCS (Massive Open Online Courses), 18, 89–90
MP3, 28, 29, 101, 102, 103, 104, 225
music, 17, 21, 28, 29, 30, 62, 68, 101, 102, 103, 181
digital, 27, 28, 29, 101, 103
music industry, 17, 30, 104, 178

N

name, 44–45, 78, 81, 91, 93, 94, 100, 134, 152, 153, 179, 181, 183, 186, 204
Napster, 27, 28, 29, 103, 181, 206
Net, 7, 19, 24, 26, 27, 47, 84, 90, 152, 170, 172, 174, 177, 194, 198
net attitude, 4, 14–15, 54–55, 151, 169, 170, 171, 172, 190, 191, 203, 209, 214, 216–17, 221

good, 159, 172, 181, 193
lack of, 171, 201
netattitude.org, 179, 222–23
Netiquette, 172, 174
Netscape, 133, 134, 192
networking, 143, 148, 225, 227
networks, 11, 12, 70, 80, 126, 127, 135, 137, 157, 182, 192, 198, 211
Next Generation, 11, 13, 51, 53, 54, 56, 95, 101, 105, 107, 108, 109, 202, 209, 213
Next Generation Internet, 3, 11, 13, 15, 121
notebook computers, 21, 72, 214

O

OASIS, 116–17
opening, 48, 49, 148, 152, 206, 210
organizations, 7, 14, 22, 43, 120–21, 148, 178, 179, 181, 182, 193, 209, 210, 211, 212–16
formal, 189–90
large, 14, 22, 25
larger, 187, 188

P

packaging, 47, 48, 49
packets, 56–57, 67, 70, 157, 182
pages, 37, 63, 65, 70, 79, 100, 114, 115, 121, 122, 123, 133
participants, 8, 94, 95, 188, 190, 197, 208
password, 74, 81, 135, 158, 160–64
Patrick, 5, 35, 37, 40, 45, 177, 225, 226, 227–28

PayPal, 50–51, 153
PC, 27, 28, 30, 63, 69, 73, 74, 78, 101, 130, 131, 135, 143, 144, 163
PDA (personal digital assistants), 12, 74, 75, 78, 79, 80, 83, 84–85, 101, 102, 146
peer-to-peer, 30, 180, 181
personal digital assistants. *See* PDA
phone, 37, 38, 40, 41, 42, 43, 71, 80, 81, 82, 83, 100, 137, 138, 175
phone display, 83
pictures, 12, 20, 56, 64, 82, 104, 105, 118, 176, 203–4
population, world's, 18, 19
portals, 119, 120
specialized, 119
post office, 50, 165
potato chip, 46, 47, 48
power, 9, 15, 17, 20, 21–24, 26–27, 30, 31, 41, 134, 136, 144, 209, 211, 222
power receptacle, 73
power to the people, 17, 18, 22, 24, 27, 31, 90, 131, 168, 170
Presidential Information Technology Advisory Committee, 11, 144
press, 7, 24, 31, 43, 44, 81, 117, 171, 176, 210
principles, 17, 33, 53–54, 151, 169, 170, 209, 210, 211, 212
privacy, 13, 25, 45, 92, 151, 152, 154, 155, 156, 159, 163, 164, 168, 183
privacy policy, 152, 156, 212
privacy preferences, 156, 163
private foundations, 218, 219
problem, 4, 6, 23, 33, 36, 37, 39, 42, 45, 47, 92, 126, 160, 187, 197

products, 8, 38, 44, 48, 102, 131, 139, 177, 178, 179, 189, 191, 210–11, 213, 215

programmers, 129, 132, 133, 134, 137, 139, 141, 215

programming, 130, 132, 133, 134, 137, 138, 198

programming language, 130, 132, 133, 134, 139, 140

programs, 21, 27, 67, 73, 91, 100, 108, 131, 133, 135, 138, 140, 147, 216

projects, 45, 61, 94, 95, 118, 120, 121, 186, 187, 188, 189, 191, 192, 205, 207

Q

Quicken, 129, 135

R

radio, digital, 103, 104, 225

S

Sametime, 93, 94

Sash, 136, 137, 141

security, 10, 13, 22, 25, 144, 151, 152, 157, 158, 159

server room, 158

servers, 24, 27–28, 62–63, 70, 71, 115, 135, 140, 141, 155, 158–60, 181, 194, 196, 198

shifts, 15, 27, 77, 78, 143, 144, 175

signature, 5, 6, 25, 45, 46, 166

site, 33, 34, 35, 37, 41–42, 71, 119, 120, 152–53, 155, 156, 177, 178, 195, 198

Skunk Works, 14, 143, 185, 186, 187, 188–89, 212

slides, 48, 94, 110

Social Networking Websites, 225, 227

software, 21, 23, 37, 38, 127, 130, 134, 137, 138–39, 142, 145, 146, 148, 165, 166

speech, 105, 106, 107, 126, 154, 176

spending, 126, 129, 177, 178

stamps.com, 49, 50

standards, 25, 130, 137, 139, 140, 141, 143, 144, 151, 167, 168, 173, 182, 183, 188

open, 140, 167, 168, 199, 212

students, 12, 23, 64, 69, 90, 97–98, 142, 145, 146, 185, 205, 206, 207

supercomputer, 107, 113, 124, 195

survey, 34–35

T

TCP, 114, 143, 144, 192

team, 64, 101, 108, 169, 172, 185, 187–88, 194, 195, 207, 221

telephone companies, 57–61, 72

terrorists, 18, 31

ThirdAgers, 207–8

threats, 58, 59, 104, 140

tools, 23, 27, 30, 91, 92, 94, 95, 115, 129, 131, 133, 155, 156, 186

trust, 25, 45, 50, 152, 153–54, 156, 157, 160, 163, 166, 167, 168, 187

U

Ubique, 91, 93
UCAID (University Corporation for Advanced Internet Development), 61
United Parcel Service (UPS), 49, 196
universities, 14, 31, 34, 69, 89–90, 97, 98, 143, 145, 160, 170, 182, 205, 210
University Corporation for Advanced Internet Development (UCAID), 61
URL, 41, 42, 179, 196
users, 27, 39, 73, 91, 108, 121, 122, 133, 137, 138, 148, 156, 180, 193, 196

V

video, 24, 29, 58, 63, 65, 79, 82, 97, 101, 105, 109, 176, 213
vocabulary, 115, 172, 173–74
VP Buddy, 89, 91, 92

W

weather, 69, 71, 74, 78, 80, 82, 99, 148
web applications, 137, 138, 139, 141
webpage developers, 132, 133, 134
web server, 6, 13, 159, 160, 197, 198
web services, 12, 138, 139, 140, 141
web services standards, 139, 140, 141
windows, 45–46, 58, 61–63, 69, 70, 105, 121, 129, 136, 144, 148, 149, 168
wireless companies, 59
wireless technology, 72, 73, 74

X

XML, 12, 113, 114–18, 122, 137, 151, 168, 213

[Created with **TExtract** / www.Texyz.com]